Questions & Answers

EVIDENCE

Keeping you afloat through your exams

QUESTIONS & Answers

Ask anyone for exam advice and they'll tell you to *answer the question*. It's good advice but the Q&As go further by telling you how to answer the questions you'll face in your law exams.

Q&As will help you succeed by:

- ✓ identifying typical law exam questions

- ✓ demonstrating how to structure a good answer

- ✓ helping you to avoid common mistakes

- ✓ advising you on how to make your answer stand out from the crowd

- ✓ giving you model answers to up to 50 essay and problem-based questions

Every Q&A follows a trusted formula of question, commentary, answer plan, examiner's tips, and suggested answer. They're written by experienced law lecturers and experienced examiners to help you succeed in exams.

'What a brilliant revision aid! With summaries, tips, and easy-to-understand sample answers, Q&As really help with exam technique and how to structure answers. A great help not only during the revision process, but also throughout the course.'
Kim Sutton, Law student, Oxford Brookes University

LAW OF TORTS
2013 and 2014

PUBLIC LAW
2013 and 2014

LAND LAW
2013 and 2014

LAW OF CONTRACT
2013 and 2014

EU LAW
2013 and 2014

FAMILY LAW
2013 and 2014

Titles in the series cover all compulsory law subjects and major options.

Buy yours from your campus bookshop, online, or direct from OUP

www.oxfordtextbooks.co.uk/law/revision

Additional online resources accompany the Q&A series.
Visit: **www.oxfordtextbooks.co.uk/orc/qanda/**

Questions & Answers

EVIDENCE

Eighth edition

Maureen Spencer
MA (Oxon), MA (Open), LLM, PhD

John Spencer
MA (Oxon), LLM, MMath, Barrister

2013 and 2014

OXFORD
UNIVERSITY PRESS

OXFORD

UNIVERSITY PRESS

Great Clarendon Street, Oxford, OX2 6DP,
United Kingdom

Oxford University Press is a department of the University of Oxford.
It furthers the University's objective of excellence in research, scholarship,
and education by publishing worldwide. Oxford is a registered trade mark of
Oxford University Press in the UK and in certain other countries

© Maureen Spencer and John Spencer 2013

The moral rights of the authors have been asserted

Fifth edition 2007
Sixth edition 2009
Seventh edition 2011

Impression: 1

Contains public sector information licensed under the Open Government Licence v1.0
(http://www.nationalarchives.gov.uk/doc/open-government-licence/open-government-licence.htm)

Crown Copyright material reproduced with the permission of the
Controller, HMSO (under the terms of the Click Use licence).

British Library Cataloguing in Publication Data

Data available

ISBN 978–0–19–966195–4

Printed in Great Britain by
Ashford Colour Press Ltd, Gosport, Hampshire

CONTENTS

Key features

The Q&A series provides full coverage of key subjects in a clear and logical way. This book contains the following features:

- Questions
- Commentary
- Bullet-pointed answer plans
- Examiner's tips
- Suggested answers
- Further reading suggestions

online resource centre

www.oxfordtextbooks.co.uk/orc/qanda/

Titles in the Q&A series are supported by additional online materials to aid study and revision.

Online resources for this title are hosted at the URL above, which is open-access and free to use.

'So what's the answer?' said Laura, a rather literal-minded girl who wrote down everything Robyn said in tutorials. 'Is it a train or a tram?'

'Both or either,' said Robyn. 'It doesn't really matter. Go on Marion.'
'Hang about,' said Vic. 'You can't have it both ways.'

Nice Work by David Lodge (Secker & Warburg, London, 1988)

Like David Lodge's fictional English Literature tutor, Evidence teachers are fonder of setting questions than giving answers. But in these days of modularisation and semesterisation, not to mention larger classes, students do sometimes need ready access to the answers outside the lecture theatre or the seminar room. The authors believe there is a place for modest study aids like this book. It does not pretend to replace the standard Evidence textbooks or the great practitioners' manuals as a source of authoritative information, yet will be more portable and perhaps more accessible to the student in a hurry.

This eighth edition takes full account of changes in Evidence law over the last two years. It covers the key developments in the law on hearsay and reflects the law as it is in July 2012. We thank the ever-patient editors and production staff at OUP, particularly Kirsten Shankland and Sarah Stephenson.

Maureen Spencer
John Spencer
August 2012

New to this edition

- New special measures for vulnerable witnesses and defendants introduced in the Coroners and Justice Act 2009.

- Application of witness anonymity provisions in the Coroners and Justice Act 2009.

- Recent cases on hearsay including the Grand Chamber decision in *Al-Khawaja and Tahery v UK* Applications nos 2766/05 and 2222/06, 15 Dec 2011.

- Recent cases on admissibility of evidence from mobile phones.

TABLE OF STATUTES

TABLE OF STATUTORY INSTRUMENTS

1 Introduction

Evidence is often regarded as one of the trickier subjects studied in undergraduate law courses. It is a mixture of arcane old rules and opaque new statutes and sometimes seems to offend common sense. Technical precepts are intermingled with judicial discretion and matters of high constitutional principle. The subject covers such areas as the defendant's right to silence, the treatment of witnesses, the role of the presumed victim in the trial process, whether or not intercept evidence should be used in court, the extent of judicial discretion in admitting evidence, for example of the complainant's sexual history in rape trials. Since we started producing this book nearly 20 years ago, there has been a great deal of legislative activity in the field of evidence, much of it dealing with questions which are politically controversial. The courts have struggled to digest complex new law while upholding the human rights of the various parties to litigation, both criminal and civil. The **Human Rights Act** and the application of **art. 6** has had a powerful impact on defendants' rights in areas such as the admissibility of improperly obtained evidence and the allocation of the burden of proof. On the other hand, there has been a parallel improvement in making prosecutors protectors of victims. Indeed, the Government in 2002 proclaimed its aim to put victims 'at the heart' of the criminal justice system (Home Office, *Justice for All* (Cm 5563, 2002), para. 0.2). One outcome was the **Criminal Justice Act 2003**, especially the provisions on character and hearsay evidence. As well as absorbing his or her course material, the alert student will follow the debates over these developments both in the general media and in legal journals.

Question and Answer books are not a substitute for learning the law. They are at best a supplementary aid to coursework preparation and particularly to revision for examinations and coursework. These are not model answers to be slavishly imitated (of course, this would constitute plagiarism), but rather examples to help the student understand the topic and see how it might be approached.

Put crudely, the examinee's objective in any examination is to accumulate in the time allowed as many marks as possible. To be manageable this task needs to be broken down into three stages: planning, execution and review.

First, planning. Make sure you arrive at the examination hall in time, with adequate equipment, including statute books if these are allowed in the hall. When you are given the examination paper, read it, read the rubric (the instructions at the top of the paper) carefully, then take five minutes to read the paper itself right through. Turn it over to make sure there's nothing on the back you have missed. You will usually be required to answer a set number of questions (say four out of ten). You must answer the number of questions required. A surprising number of candidates fail because they answer fewer questions than required.

Having chosen the required number of questions try and sketch out in telegraphic note form your answer to each. In problem questions in law examinations this is very often a matter of spotting the issues, as several different areas of the subject are mixed together. If at this point you can recall the names of the cases which are authority for particular propositions in the area concerned, all the better. If you can't, pass onto the next of your chosen questions. By the end of this process, which should not take more than perhaps 20 minutes, you will have sketched out in rough form your answer to each of your chosen questions. Many of your fellow examinees will already be scribbling frantically. Don't panic. Before you go to the stage of execution make a simple calculation. Take the length of the examination in minutes (180 minutes for the classic three-hour examination). Subtract the time you have spent on the planning stage (perhaps 25 minutes) and allow five minutes review time for the end of the examination. Then divide the remainder equally between the questions you have chosen.

Now you can start writing your first answer. Bear in mind that there is often no obvious right answer to a practical question. The authorities may conflict, or you may need to point out that more information is needed than the question provides. What is important is not so much arriving at a conclusion as demonstrating clearly in your reasoning that you appreciate the complexities and sometimes ambiguities of the law. Break your answer into paragraphs, underline the names of cases and don't write in the margins.

It is very important to remember that the examiner is interested in what you do know, not what you don't know. So if you are uncertain about a particular point, it is generally better to put down what you think is the answer, provided it is relevant to answering the question. If you are right, you will gain marks, if you are wrong you will usually not have marks taken away. Don't be tempted to exceed your time limit. You are more likely to pick up marks at the beginning of your answer than at the end. Once your self-imposed time limit is up, stop writing and go on to the next question.

About half way through the examination your concentration may start to sag. It is at this point that you will appreciate having made your sketch answer to your third question at the beginning of the examination period. Your fellow examinees who rushed to get pen to paper at the start of the examination will be flagging too, but they won't have tried to think through the issues in the question when they were fresh. Your aim will be to get as many marks for your last answer as for your first.

The approach required to answering questions will vary with the type of question. There are broadly two types you will encounter in Evidence examinations: problems and essays. Briefly, in answering problem questions, the student must first identify the areas of law in which the problem falls. Almost invariably, there will be more than one issue and it is important that you identify them at the start. Having done so, you should be able to outline the legal principles which are relevant to the issues in the problem, citing the relevant cases and statutes. The next stage is to apply these authorities to the facts. This involves discussion of the facts in the light of the relevant principles, analysis of the facts to select which are significant, and, where appropriate, a comparison of the problems' facts with those of the authorities, in such a way as to support your argument. Finally, come to a practical conclusion, which need not be a definitive answer, may suggest more than one alternative and should where necessary indicate what additional factual material would be required to give a definitive response.

A different approach is required when answering essay questions. These are likely to figure largely in your coursework and to be related to current controversies in the field. The good student will have spent time during the year dipping into such publications as the *International Journal of Evidence and Proof*, *Criminal Law Review*, *New Law Journal*, *Law Quarterly Review* and *Solicitors' Journal*. Even if you are not of their number, it is well worth spending a few hours of revision time before the examination in the library looking through recent issues and making a note of evidence topics which have drawn academic comment. In many cases this is where the examiner will have looked when drafting the exam paper. Background reading will help you to see what the question-setter is looking for in answer to essay questions. You should analyse the question to establish whether you are asked to discuss, explain or criticise a particular area of the law.

These days law examinations can take different forms, including seen questions, open book exams and so on. To take account of this, we have included among the essay answers in this book some which are closer to more fully researched pieces rather than to off-the-cuff answers in a traditional exam. Many courses now require coursework as well as exams and we have tried to supply some material which might help students faced with assessments other than by three-hour unseen examination. You therefore will notice, particularly in the essay questions, much lengthier quotations are given than you could possibly remember in an examination. We have included them because it is artificial for us not to check the exact wording. We would recommend that at least you try to recall comments from academic writers in your answers to essay questions, although clearly you will mostly paraphrase (of course acknowledging the source) rather than quote verbatim. Perhaps perversely, examiners often award more marks for a student's recall of and comment on how an academic deals with a problem of legal analysis rather than the student's intuitive response. Of course it is also expected that you will include your own analysis, particularly in essay questions, but this must be evidence-based! Do not be tempted to write an editorial giving simply your critique without first reviewing academic comment in the area.

Recommended further reading is given at the end of each chapter. The more general texts are listed in the **Selected bibliography** at the end of the book on p. 249.

2

Burden and standard of proof; presumptions

Introduction

The allocation of the burden of proof in both civil and criminal trials depends on the decision as to who should bear the risk of losing the case. That allocation is decided by common law and by statute. In criminal trials the 'presumption of innocence' means that the burden of proof will be on the prosecution, unless this is reversed by some express or implied statutory provision. Here the law of evidence safeguards what in some other jurisdictions is a matter of individual civil rights backed up by a tenet of the constitution.

In answering questions in this area, you must understand the difference between the legal and the evidential burden and the occasions where they are separately allocated. It is helpful to see the evidential burden primarily as an aspect of the sensible proposition that there must be a degree of evidence on asserted issues before they can be a matter for the trial. It is for the judge then to decide whether the assertion can go before the jury. Thus the prosecution has to adduce enough evidence of the guilt of the accused for the judge to be satisfied that there is a case to answer. In other words, it has the evidential burden. Here, the prosecution also has the legal burden on the same matter and this is the normal state of affairs directed at convincing the jury of the defendant's guilt beyond reasonable doubt (the criminal standard). The tricky areas are those where there is a divorce of the legal and evidential burden. These arise primarily in situations where the prosecution cannot be expected to put up evidence to anticipate every specific defence the accused may present. Thus in order to plead self-defence the accused will have to provide some evidence to enable the court to consider the matter. The legal burden stays with the prosecution.

It is somewhat misleading to refer to a single burden of proof in a trial. The burden may relate to several different specific facts in issue. Burdens may be allocated between the parties in relation to these different facts in issue. This is particularly so in civil cases but may also occur in criminal cases. In civil cases the principle 'He who asserts must prove' means that the burden may shift according to who is trying to establish a relevant fact in issue. In criminal cases the presumption of innocence means that as a general principle the burden of proving *actus reus* and *mens rea* lies on the prosecution. Statutes may impliedly or expressly shift that burden, however. The enactment of the **Human Rights Act 1998** has affected the allocation of the burden of proof in criminal cases. It is arguable that to place the burden on the accused violates the presumption of innocence in **art. 6(2) of the European Convention on Human Rights**. The Strasbourg case law suggests, however, that placing the burden on the prosecution is not an absolute rule. See **Table 1**. The standard of proof is a less complex topic. In this area, as in all areas of evidence, you must be careful to apply the appropriate rules according to whether the case is a civil or a criminal one.

Presumptions can obviate the need for proof, or make the process easier; on occasions they are irrebuttable. The word presumption has been used in various ways. Evidence courses nowadays usually concentrate on what are known as 'rebuttable presumptions of law', i.e., those of death, legitimacy, marriage and here we deal only with them. Other presumptions, including 'irrebuttable presumptions of law', such as the age of criminal liability, belong more properly to the substantive law. Finally 'presumptions of fact' are really aspects of logical reasoning. Since questions on presumptions are not commonplace in Evidence examinations, only one is included here. A second is available on the website.

Example of allocation of burden of proof in a criminal case

Joan is accused of growing an illegal drug in a window box at her flat, contrary to **ss. 5 and 28 of the Misuse of Drugs Act 1971**. She pleads not guilty, arguing that she thought the plants she was growing were tomato plants since they looked similar to a picture she had in a book *Growing Tomatoes in Small Places*. See **Table** 2.

Example of allocation of burden of proof in a civil case

Cowboys Ltd are engaged to transport a racehorse, Diana, belonging to Sam Sloane. The contract specifies that Cowboys will not be liable for damage caused to Diana in transit if Sloane has not organised to have her given a clean bill of health by a veterinary surgeon before the journey. Diana dies of a heart attack during the journey. Sloane is suing Cowboys Ltd for breach of contract. Cowboys rely on the exclusion clause. See **Table** 3.

Table 1 The Human Rights Act and the burden of proof

A. Evidential and legal burden on accused

Case	Court	Statute
R v Ali and Jordan [2002] 2 AC 545 (joined with ***R v Lambert***, see later)	HL	**Homicide Act 1957 s. 2**
R v Chargot Ltd [2009] 1 WLR 1	HL	**Health and Safety at Work Act 1974 s. 40**

Case	Court	Statute
R v Johnstone [2003] 1 WLR 1736	HL	Trade Marks Act 1994 s. 92(1)(b) and s. 92(5)
Attorney General's Reference (No. 1 of 2004) [2004] 1 WLR 2111	CA	(i) **Insolvency Act 1986 s. 353** (ii) **Protection from Eviction Act 1997 s. 1(2)** (iii) **Homicide Act 1957 s. 4** (iv) **Criminal Justice and Public Order Act 1994 s. 51(1)**
L v DPP [2003] QB 13	Divisional Ct	**Criminal Justice Act 1988 s. 139(4)**
Sheldrake v DPP [2004] UKHL 43	HL	**Road Traffic Act 1988 s. 5(2)**

B. Evidential burden only on accused

R v Lambert [2002] 2 AC 545 (joined with *R v Ali and Jordan*, see earlier)	HL	**Misuse of Drugs Act 1971 s. 28(3)**
Attorney General's Reference (No. 1 of 2004) [2004] 1 WLR 2111	CA	**Insolvency Act 1986 s. 357**
Attorney General's Reference (No. 4 of 2002) [2005] 1 AC 264	HL	**Terrorism Act 2000 s. 11(1) and (2)**

Table 2 Burden of proof—criminal cases

Elements of the offence	Who has evidential burden?	Who has legal burden?	What is the standard of proof of the legal burden?
1. Possession of window-box	Prosecution	Prosecution	Beyond reasonable doubt
2. Defendant's knowledge of possession of window-box	Prosecution	Prosecution	Beyond reasonable doubt
3. Identity of plant as cannabis	Prosecution	Prosecution	Beyond reasonable doubt
4. Defendant's knowledge of identity of plants	Defence*	Prosecution*	Beyond reasonable doubt

* Following *R v Lambert* (2002).

Table 3 Burden of proof—civil cases

Fact in issue	Who has legal burden?	Who has evidential burden?	What is the standard of proof on legal burden?
Existence of contract	Sloane	Sloane	Balance of probabilities
Death of Diana	Sloane	Sloane	Balance of probabilities
Absence of veterinary surgeon's examination	Cowboys	Cowboys	Balance of probabilities

Question 1

'In order to merit its reputation as a fundamental constitutional guarantee, the presumption [of innocence] must be reasonably extensive and not too easily defeated.'

(Roberts and Zuckerman, *Criminal Evidence* (Oxford: OUP, 2010), p. 223.)

How far does the current law in this area meet the requirements set out by Roberts and Zuckerman?

Commentary

The question requires you to analyse why the presumption of innocence should be regarded as a constitutional right and how far it is safeguarded in current law. The **Human Rights Act 1998** has played a part in generating an increasingly jurisprudential approach to the law of Evidence and this question requires you to demonstrate your appreciation of the principles enshrined in the technically somewhat complex law relating to the presumption of innocence. This presumption is also fully acknowledged by the common law. Your answer will therefore have to examine the law before and after the **1998 Act** and the extent to which inroads into the presumption were and are currently allowed. You should be aware of the leading cases in this area including: *Woolmington v DPP* **[1935] AC 462**, *R v Hunt* **[1987] AC 352**, *R v Lambert, Ali and Jordan* **[2002] 2 AC 545** and *Sheldrake v DPP; Attorney General's Reference (No. 4 of 2002)* **[2005] 1 AC 264**. (See **Table 1**.)

Answer plan

- Outline the reasons why the presumption of innocence is a constitutional guarantee and why it has a place in ensuring a fair trial.
- Outline the evolution of the principle in English law demonstrating how it was never an absolute right.

- Consider the impact of the **European Convention on Human Rights** and the pragmatic approach taken in **Salabiaku** and the continuing problem of strict liability offences; see **R v G (2008)**.
- Trace the impact of the **Human Rights Act** in leading cases, e.g. **Lambert**.
- Conclude with a review of the jurisprudential issues involved such as the overlap of substantive and procedural rights, and the possibility of decriminalising regulatory offences.

 Examiner's tip

It is important that you avoid giving an answer based on a narrative account of the case law. You must try and derive an analysis of the constitutional principle of the presumption of innocence and explain the difference between a procedural and a substantive right.

 Suggested answer

A criminal conviction and subsequent state-imposed punishment subjects individuals to moral denunciation and physical hardship. The constraints imposed by the law of evidence on the trial process exist in large part to try to ensure that only the guilty are convicted and that the trial process is fair. In other words trials should have factual and moral legitimacy. The presumption of innocence is recognised in many jurisdictions as one of the most important constitutional foundations of this legitimacy. Its constitutional significance is that it recognises the vulnerability of the defendant faced with state prosecution and concomitant 'inequality of arms'. The individual liberty of the subject is safeguarded by placing the task of proving the case firmly on the prosecution. The prosecution, in other words, has the burden of proof, must carry out the task of amassing and presenting the evidence and in order to succeed has to do this to an exacting standard. The defendant is entitled to receive the benefit of reasonable doubt. The prosecution bears the risk of losing. Reference to the presumption of innocence is to be found in all major international human rights treaties but until the enactment of the **Human Rights Act 1998** its acknowledgement by English law is to be found in judicial observations. Viscount Sankey's 'golden thread' speech in **Woolmington v DPP [1935] AC 462** is one of the most celebrated passages in English criminal law: 'No matter what the charge or where the trial, the principle that the prosecution must prove the guilt of the prisoner is part of the common law of England and no attempt to whittle it down can be entertained.'

The question raises an important principled point, namely what is meant by a 'fundamental constitutional guarantee' and whether it is a procedural or a substantive right. Dennis (2005, p. 917) argues that English courts concentrate more on the effect of decisions rather than the processes of achieving them. It follows therefore that questions of moral blameworthiness should be on the prosecution.

Burden of proof not historically always on prosecution

Closer examination reveals that the *Woolmington* principle itself has never been absolute. Indeed, if it is so much part of the common law of England, it does seem strange that a trial judge and the Court of Criminal Appeal as late as the twentieth century could have made so fundamental an error as to place the burden of proving lack of *mens rea* on the defendant. In fact, the concept that the prosecution bears the legal burden on *mens rea* and *actus reus* was still somewhat undecided until the last century. For example, the common law recognised the principle that if the defendant has possession of facts known only to him, it is for the defendant to produce the relevant evidence. Furthermore, *Woolmington* itself cited exceptions to the principle, notably the common law defence of insanity and statutory reversals of the burden. The constitutional principle of parliamentary sovereignty meant that Parliament could expressly shift the burden of an element of the offence to the defendant. Research by Ashworth and Blake (1996) revealed that the 40 per cent of offences triable in the Crown Court appeared to violate the presumption of innocence by placing a legal burden of proof on the defendant or imposing a form of strict liability. Doubtless the number has much increased in the subsequent years. The justification for this is the consequentialist argument that on occasion the social good of crime reduction achieved by reducing the burden on the prosecution takes precedence over the defendant's rights. Particular controversy arose, however, over the clearer acknowledgement, post-*Woolmington*, of a third exception to the 'golden thread', namely implied statutory exceptions. Historically the starting point was what is now **s. 101 of the Magistrates' Court Act 1980**, which covers situations where a defendant relies for his defence on an 'exception, exemption, proviso, excuse or qualification' whereby specified conduct is allowed in permitted circumstances. In such situations it was for the defendant to prove that he falls within the exception, etc.

Regulatory offences

The objective of such legislation was to make it easier for the authorities to prosecute certain regulatory offences, such as driving without a licence. The approach of the courts, however, was to extend the possibility of shifting the burden to the defendant in a wider range of circumstances. This was illustrated in the landmark cases *R v Edwards* [1975] QB 27 and *R v Hunt* [1987] AC 352. In both cases it is arguable that the constitutional principle of the presumption of innocence was secondary to policy considerations. Thus in *Edwards* the Court of Appeal adopted what Stein (1991, p. 1) called a 'syntactical approach' and classified defences on their syntactical status or sectional location in the statute. It held statutes could be interpreted to have impliedly shifted the burden for trials on indictment as well as summary offences, and that where the burden shifted it would be the legal, not simply the evidential, burden. One safeguard was that the standard imposed on the defendant was only the balance of probabilities. In the subsequent case of *Hunt* the House of Lords set out more fully the circumstances in which the courts would interpret legislation as permitting placing the legal burden on the defendant. Stein (1991) points out that the House of Lords in *Hunt*, while upholding *Edwards*, saw the issue as more complex. Attention should be paid not only to the linguistic structure of the Act but also to the mischief at which it was aimed and various practical matters which affect the burden of proof.

As regards general guidelines these were as follows. First, the courts should recognise that Parliament can never lightly be taken to have intended to shift the burden of proof onto the defendant. Secondly, a factor of great importance was the ease or difficulty that parties met in discharging the probative burden. Here the courts drew on the House of Lords decision in *Nimmo v Alexander Cowan & Sons Ltd* [1968] AC 107, where the plaintiff employer was allocated the burden of proof on the issue of whether it was 'reasonably practicable' to observe health and safety standards. Finally, the gravity of the offence should be borne in mind.

In *Hunt* itself the House of Lords reversed the Court of Appeal and held that on the proper construction of the statute, the composition of the alleged prohibited drug was an element of the offence which the prosecution should prove. However, a number of critics, while applauding the actual decision, pointed out its dangerous implications. By abdicating on the matter of principle the House arguably opened the door to serious inroads on the presumption of innocence. In cases of ambiguity in the statute, instead of relying unequivocally on the presumption of innocence, their Lordships were prepared only to see the necessity of avoiding the imposition of 'onerous burdens' on the defendant.

Human Rights Act

If *Hunt* and *Edwards* marked a retreat from constitutional principle then the **Human Rights Act 1998** clearly signalled a return and, as Roberts and Zuckerman advocate, the courts have set clearer limits to the shifting of the burden in interpreting statutes. The Act requires the courts to take account of the Strasbourg jurisprudence in interpreting legislation. The outcome has been to a large extent a return to the *Woolmington* principled approach. This has been examined by the House of Lords in several landmark cases. First, in *R v DPP, ex parte Kebilene* [2000] 2 AC 326 the House of Lords was asked to consider, inter alia, whether **s. 16A of the Prevention of Terrorism (Temporary Provisions) Act 1989** violated the principle of the presumption of innocence guaranteed by **art. 6(2) of the European Convention on Human Rights**. It held that it was open to the accused on a prosecution under that section to argue that no more than an evidential presumption had been raised which could be displaced by the raising of a reasonable doubt as to guilt rather than a reverse onus of persuading the jury as to guilt or innocence. Lords Cooke, Hope and Hobhouse held that it was open to argument that **art. 6(2)**, although expressed in absolute terms, was not to be regarded as imposing an absolute prohibition on reverse onus provisions. The House considered some of the Strasbourg cases which indicated that reverse onus of proof provisions are not necessarily a violation of the Convention. In *Salabiaku v France* (1988) 13 EHRR 379, for example, the Strasbourg Court accepted that there was no objection in principle to the operation of strict liability in criminal law. However, it clearly indicated that a powerful consideration will be the question of proportionality since presumptions of fact or law were not to be regarded with indifference in criminal cases. States should confine them within reasonable limits which take into account the importance of what is at stake and maintain the rights of the defence. In *Kebilene* Lord Bingham in the Divisional Court had held that **s. 16A of the 1989 Act** undermined in a blatant and obvious way the presumption of innocence. Although the House of Lords did not pronounce on the matter in *Kebilene*, it is clear that courts will have now to weigh a number of considerations in applying statutes which appear to place the onus of proof on the defendant. Following *Hunt* they were not restricted to the form or wording of the statutory provision but must consider also policy matters. *Pepper v Hart* [1993] **1 All ER 42**, of course, allows recourse to Hansard as a means of statutory interpretation. The **Human Rights Act** has now, however, reasserted the *Woolmington* principle. In the **Terrorism Act 2000**, replacing the **1989 Act**, Parliament, by **s. 118**, converted some but not all reverse legal burdens in the Act to evidential burdens.

R v Lambert (2001)

This is even clearer in the second of this series of House of Lords cases namely, *R v Lambert, R v Ali, R v Jordan* [2002] 2 AC 545. By a majority of four to one the House decided that in the context of reverse burdens of proof, 'prove' in a statute could be interpreted as imposing an 'evidential burden'. Lord Steyn, in giving the majority judgment, stated that 'legislative interference with the presumption of innocence requires justification and must not be freer than necessary. The principle of proportionality must be observed.' A transfer of the legal burden would amount to a disproportionate interference with the presumption of innocence. Ashworth (2001, p. 865) favourably contrasted *Lambert* with that of the Strasbourg Court in *Salabiaku v France* (1988) 13 EHRR 379. In the latter case the Court accepted that legislatures may reverse the burden of proof 'within reasonable limits which take into account the importance of what is at stake and maintain the rights of the defence.' Ashworth comments that it 'must be said that the Strasbourg jurisprudence on **art. 6(2)** is underdeveloped, not to say flaccid, and it is British judges, taking their cue from Commonwealth constitutional courts, who have sought to give greater sharpness to the right and any exceptions.'

In *R v Johnstone* [2003] UKHL 28 the House of Lords gave fuller guidance on reverse burden provisions. They were permitted so long as they were confined within reasonable limits that took account of the importance of what was at stake and maintained the rights of the defence. The case involved an offence under **s. 92(6) of the Trade Marks Act 1994** and the section concerned with the burden of proof read, 'it is a defence for a person charged with an offence under this section to show that he believed on reasonable grounds that the use of the sign in the manner in which it was used, or was to be used, was not an infringement of the registered trademark.' Lord Nicholls gave the majority judgment, cited a number of policy reasons why there should be a legal burden on the case and also identified **s. 92** as imposing an offence of almost strict liability. Subsequent case law has demonstrated that the courts place much importance on the nature of the offence and are more ready to allow a shift of the burden in the case of regulatory offences. Reverse legal burdens were probably justified if the overall burden remained on the prosecution but Parliament had for significant reasons concluded that it was fair and reasonable to make an exception in respect of a particular aspect of the offence (*Attorney General's Reference (No. 1 of 2004)* [2004] EWCA 1125). However, Parliament's intentions may be disregarded if the fairness of the trial is threatened (*Attorney General's Reference (No. 4 of 2002)* [2004] UKHL 43). In the latter case there was no doubt that Parliament in the **Terrorism Act** intended to shift the legal burden but 'it was not the intention of Parliament in the **1998 Act**' (para. 51) and the House imposed only an evidential burden on the accused. It held that both *Lambert* and *Johnstone* were leading cases on reverse burdens and that, despite the statement of Lord Woolf in *Attorney General's Reference (No. 1 of 2004)*, *Johnstone* did not depart from *Lambert*.

Uncertainty

Lambert itself left a number of unanswered questions. First, Lord Hutton argued in a powerful dissenting speech that the effect of upholding the defendant's right was to endanger society. Defendants would now easily be able to raise defences under the statute. He stated that 'the threat of drugs to the well-being of the community and the peculiar difficulty of proving knowledge in such cases justifies an exception to the general principles . . . In my opinion, it is not unprincipled to have regard to practical realities where the issue relates to knowledge in a drugs case.'

Secondly, the law is left in a state of some uncertainty. As Munday argues (2011, p. 110) 'One ought not to run away with the idea that *Lambert* and subsequent decisions has led to wholesale abandonment of the idea that Parliament can legitimately cast a legal burden of proof on a defendant.' He pointed out that in *L v DPP* [2003] QB 137 the Divisional Court interpreted **s. 139(4) of the Criminal Justice Act 1988** as amended as placing a legal burden on the accused 'to prove that he had good reason or lawful authority for having [an offensive weapon] with him in a public place.' This interpretation struck the correct balance between protecting society on the one hand and the rights of the defendant on the other. Here, by contrast to *Lambert*, derogation from the principle of the presumption of innocence was acceptable. As Munday (2011, p. 114) commented; 'whenever construing a statutory provision that would purport to impose a legal burden of proof upon a defendant, the court will find itself wandering in Tennyson's "wilderness of single instances (see *Aylmer's Field*)".' It is difficult to square the uncertainty generated by the decisions in these cases in relation to allocating the burden of proof with the need for a recognition of a degree of absolutism in discussing constitutional principles. As Tausz and Ashworth (2005, p. 219) observe, 'The only certainty is that courts should use s3 of the Human Rights Act 1998 fully, and should not defer to the intention of Parliament, least of all where there is no evidence that the legislature had the presumption of innocence in mind.'

Substantive or procedural right?

On the other hand, some commentators argue that too robust an attachment to applying the presumption of innocence can make for a poor constitutional outcome. For example, Roberts and Zuckerman (2010, pp. 286–287) comment that by using, as they did in *Lambert*, art. 6(2) to apply to affirmative defences as if they were elements of the offence, the courts are opening the door to Parliament extending the ambit of strict liability offences. They write, 'Rewriting criminal prohibitions under the aegis of **Article 6(2)** is neither transparent nor predictable. If the courts routinely blur the conceptual distinction between affirmative criminal law defences and onus-reversing evidentiary presumptions, treating both as equally amenable to **Article 6(2)** analysis, Parliament is unlikely to reform its bad habits of loose drafting or try harder to be more careful in its use of statutory language.' Roberts is critical of the reasoning in *Lambert*. He commented (2002(a), p. 36) that the courts were in effect using the evidential principle of the presumption of innocence to undermine the substantive law in relation to strict liability offences. There is a clash of the two constitutional principles, parliamentary sovereignty and the presumption of innocence. Roberts argued that the legislative precursors of the **1971 Act** created absolute liabilities for possessing drugs and that this was 'wholly dispositive' of art. 6(2) issues.

Moreover, there are limitations to the application of *Lambert* and the acknowledgement of art. 6 rights particularly if the relevant statute appears to be upholding art. 8 rights. Emson (2010, p. 62) is critical of the restrictive and deferential position of the English courts in relation to strict liability and suggests they are not upholding the rights of the defence to the extent that even *Salabiaku* does. He cites the case of *R v G* **[2008] 1 WLR 1379** where a 15-year-old defendant was convicted of the statutory rape of a child under 13 contrary to **s. 5 of the Sexual Offences Act 2003**. It had been accepted that the girl told him she was 15. The House of Lords held that strict liability offences could not be challenged under **art. 6(2)** since the article concerned procedural matters not the substantive law. The Strasbourg Court ruled a referral inadmissible. Ashworth (2012) comments that the 'permissible limits' which in *Salabiaku* are proper for strict liability are left unclearly defined. He is also critical of the judgment in that it cited the **art. 6** rights of the victim but not the child defendant who arguably would have been better prosecuted under the less serious charge in **s. 9 of the Sexual Offences Act 2003**. Ashworth (2006) had called for an application to the substantive law of the principle that there should be no criminal liability without fault.

Parliament and the courts

These observations illustrate the difficulty of deciding the parameters of a 'fundamental constitutional guarantee' and that the courts have not taken an absolutist stance. They have been prepared, however, on occasion to depart from the intention of Parliament, which does suggest that the presumption of innocence may override the popular will. The constitutional significance of the presumption of innocence was at the heart of Lord Bingham's rejection of the Court of Appeal's reasoning and refusal to accept the ten guiding principles in *Attorney- General's Reference (No. 1 of 2004)*, case conjoined with *Sheldrake v DPP* [2004] 1 AC 264. As Tausz and Ashworth (2005, p. 218) comment, there 'Lord Bingham expressly rejected one of the less satisfactory principles, the assumption that Parliament would not have made an exception (to the presumption of innocence) without good reason.' Lord Bingham stated (para. 9) that '. . . it is repugnant to ordinary notions of fairness for a prosecutor to accuse a defendant of crime and for the defendant to be then required to disprove the accusation on pain of conviction and punishment if he fails to do so.'

This principled approach was followed by the Court of Appeal in *R v Keogh* [2007] 1 WLR 1500. There the reverse-onus defences in **ss. 2(3) and 3(4) of the Official Secrets Act 1989** were interpreted to apply only to the evidential burden.

Thus in English law, as in the Strasbourg jurisprudence, the presumption of innocence is not quite an absolute. In *Lambert*, however, the Court moved closer to the *Woolmington* principle by requiring close examination of all statutory reverse onus provisions. But reverse onus provisions will still exist either by virtue of unambiguous wording of the statute or judicial interpretation of ambiguous statutes. As the analysis has shown, the current position has left some uncertainty and theoretical incoherence. One way forward suggested by Roberts and Zuckerman (2010, p. 289) is a 'planned programme of de-criminalisation' of the regulatory offences which are most often at issue in this area of statutory interpretation. Such criticisms are endorsed by Padfield (2005). The legal landscape in relation to the presumption of innocence thus demonstrates that the position advocated by Roberts and Zuckerman is difficult to achieve. The courts and Parliament, particularly by the mechanism of separating the evidential and legal burdens on occasion, acknowledge that public policy considerations impact on constitutional rights to a fair trial.

The presumption of innocence, together with the high standard of proof required, is generally regarded as a necessary right, safeguarding the citizen against an all-powerful state. This account has illustrated, however, that it is also accepted that there may be compromises to this principle. Some parts of the burden may be shifted to the defendant in some cases. This has been imposed by both Parliament and the judges. In *Lambert* the House of Lords, stretching the linguistic interpretation somewhat, signalled a return to the principled approach of *Woolmington* away from the pragmatism of *Hunt*. The principles should, the majority held, not be easily defeated. Public interest arguments for the opposite stance did not prevail, a stance that showed more respect for the presumption of innocence than Strasbourg showed in *Salabiaku*. However, principle and pragmatism currently go hand in hand, creating what Roberts and Zuckerman have called (2010, p. 281) a 'blizzard of single instances'.

Question 2

Answer all parts:

(a) Harry is refused entrance to a nightclub by a bouncer called George. A scuffle breaks out and George suffers a broken nose. Harry is prosecuted for assault and claims that George struck the first blow. In her summing up the judge says, 'Ladies and gentlemen of the jury you have heard the defendant claim that he acted in self-defence. It is for the prosecution to prove however that he did not act in self-defence.'

Comment on the judge's summing-up.

(b) 'Are we to infer that *M'Naghten* (and *Woolmington*) have been overruled, to the extent that the accused no longer has to prove insanity (on the balance of probabilities) but only to raise enough evidence to pass the judge?'

> (P. Roberts, 'Criminal Procedure, Drug Dealing and the Presumption of Innocence: The Human Rights Act (Almost) Bites' (2002) 6(2) *International Journal of Evidence and Proof* 17 at p. 37.)

Comment.

(c) Janet is facing two charges under the (imaginary) Tenant Protection Act 2010. Section 1(1) reads 'it is an offence to include car parking space in the tenancy except where the landlord has a licence from the local authority'. Section 1(2) reads: 'it is an offence for a landlord to enter a tenanted room after 10.00 p.m. without permission from the tenant and without a reasonable excuse'. The prosecution allege that Janet let a parking space to her tenant Zara without a licence. They also allege that Janet entered the flat of her tenant Abdul while he was away and without his permission at 2.00 a.m. Janet claims she had an anonymous phone call about a smoke alarm.

Advise Janet on the burden and standard of proof on both these charges.

 Commentary

These three questions require you to be familiar with situations where the burden of proof may shift in criminal trials. You will need some knowledge of the evolution of the law in this area and the impact of recent case law under the **Human Rights Act 1998**. You must be careful to use the correct terminology and in particular to understand the difference between the legal and the evidential burdens. The legal burden is the obligation placed on a party to prove a fact in issue, whereas the evidential burden (the 'burden of passing the judge') is that placed on a party to adduce sufficient evidence on a fact which is asserted for it to become an issue in the trial. There is a significant amount of academic literature in this area and your answers would be improved by familiarity with it.

 Answer plan

(a) This part requires an outline of the evidential rules concerning a claim of self-defence.

- Trace the common law position through the case law.
- Distinguish the evidential and legal burdens and the standard of proof in both.

(b) In this article Paul Roberts is critical of the logic behind the majority ruling of the House of Lords in ***Lambert***. He outlines the uncertainties it has created in the law over reverse onus clauses, including the defence of insanity.

- State the **Woolmington** position on insanity.
- Discuss the potential impact of the **Human Rights Act** in this area.
- Law Commission reform proposals.

(c) Your answer requires knowledge of the nature of implied statutory exceptions in relation to the burden of proof. The law in this area has been dominated by the cases of **R v Hunt** and **R v Edwards**. In your answer you should demonstrate an academic knowledge of the historical development of the law but concentrate on giving practical advice in the light of some more recent cases since 2000. It is important to show you understand that there may be several elements to an offence and the allocation of the legal and evidential burdens of proof will not be the same for all of them.

- Identify the elements of the *actus reus*.
- Refer to **s. 101 of the Magistrates' Court Act**, **Hunt** and **Edwards**.
- Assess the impact of the **Human Rights Act** and the possibility of construing a statutory provision to place an evidential burden on the defendant.
- Show some familiarity with relevant recent case law, **Sheldrake v DPP [2004] 3 WLR 976** and **L v DPP [2003] QB 13**.

Suggested answer

(a) Comment on the judge's summing-up

The judge in her summing-up has directed the jury's attention to Harry's use of self-defence based on the common law. It is a well-established principle that the prosecution does not have to anticipate every claim the defendant makes. If the defendant wishes to plead self-defence then he must adduce sufficient evidence to convince the judge that this can be a live issue at the trial. In other words the defendant has what is popularly known as the evidential burden. As Roberts (2002(a), p. 34) points out the 'evidential burden is not a burden of proof at all, but only a burden of adducing evidence'. The judge therefore does not have to refer to the evidential burden in her summing-up because it is not a matter for the jury at all. Here the judge is correct to point out that the legal burden remains with the prosecution on this issue (*Lobell* [1957] 1 QB 547). A failure to do this could lead to an appeal (*R v Moon* [1969] 1 WLR 1705). More recently in *R v O'Brien* [2004] EWCA Crim 2900 the Court of Appeal held that a failure by the judge to direct the jury that it was the task of the prosecution to prove the defendant was not acting in self-defence was 'an important misdirection in relation to a very significant aspect of the law of self-defence'. In the question set there is no reference to the standard of proof in the summing-up. There is considerable case law on the words judges should use in directing juries on the standard of proof. Where the prosecution bears the legal burden the standard of proof required for conviction is beyond reasonable doubt. The Judicial Studies Board has drafted a model direction as follows:

> How does the prosecution succeed in proving the defendant's guilt? The answer is—by making you sure of it. Nothing less than that will do. If after considering all the

evidence you are sure that the defendant is guilty you must return a verdict of 'Guilty'. If you are not sure your verdict must be 'Not Guilty' (www.jsbni.com/Publications/BenchBookRevisedApr2010.doc).

The judge would therefore be expected to include in her summing-up a direction along those lines. The Court of Appeal has over the years pronounced on unacceptable judicial directions in this area. In *R v Yap Chuan Ching* (1976) 63 Cr App R 7, 11 Lawton LJ observed that 'if judges stopped trying to define that which is almost impossible to define there would be fewer appeals'. In this case, however, the Appeal Court stated that judges should avoid defining 'reasonable doubt'. Lord Denning in *Miller v Minister of Pensions* [1947] 2 All ER 372, 373 gave a celebrated definition:

> Proof beyond reasonable doubt does not mean proof beyond a shadow of a doubt. The law would fail to protect the community if it admitted to fanciful possibilities to deflect the course of justice. If the evidence is so strong against a man as to leave one a remote possibility in his favour which can be dismissed with the sentence, 'of course it is possible, but not in the least probable,' the case is proved beyond reasonable doubt but nothing short of that will suffice.

Thus the judge's summing-up in this instance is correct on the burden of proof but incomplete on the question of the standard of proof.

(b) Proof of insanity

The classic common law summary of the burden of proof in criminal cases is given in *Woolmington*. Lord Sankey identified two exceptions to the placing of the burden of proof on the prosecution, namely statutory exceptions and that created in *M'Naghten's Case* (1843) 10 Cl & Fin 200. The latter specifies that where the defendant in a murder trial makes a plea of insanity the burden of proving insanity is on him.

The quotation in this question acknowledges the importance of this exception to the 'golden rule' while at the same time acknowledging its status may be under threat from current judicial attitudes. To take the first point it is salutary to realise that, as Roberts and Zuckerman point out, the insanity exception is 'of limited practical significance' (2010, p. 266). They point out that a finding of 'not guilty by reason of insanity' meant 'mandatory detention in a secure hospital', and although other sentencing options are now available, 'a plea of insanity remains an unattractive option for most accused, and the defence is seldom raised'.

In the article cited in the question, however, Roberts goes further by outlining the shaky intellectual basis for the exception. The House of Lords in *Lambert*, argues Roberts, is close to saying that the only burdens on the defence should be evidential ones. He finds the reasoning in this case doctrinally incoherent, 'with scant regard for established evidentiary concepts and taxonomies'. In particular he criticises the judgment because the analysis fails to acknowledge the conclusive nature of the specific statutory section, namely that it creates an offence of strict liability and therefore the discussion on burden of proof in relation to guilty knowledge is theoretically incoherent.

This approach leads Roberts to speculate about the possible implications for other seemingly entrenched doctrines, including the burden of proof on an insanity defence.

He mentions that the Canadian courts have re-examined the approach to this in the light of fair trial right considerations, although this is not specifically included in the House of Lords' *Lambert* ruling. Roberts points out, however, that the Canadian courts have acknowledged that the traditional reverse onus clause in relation to insanity was upheld as a justifiable derogation from the presumption of innocence under the general saving clause, **s. 1 of the Canadian Charter of Rights and Freedoms**. He adds that there is no comparable provision in **art. 6 of the European Convention on Human Rights**.

In short, Roberts is arguing that the implications of the *Lambert* judgment are far-reaching. Although putting an evidential burden rather than a legal burden on the defence might be welcome from a human rights standpoint, the uncertainty and intellectual confusion the judgment has prompted is troubling.

In fact, since Roberts penned this observation the courts have retreated somewhat from an overly robust readiness to refuse to interpret reverse onus clauses so that the legal burden is not placed on the defence and have adopted a case-by-case approach. This, however, succeeds only in perpetuating the uncertainty, as a number of commentators have pointed out (Choo (2012, p. 36) for example, comments in relation to the leading case *Sheldrake v DPP; Attorney General's Reference (No. 4 of 2002)* [2005] 9 1 AC 264 that it has 'served to bring the problem of uncertainty and unpredictability into even sharper focus').

With regard to the principled question in relation to insanity, namely should the burden of proof be on the defendant, it is certainly arguable that the *M'Naghten* decision itself is a historical anomaly and is arguably difficult to justify in the light of **art. 6** provisions. The European Court of Human Rights has held, however, that the rule does not violate the presumption of innocence, *H v UK* **(1990) App No 15023/89**. Jones (1995, p. 475), however, cites arguments that the burden on the defence should be evidential only. Jones acknowledges that the courts are just as concerned with social protection as they are with issues of individual fairness or responsibility and that 'there is a constant tension between these two competing values, which goes some way to explaining (but not justifying) the complexities and paradoxes which pervade this area of law'. The Law Commission has produced a draft report on the issue, the *Draft Criminal Code: Criminal Liability and Mental Disorder* (2002). It proposed that the general law relating to mental illness should be rationalised and a new term 'mental disorder' should replace 'insanity'. The burden of proving the defence would remain on the accused on the balance of probabilities.

Loughran (2007) has suggested that a concept of 'manifest madness' may provide a theoretical frame for interpreting the evidentiary and procedural aspect of the defence. She suggests that the defence is in effect limited to cases where the madness is encoded in the defendant's acts and its nature is intelligible to lay observers.

(c) Express and implied statutory exceptions

The elements of the first offence are letting a parking space for a tenant without a licence. The courts will be likely to consider this scenario as being covered by **s. 101 of the Magistrates' Courts Act 1980**. This provides that 'where the defendant to an information or complaint relies for his defence on any exception, exemption, excuse or qualification, whether or not it accompanies the description of the offence or matter of complaint in the enactment creating the offence or on which the complaint is founded, the burden of proving the exception, exemption, proviso, excuse or qualification shall be on him, and this notwithstanding that the information or complaint contains an allegation negativing the exception, exemption, proviso, excuse or qualification'. Janet should be advised that it is immaterial in relation to this provision whether the trial takes place in the magistrates' court or the Crown Court. It is a fundamental rule that the burden of proving the defendant's guilt rests on the Crown which will have to prove the *actus reus* of letting the car parking space and, presumptively, the *mens rea* of doing it knowingly. Janet should be advised, however, that the court is likely to decide that she has the burden of proving the existence of a licence rather than the prosecution its non-existence. The use of the word 'except' clearly signals that the existence of the licence would be an 'excuse', 'proviso' or 'exception' which would provide a defence to criminal liability. Janet will have to prove the existence of the licence on the balance of probabilities.

The wording of the second offence brings into play the possibility of an alternative statutory construction. The court will examine whether 'without reasonable excuse' constitutes an exception which must be proved by the defendant. On its face the statute is not apparently worded to clearly indicate that **s. 101 of the Magistrate's Courts Act 1980** should apply. The leading cases of *Hunt* and *Edwards* indicate a move away from an overly semantic or grammatical approach to statutory interpretation to one where police considerations apply. Following the **Human Rights Act 1998** the courts will apply a series of tests to decide if a reversal of the burden of proof in a statute is a proportionate response. In *Sheldrake v DPP* [2005] 1 AC 264, the House of Lords examined the status of the burden of proof in a case involving the application of the **Road Traffic Act 1988**. At issue was whether, where the defendant was on trial for being in charge of a car while intoxicated, the defence under s. 5(2) placed the burden on him or on the prosecution. The defence was held to be available on proof that there was no likelihood of the defendant driving his car. In giving the lead judgment, Lord Bingham referred to Lord Griffith's statement in *R v Hunt*. This stated that if the statute was unclear the court should look to other considerations to determine the intention of Parliament. These included the mischief at which the Act was aimed and practical considerations affecting the burden of proof including the ease or difficulty the parties would find in discharging the burden. In *Sheldrake* the House placed the burden on the defendant. In *L v DPP* [2002] QB 13 the Divisional Court interpreted **s. 139(4) of the Criminal Justice Act 1988** so as to place the legal burden on the accused to prove he had a good reason or lawful authority as a defence to a charge under s. 139(1). The *actus reus* was having a bladed article in his possession in a public place. The prosecution had to prove possession, and that the accused knew he had the relevant article. The court agreed that there was a strong public interest in suppressing this crime. The accused was being asked to prove something within his knowledge. Placing the burden on him as a proportionate response which maintained the balance between the public interest and individual rights. The prosecution will argue therefore that Janet should have the burden since the existence of the phone call was within her knowledge and there was a strong public interest in protecting the privacy of tenants. The offence appears to be a regulatory one, not one where there would be limited moral opprobrium. Even if there is moral blameworthiness the prosecution may additionally rely on *R v Johnstone* [2003] UKHL 28 and *R v Davies* [2002] EWCA Crim 2949, CA. In those cases the perpetrator engaged in a regulated activity but there was some element of moral blame-worthiness, such as breaching the **Trade Marks Act 1994.** Dennis (2005, p. 920) analyses these cases as involving the 'voluntary acceptance of risk' principle where the alleged offender obtained a benefit and so he, not the prosecution, should prove exculpation from the apparently wrongful acts. Janet as landlord gets to inspect her property by breaching the time regulation. On the other hand Janet may rely on *R v Charles* [2010] **Crim LR 303.** The case turned on the interpretation of **s. 1(10) of the Crime and Disorder Act 1998** which provided that 'if without reasonable excuse a person does anything which he is prohibited from doing by an anti-social behaviour order, he is guilty of an offence . . .' The Court of Appeal held that the prosecution must prove a breach of the order to the criminal standard. If the defendant raises the evidential issue of reasonable excuse it is for the prosecution to prove lack of reasonable excuse. Not all of the require-ments under an ASBO were criminal offences and the court held that Parliament could not have intended to put the burden of proof on the defendant in **s. 1(10)** which crimi-nalised conduct that Parliament had not criminalised. The statute in question here does not expressly create an 'excuse', 'proviso' or 'exception'. The court will be likely to take a pragmatic approach and hold that placing the legal burden on Janet would embrace conduct that would be very broad in nature and undermine the fairness of the trial. Placing the evidential burden only on Janet would preserve the *Woolmington* principle.

If the legal burden is placed on the defence, the standard of proof will be the balance of probabilities.

? Question 3

The owners of Legacy Athletics Arena (LAA) are suing Arnold, a former employee.

They claim that he took away a sports bag of equipment when he left their employment. Arnold defends the claim for fraudulent conversion and relies on a clause in his contract which exempted him from liability for returning the sports bag provided he had introduced 20 new members to the LAA in the 12 months before his employment ended.

In a separate action the chief officer of police has applied for a civil banning order under the (imaginary) Athletics Arenas Protection Act 2012 under which spectators may be banned from attending athletics meetings if there is reasonable cause to suspect that a banning order will help prevent disorder or violence. Arnold has just been convicted of sending threatening offensive tweets to members of a team visiting the LAA for a competition.

Advise the parties on burden and standard of proof in the civil proceedings.

Commentary

Questions on the burden and standard of proof in civil cases do not raise as many controversies as those in criminal cases. The simplest approach is to realise that the burden generally lies on the party who pleads an issue. Three problematic issues arise here: the first is whether the principle that the standard of proof in civil proceedings still applies when there is an allegation of a quasi-criminal nature. The LAA are alleging fraudulent retention by Arnold of property not owned by him. Secondly there is the issue of the burden in the exemption clause and its proviso. This will arguably shift from one to the other as assertion meets counter-assertion. The third issue concerns the application for a banning order which will be made in a civil court. but the question arises as to whether this is akin to a number of exceptions to the principle of the standard of proof being the balance of probabilities.

Answer plan

- General principle in civil cases, he who asserts must prove. The LAA has the burden on the issue of the removal of the bag. Arnold has the burden of proving his defence and that he falls within the exemption clause (see ***Munro Brice and Co. v War Risks Association*** **[1918] 2 KB 78**); both burdens are legal and evidential.
- A case may be decided on burden of proof—***Rhesa Shipping Co. SA v Edmunds*** **[1985] 1 WLR 948**.
- General rule that civil standard of proof is balance of probabilities. Examine cases where quasi-criminal accusation is made in a civil case; despite some deviation from balance of probabilities the House of Lords has decided there is no third standard—***Re B (Children) FC*** **[2008] UKHL 35**.

Examiner's tip

This is a problem question and you are not asked to comment on the strength or weakness of the law. It would gain you no marks therefore to discuss possible reform proposals here.

Suggested answer

Burden and standard of proof on fraudulent conversion claim

The general principle in civil litigation is that the burden of proof lies on the asserter of a claim. The incidence of the legal burden of proof will decide the outcome of the case if the tribunal is not able to come to a decision which to prefer. In ***Rhesa Shipping Co. SA v Edmunds*** [1985] 1 WLR 948 the House of Lords, overturning the Court of Appeal, held that the judge had not been obliged to choose between two versions merely because the defendants had chosen to put forward their explanation of events.

It is thus for the LAA to prove the removal of the sports bag. The incidence of the burden is thus here a matter of substantive law and the House of Lords held that it is usually clear from the pleadings: *Wilsher v Essex Area Health Authority* [1988] AC 1074. The LAA therefore have the legal burden of proof on this issue. They also have the evidential burden in the sense that they must put in some evidence to convince the court there is a case to answer. Arnold may simply deny liability but he runs the risk tactically of losing. He appears, however, to be putting up a specific defence, namely that the sports bag was due to him for introducing new members to the LAA. He has the legal and evidential burden of mounting this defence and the standard of proof is on the balance of probabilities. There is a possible further consideration in that the LAA are alleging that Arnold held the bag fraudulently.

The Bar's Code of Conduct provides that counsel may not draft an allegation of fraud without specific instructions and unless he or she has reasonably credible material which, as it stands, establishes a prima facie case of fraud.

There have been some examples in civil cases where courts have held that certain matters must be proved to the criminal standard of proof, in *Re a Solicitor* [1992] QB 69 for example. The issue was the standard of proof in a case before a solicitors' disciplinary tribunal, where allegations of professional misconduct were made. The Divisional Court held that since what was alleged was tantamount to a criminal offence the criminal standard should apply. However, this has not been generally followed. In *Hornal v Neuberger Products Ltd* [1957] 1 QB 247, a case involving an allegation of fraudulent misrepresentation, the Court of Appeal rejected the view that there was a higher standard necessary than balance of probability but rather puzzlingly commented per Denning LJ at p. 258 'the more serious the allegation the higher the degree of probability that is required' and per Morris LJ at p. 266 'the very elements of gravity become a part of the whole range of circumstances which have to be weighed in the scale when deciding as to the balance of probabilities.' In *Re H and Others (Minors) (Sexual Abuse: Standard of Proof)* [1996] AC 563 the House of Lords in a majority decision rejected the concept of a third standard in civil cases of this sort.

The issue seems to have been conclusively settled by subsequent House of Lords decisions, see *Re B (Children)* [2008] UKHL 35. On the facts as they are given here it is likely that the position stated in *Re B* should be applied and that the standard of proof required will be on the balance of probabilities but that cogent evidence of Arnold's alleged fraud will be required.

As regards the exclusion clause it is for Arnold to prove the bag falls within the exemption clause, although this is a matter of construction for the court: *Munro Brice and Co. v War Risks Association* [1918] 2 KB 78. However, it is arguable that if a claimant relies upon a proviso to an exemption clause the burden of proving that the facts fall within the proviso may be on the claimant: *The Glendarroch* [1894] P 226. Arnold may argue by analogy with this reasoning that the LAA will have to prove that he did not secure 20 new members.

Athletics Banning Order

The application for a banning order will take place in a civil court but the question is whether the (imaginary) Athletics Arenas Protection Act 2012 is analogous to those statutes where the courts have held that a standard of proof which is in effect identical to the criminal standard applies. Thus, for example, in *R (McCann) v Crown Court at Manchester* [2003] 1 AC 787 the House of Lords held that applications for anti-social behaviour orders under **s. 1(1)(a) of the Crime and Disorder Act 1998** should only be made where the preliminary conditions had been proved beyond reasonable doubt. See also *Gough v Chief Constable of the Derbyshire Constabulary* [2002] QB 1213 in relation to football banning orders under **s. 14B of the Football Spectators Act 1989.** It is likely that the banning order will only be made against Arnold if it can be proved beyond reasonable doubt that he is likely to cause violence. The earlier conviction will be relevant evidence.

Question 4

Jane and Harry are legally married in 1960 in Birmingham. In 1961 Harry leaves to join a revolutionary group in Bolivia, but tells Jane he will return in a year. In fact Jane does not hear from him again and in 1963 gets a letter from the group leader saying Harry has been missing for six months following an expedition against counter-revolutionaries. Jane hears no more and in 1972 marries Oliver, an older man, in Paris. In 1973 Jane gives birth to twins Barry and John and in 1975 to Margaret. In 1995 Jane and Oliver are both killed instantly in a car crash. Shortly before he was killed Oliver told John that Margaret could not be his child because he had not had intercourse with Jane for a year before her birth. At the funeral, Alan, an old college friend of Jane and Harry's, who has been out of touch for years, tells John that he saw Harry in a cafe in La Paz in 1971 but says Harry disappeared before he could speak to him. Jane's will said that if she died after Oliver her estate should be divided between her children and a charity for distressed Bolivian revolutionaries. Oliver's will left all his property to his 'legitimate children'. When John and Margaret, after the car crash, look through old photographs in the attic they come across one showing Oliver and an unknown woman. On the back is noted 'Wedding day, 29 March 1969'.

Advise whether Margaret can claim under Oliver's will and whether all children can succeed under Jane's will.

Commentary

Presumptions do not figure in all evidence courses, so you should check your syllabus. This is conceptually quite a tricky area and you need to keep in mind the difference between presumptions in civil cases and criminal cases and the traditional classification of irrebuttable presumptions of law, rebuttable presumptions of law and presumptions of fact. It is mainly the second with which you need to be concerned in this question. In addition, you will need to distinguish persuasive presumptions, that is those where the effect of the presumption is to put the legal burden of disproof on the party who wishes to challenge it, and evidential presumptions where the evidential burden only is placed on the party against whom it operates. As regards criminal cases it is generally accepted that presumptions can place an evidential burden on the accused only. Thus, for example, the Privy Council held that the prosecution could not rely on the presumption of regularity in **Dillon v R [1982] AC 484**. In this question, the examiner is looking for a clear application of the law on presumptions to the facts, rather than discussion on the rationale of presumptions more appropriate to an essay question. You should begin by listing the events in chronological order and stating the relevant presumptions. In your approach to presumptions, you must first acknowledge that the primary facts must first be proved; if they are, the specific presumption must be drawn from them, although it may be rebutted by other conflicting facts. Thus you must first see if the presumptions apply and then see if they can be rebutted.

 Answer plan

- 1960 Jane and Harry marry—presumption of validity of marriage.
- 1972 Jane and Oliver marry—does presumption of Harry's death operate?
- What is the effect of the 1971 sighting of Harry? Is validity of marriage challenged by 1969 'wedding photograph' of Oliver and unknown woman?
- Does it matter marriage takes place in Paris?
- 1973 John and Barry born.
- 1975 Margaret born—presumption of legitimacy but does what Oliver told John rebut presumption of Margaret's legitimacy? Does the 'wedding photograph' affect all children's legitimacy?
- 1995 Jane and Oliver killed—presumption of order of death and effect on inheritance.

 Suggested answer

The order of death of Jane and Oliver is determined by their seniority (**Law of Property Act 1925, s. 184**, but see **Administration of Estates Act 1925, s. 46(3), Intestates' Estates Act 1952** and **Law Reform (Succession) Act 1995**). As Jane is the younger of the two, Oliver will be presumed to have died first, thus in accordance with the terms of her will her estate is divided between John, Barry and Margaret and the Bolivian charity.

Oliver's estate raises more complicated issues. John, Barry and Margaret can inherit only if they are legitimate. The validity of the marriage between Jane and Oliver could affect the legitimacy of all three. The validity of the marriage is threatened by two pieces of evidence. One is the evidence of Alan that Harry may have been alive after he was presumed to have died. The other is the photograph which suggests that Oliver was not free to marry Jane. The presumption of the validity of a marriage is a very strong one. There are two presumptions which may be operative here. On proof of the celebration of a marriage ceremony, that is one which is capable of producing a valid marriage, the law will presume the formal validity of the marriage, that is to say that the formalities have been complied with. The primary facts thus are the evidence of the ceremony that is valid according to local law. In *Mahadervan v Mahadervan* [1964] P 233 it was argued that the presumption did not apply in favour of a foreign marriage but Sir Jocelyn Simon P said (at p. 247):

> To accept it would give expression to a legal chauvinism that has no place in any rational system of private international law. Our courts in my view apply exactly the same weight of presumption in favour of a foreign marriage as of an English one, and the nationality of any later marriage brought into question is quite immaterial.

It is not significant therefore that the marriage took place in Paris.

This presumption is a persuasive one and there is a legal burden on the party seeking to rebut formal validity. The standard of proof to be met by that party is high. In *Mahadervan* Sir Jocelyn Simon P held that the presumption can only be rebutted by evidence which establishes beyond reasonable doubt that there was no marriage.

On proof of the celebration of a marriage ceremony, relying on the same primary facts, the 'essential validity' of the marriage will be assumed. This is that the parties had the necessary capacity of marrying and that their respective consents were genuine. There appears to be little doubt about the formal validity of the marriage of Jane and Oliver: the issue is its essential validity, in other words, were the parties free to marry? Again in civil proceedings the presumption is persuasive rather than an evidential presumption, but the standard of proof is lower than that in the case of the presumption of formal validity. In *Re Peete, Peete v Crompton* [1952] 2 All ER 599 the issue arose as to the essential validity of a formally valid marriage in 1919. There was some evidence of the existence of an earlier marriage and the presumption of validity of the 1919 marriage failed. Even so, the photograph in itself is unlikely to be sufficient evidence to undermine the presumption that Oliver was free to marry Jane.

The issue whether Jane was free to marry is more complicated. Evidently, she relied on the presumption that Harry was dead when she went through the ceremony with Oliver. The rules relating to presumption of death were set out in *Chard v Chard* [1956] P 259. Harry is presumed dead when four circumstances apply: there is no acceptable evidence that he has been alive for at least seven continuous years; there are persons likely to have heard of him, had he been alive; who during that period have not so heard; all due enquiries have failed to locate him. We aren't told whether Jane made enquiries about Harry after his disappearance, but assuming she did she was entitled to presume his death by 1970. Had she been properly advised she would have followed the special procedure laid down by **s. 19 of the Matrimonial Causes Act 1973**, petitioning for a decree dissolving the marriage and presuming the death of the spouse. This does not require that enquiries be made, takes no account of the likelihood that the petitioner would have heard of the person had they been alive and restricts the issue whether the petitioner had no reason to believe in the spouse's continued existence to events taking place in the last seven years.

If she had married Oliver without petitioning for a **s. 19** decree, the marriage would not necessarily have been an act of bigamy since she could still rely on the common law presumption. Those wishing to challenge the presumption will have the evidential burden. In *Prudential Assurance Co. v Edmonds* **(1877) 2 App Cas 487**, a niece standing in a crowded street in Australia had briefly caught sight of a man she recognised as her uncle. The judge had first to decide whether or not she was mistaken. If she was, it made no difference to the presumption. If she was not, the onus was on the side claiming that he was dead to establish that he was. The House of Lords held that it was for the tribunal of fact to decide whether or not to accept the niece's evidence and that if the jury had been satisfied that she was mistaken the basic facts giving rise to the presumption were established. Here Alan is available for cross-examination and the preliminary issue is ultimately one of fact.

The next issue concerns Margaret. Does what Oliver told John affect her legitimacy and claim under Oliver's will? There is a presumption that a child born to the wife in lawful wedlock and conceived while the husband was alive is legitimate. This persuasive presumption can be rebutted by evidence which shows that it is more probable than not that the person is illegitimate and it is not necessary to prove that fact beyond reasonable doubt: **Family Law Reform Act 1969, s. 26** and *S v S* **[1972] AC 24**. Oliver's remark to John (admissible under the **Civil Evidence Act 1995**; see **Chapter 5**) is evidence which might be capable of rebutting the presumption that Margaret is legitimate. The presumption is a persuasive one, so the legal burden of disproof falls on John and Barry, assuming it is they who are challenging Margaret's claim. However, against the remark should be set the provisional presumption (or presumption of fact) that sexual intercourse between husband and wife is likely to follow where opportunities for it occur. This is a weaker presumption: *Piggott v Piggott* **(1938) 61 CLR 378**, probably destroyed here by the remark itself. John and Barry have only the tactical burden of disproving it. Finally the issue might be resolved by DNA testing.

Further reading

Ashworth, A., 'Criminal Proceedings after the Human Rights Act: The First Year' [2001] Crim LR 855.

Ashworth, A., 'Four Threats to the Presumption of Innocence' (2006) 10 E & P 241.

Ashworth, A., ' Case Comment, *G v UK*' [2012] Crim LR 46.

Ashworth, A. and Blake, M., 'The Presumption of Innocence in English Criminal Law' [1996] Crim LR 306.

Ashworth, A. and Rees, T., 'Burden of Proof: Reverse Burden of Proof' [2004] Crim LR 832.

Dennis, I., 'Reverse Onuses and the Presumption of Innocence' [2005] Crim LR 901.

Dingwall, G., 'Statutory Exceptions, Burden of Proof and the Human Rights Act 1998' (2002) 65 MLR 450.

Hamer, D., 'The Presumption of Innocence and Reverse Burdens: A Balancing Act' (2007) 66 CLJ 142.

Jones, T.H., 'Insanity, Automatism and the Burden of Proof on the Accused' (1995) 111 LQR 475.

Lewis, P., 'The Human Rights Act 1998: Shifting the Burden' [2000] Crim LR 667.

Loughran, A., '"Manifest Madness": Towards a New Understanding of the Insanity Defence' (2007) 70 MLR 379.

Padfield, N., 'The Burden of Proof Unresolved' (2005) 64 CLJ 17.

Roberts, P., (a) 'Drug Dealing and the Presumption of Innocence: The Human Rights Act (almost) Bites' (2002) 6 E & P 17.

Roberts, P., (b) 'The Presumption of Innocence Brought Home? *Kebilene* Deconstructed' (2002) 118 LQR 41, Part VIII.

Smith, J.C., 'The Presumption of Innocence' (1987) 38 NILQ 223.

Stein, A., 'After *Hunt*: The Burden of Proof, Risk of Non-persuasion and Judicial Pragamatism' (1991) 54 MLR 570.

Tadros, V. and Tierney, S., 'The Presumption of Innocence and the Human Rights Act' (2004) 67 MLR 402.

Tausz, D. and Ashworth, A., 'Case Comment, *Sheldrake v DPP* [2004] UKHL 43' (2005) Crime LR 215.

3 Witnesses: competence and compellability; special measures

Introduction

Witnesses are a principal source of evidence in a trial and the rules relating to their attendance indicate their importance. The starting point is that all witnesses with relevant information are assumed to be competent to give evidence. This is now reinforced by **s. 53(1) of the Youth Justice and Criminal Evidence Act 1999 (YJCEA)**, which states that at every stage in criminal proceedings all persons are (whatever their age) competent to give evidence. Such witnesses are also usually compellable to give evidence, in that the court may summon them to attend. Other interests of the witness are secondary to the need for the court to have all the necessary information. The exceptions to compellability are predominantly to be found in criminal law.

Some witnesses who are competent may, however, claim a privilege not to give evidence; thus they are not in contempt of court if they refuse to appear or if they do appear but refuse to answer certain questions. These witnesses include defendants on their own behalf, although the evidential consequences of their failure to testify under **s. 35 of the Criminal Justice and Public Order Act 1994 (CJPOA)** should be borne in mind.

The other main group of witnesses that has to be considered is spouses or civil partners testifying for the prosecution, particularly a rule based on the rather quaint idea that any compulsion may lead to marital discord. However, lack of compellability is subject to a number of important exceptions set out in the **Police and Criminal Evidence Act 1984 (PACE), s. 80(3)**.

Tables 4 and **5** may help you remember the various permutations of the status of witnesses with regard to competence and compellability in criminal trials. Note under the **Criminal Justice Act (CJA) 2003** the defendant who elects not to testify will face the same risk of having previous convictions admitted as one who testifies (see **Chapter 4**).

Table 6 gives an outline of the Special Measures Directions for certain categories of vulnerable witnesses introduced in the **YJCEA 1999** and the **CJA 2003**. Further changes were introduced under the **Police and Justice Act 2006** and the **Coroners and Justice Act 2009** for child witnesses, child and vulnerable defendants and complainants of sexual assault.

Note also the **Coroners and Justice Act 2009** which provides for witness anonymity in certain cases.

Table 4 Competence and compellability: single defendant and co-defendant situations

	For prosecution		For own defence		For co-defendant	
Witness	Comp't	Comp'able	Comp't	Comp'able	Comp't	Comp'able
Defendant where no co-defendant	No. **YJCEA, s. 53(4)**	No	Yes. **YJCEA, s. 53(1)**	No. **CEA 1898, s. 1(1)**	n/a	n/a
Co-defendant pleading not guilty	No. **YJCEA, s. 53(4)**	No	Yes. **YJCEA, s. 53(1)**	No. **CEA 1898, s. (1)**	Yes. **CEA 1898, s. 1(1)**	No. **CEA 1898, s. 1(1), PACE, s. 80(4)**
'Ex-co-def', i.e. pleading guilty, acquitted or *nolle prosequi* entered	Yes. **YJCEA 1999, s. 53(5)**	Yes	n/a	n/a	Yes. *R v Boal* **[1965] QB 402;** *R v Conti* **[1973] 58 Cr App R 387**	

Table 5 Competence and compellability: spouse and civil partner of defendant

	For prosecution		For spouse's defence		For other co-defendant	
Witness	Comp't	Comp'able	Comp't	Comp'able	Comp't	Comp'able
Spouse of defendant jointly charged with him or her (whether or not the same offence(s)) and pleading not guilty	No. **YJCEA, s. 53(4)**	No. **PACE, s. 80(4)**	Yes. **YJCEA, s. 53(1)**	No. **PACE, s. 80(4)**	Yes. **YJCEA, s. 53(1)**	No. **CEA 1898, s. 1(1); PACE, s. 80(4)**
Spouse of defendant not jointly charged	Yes. **YJCEA, s. 53(1)**	Only for offences in **PACE, s. 80(3)**	Yes. **YJCEA, s. 53(1)**	Yes. **PACE, s. 80(2)**	Yes. **YJCEA, s. 53(1)**	Only for offences in **PACE, s. 80(3)**

Question 1

John is charged with assaulting Fred after an argument about football in a bus queue. John claims self-defence because Fred was wearing knuckleduster rings and he was afraid he would be hurt. Fred denies he threatened John. The only other witness to the brawl was John's wife, Hilda.

Discuss whether she is competent and compellable as a witness for John or the prosecution. Critically evaluate the law of evidence in this area.

 Commentary

You need to have a clear picture of the position of spouses under **s. 80 of PACE** as amended by the **YJCEA**. You are expected to outline the law and then comment on its rationale. It is an area which previously has raised a number of controversial issues, but arguably the **1999 Act** has resolved some of these issues. Be careful not to be too expansive on the historical background of the law but it is quite appropriate to set the development of the law in context.

 Answer plan

- Presumption of competence and compellability for all witnesses.
- **YJCEA, s. 53(1)**, **PACE, s. 80** and special rules on compellability of spouses.
- Compellability of spouses for defence—Hilda.
- Compellability of spouse for prosecution only for specified offences—Hilda compellable if Fred under 16 years, **PACE, s. 80(2A)(a) and s. 80(3)(b)**.
- Comment by prosecution on failure of spouse to give evidence.
- Critical evaluation: note the competing social interests involved and arguably archaic nature of the current law. See academic comment by Roberts and Zuckerman, Laudan and Brabyn.

Table 6 Outline Special Measures Directions (SMD) in criminal cases*

Statute	Protection	Circumstances
CJA 2003, s. 51	Live link	Court must consider if it is in the interests of the efficient or effective administration of justice; relevant factors include availability of witness and need for witness to attend in person

Statute	Protection	Circumstances
CJA 2003, ss. 137, 138	Testimony video-recording	Need Crown Court trial; need for events to be fresh in witness's memory
YJCEA 1999, ss. 16–31	• Screens • Live links • Evidence given in private • No wigs or gowns • Video-recorded evidence • Use of intermediaries • Aids to communication	Apply to specific categories of witness: • Apply presumptively to all under 18 years (primary rule, note that the same provisions now apply to all child witnesses whatever the offence) or • Quality of evidence likely to be impaired by physical disability or mental disorder or • Witness in fear or distress (automatically includes complainants in sexual cases and witnesses of assaults involving knives or firearms), SMDs apply to examination-in-chief and cross-examination in sexual cases, but only examination-in-chief for other relevant offences
YJCEA, s. 32	Judicial warning so that direction does not prejudice the accused	May be given during the trial or in the summing-up

* These do not apply to defendants.

Suggested answer

Hilda as witness for defence or prosecution

The general rule is that any person is competent and compellable as a witness provided he or she is able to communicate coherently. Thus he or she may lawfully give evidence. It is for the court to decide issues as to the competence and compellability of witnesses, as the Court of Appeal held in *R v Yacoob* (1981) 72 Cr App R 313. A competent witness is generally compellable. The main exceptions apply in differing degrees to spouses, civil partners, children and those of unsound mind.

By virtue of **s. 53(1) of the Youth Justice and Criminal Evidence Act 1999 (YJCEA)**, all persons are competent to give evidence. There is no longer any necessity to consider the issue of competence in terms of the spouse being called as a witness for the prosecution or for the defence. Hence, Hilda is a competent witness for the prosecution. She is also compellable for the defence: **s. 80(2) of the Police and Criminal Evidence Act 1984 (PACE)**. But by **s. 80(2A)(b) and (3) of the 1984 Act**, she is compellable for the prosecution only if Fred was under 16 at the time of the alleged assault. If she does choose to give evidence for the prosecution, provided the right of refusal has been clearly explained to her, she can be treated like any other witness, as the Court of Appeal held in *R v Pitt* [1983] QB 25. The prosecution has the burden of establishing the competence of a prosecution witness and the standard of proof is on a balance of probabilities: s. 54(2) of the YJCEA (reversing *R v Yacoob* (1981) 72 Cr App R 313).

Section 80A of the 1984 Act as amended forbids comment by the prosecution on the failure of a defendant to call his or her spouse to give evidence. This provision originally appeared in s. 1 of the Criminal Evidence Act 1898 and in s. 80(8) of the 1984 Act. Thus, in *R v Naudeer* (1984) 80 Cr App R 9, the Court of Appeal quashed a conviction because the prosecuting counsel had told the jury it had been deliberately deprived of material evidence as the defendant had not called his wife as a witness. The case was one of shoplifting and the wife had been in the shop at the relevant time. The court may, however, correct the damage by making a relevant comment. It should be stressed that the prohibition in s. 80A is with regards to comment by the prosecution only. It does not prevent the judge from commenting on the defendant's failure to call his or her spouse, as the Court of Appeal held in *R v Gallagher* [1974] 1 WLR 1204, just as he may comment on the failure to call any witnesses.

Thus if Hilda does not give evidence for the prosecution comment by prosecution counsel is precluded.

Critical evaluation of spousal privilege

In relation to spouses, their exemption from a general duty to testify for the prosecution has been a matter of some controversy. At present, spouses are only compellable for the prosecution if the offence in question is a crime of violence or a threat to one of the spouses or a person under 16, if it is a sexual offence committed against a person under the age of 16, or it consists of an attempt or a conspiracy to commit or of aiding or abetting the commission of one of the offences stated earlier (s. 80(3) of the 1984 Act). Until the 1984 Act came into force, spouses were at common law not competent nor compellable for the prosecution. If there was a co-accused, he or she was treated as being in the same position as the prosecution and similar changes in relation to the co-accused as to the prosecution were enacted in PACE, which has since been amended by the YJCEA. A spouse could, under the Criminal Evidence Act 1898, give evidence on behalf of the accused. The reasoning for this was based on the legal fiction of the single personality of the husband and wife and the policy of attempting to preserve the institution of marriage.

It should be noted that by s. 80(9) of the 1984 Act, a spouse who testifies cannot refuse to disclose the content of marital communications even if they are confidential, nor refuse to answer relevant questions on when sexual intercourse took place.

The changes enacted (in the 1984 Act and subsequently as amended by the 1999 Act) go in some ways further than had been recommended by the Criminal Law Revision Committee in its 11th report (Cm 4991, 1972). A spouse is thus compellable even in cases involving violent or sexual offences against persons under 16 who are not members of the same household. Once the marriage is over spousal privilege ceases (s. 80(5)).

Generally, even with the changes treating civil partners as spouses, the present law can still be criticised as being too restrictive and inconsistent.

The historic reason for spousal privilege was stated by Lord Salmon in *R v Hoskyn* [1979] AC 474, at p. 495: 'This rule seems to me to underline the supreme importance attached by the common law to the special status of marriage and to the unity supposed to exist between husband and wife. It also no doubt recognised the natural repugnance of the public at the prospect of the wife giving evidence against her husband in such circumstances.' This case has been overruled by **PACE** on the facts. Spouses may now be compelled to testify if they are alleged victims of domestic assault. In cases other than those specified in **s. 80(4)** a spouse may claim exemption from testifying against the husband or wife. Roberts and Zuckerman have expressed a number of criticisms of the current law. They write (2010, p. 313): 'Marital harmony is not, to be sure, a trivial consideration. Whether it should be allowed to take priority over doing justice in contemporary society is however, another matter entirely.' They make the following points to illustrate the illogicality of the present position. First, marriages are more easily dissoluble today so a married couple are no longer so constrained to remain together. Second, non-compellable spouses have to make a morally repugnant choice between their civic duty to testify and upholding marital harmony. Third, although the exceptions to non-compellability in **PACE, s. 80(3)** are welcome, they are also illogical. There are other vulnerable groups than battered partners and children: these include older people, racial minorities, etc. Roberts and Zuckerman (2010, p. 315) cite *Cross and Tapper on Evidence* (1999, p. 222): 'The accused's wife is compellable against him if he kissed a 15-year-old . . . but not if he raped and murdered a 16-year-old.' Fourth, the position in relation to co-defendants is confused; Roberts and Zuckerman point out (p. 315) that 'It is difficult to comprehend why a wife should be compellable for her husband's co-accused when both men are jointly charged with child abuse but not in other cases. If the co-accused requires the wife's assistance to prove his innocence, the law should compel her testimony regardless of the impact on the wife's marital harmony; or at least, in the alternative, should sanction separate trials.' Munday (2011, p. 130) also points out that the scope of **s. 80(3)** 'is not necessarily as straightforward as at first might appear'. As he suggests, 'the word "involves" is not the most precise of terms'. He cites the case of *McAndrew-Bingham* [1991] 1 WLR 1897 the Court of Appeal took a broad interpretation in holding that every child abduction under the **Child Abduction Act 1984** should be taken as an assault for the purposes of the **Criminal Justice Act 1988, s. 32(2)(a)**, allowing video-recording of a child's evidence. The section has identical wording to **s. 80(3)(a)**. A further anomaly is illustrated in *R v L* [2009] **All ER (D) 137** where a statement made in a police interview by a non-compellable spouse was held to be admissible hearsay under the **Criminal Justice Act 1988, s. 114(1)(d)**. She had not been warned at the interview she was not compellable and at the trial declined to testify.

It is arguably offensive that parties who are cohabiting but are not married or civil partners are outside the scope of **s. 80** and are treated as ordinary witnesses. In *R v Pearce* (2002) Kennedy LJ stated, 'there may be much to be said for the view that with very limited exceptions all witnesses who are competent should also be compellable, and certainly the material before us does not enable us to conclude that because a concession has been made to husbands and wives proper respect for family life requires that a similar concession be made to those in the position of a husband or wife'.

Another anomaly in the current legislation is the question of permissible comment on the spouse's failure to testify. **Section 80A of PACE** states, 'the failure of the spouse or civil partner of a person charged in any proceedings to give evidence in the proceedings shall not be made the subject of any comment by the prosecution'. This prohibition is a wide one and thus prevents comment even if it may be based on logical inferences. It is perhaps surprising that it still exists since comment on the accused's failure to testify may be permissible (**s. 35 of the Criminal Justice and Public Order Act 1994**); see *R v Davy* [2006] EWCA Crim 565.

Academic comment is divided on whether the law on spousal privilege should be reformed. A critic of the current law is the neo-Benthamite American academic Laudan. He argues (2008) that the rule is based on protecting a specific relationship rather than getting at the truth in a trial. He argues for a system of free proof and the admissibility of all relevant evidence. On the other hand, Brabyn (2011) wants the law in this area strengthened. She is critical of the Court of Appeal decision *R v L* [2009] 1 WLR 626. Brabyn argues (p. 614) that the decision undermined the laudable objective of spousal privilege since '. . . it is modern society's long term interests to generally favour the institution of marriage specifically and close family relationships generally over securing the conviction of all people who commit offences.'

There is thus an acknowledgement that theoretical coherence of the current law is flawed although whether it should be strengthened or dismantled is value-laden. It is arguable that the criminal law treats spouses as witnesses in an unsatisfactory way. In civil cases, by contrast, spouses are treated as any other witness, although arguably the threat to the institution of marriage exists in these cases too. There is a powerful argument that the privilege afforded to spouses and civil partners as witnesses in criminal cases should be removed, subject to discretionary exception. As Dennis (2010, p. 57) concludes '. . . it might be preferable to abandon attempts at compromise and to adopt a general rule that a spouse should be a compellable witness in all cases.'

 Question 2

Dido is charged with causing criminal damage to some gnomes in the garden of 14 Churchill Road. The prosecution case is that she was hawking flowers door to door with her daughter Janet, aged 12. Mr and Mrs Baldwin refused to buy from Dido. As she left she allegedly kicked down the gnomes in anger. Hector, the Baldwins' 20-year-old son, who has a mental age of ten, was looking out of the window. James, aged 17, also saw the incident from the top of a bus. He is worried about testifying since he was bullied by Dido's nephew at school and is afraid he might be attacked if he testifies against Dido. The prosecution wish to call Janet, James and Hector as witnesses.

Advise on how they may give evidence. whether they are competent and compellable.

Commentary

This is a similar question on two other groups of witnesses who are to some extent a deviation from universal competence and compellability. The law relating to children in criminal cases is now relatively simple and amended after much research in this area. However, it has only reached this state after a number of statutory measures. Children are now assumed to be as competent in criminal trials as other witnesses. Adults may be incompetent to testify through drunkenness, or some physical or mental disability. In this, as in all other cases, the question of competence in any specific case remains one for the trial judge. There are a number of ways you could organise your answer. It is suggested here that you deal with each witness separately for competence, compellability and hearsay and you cover the complex Special Measures Directions by considering the witnesses together.

Answer plan

Janet

- Competence of children under **YJCEA, s. 53, s. 55(2) and s. 56**—evidence of children under 14 is unsworn.
- Pigot Committee recommendations and change in approach to children's evidence.

Hector

- Hector—mental capacity, **YJCEA, s. 53**, **s. 54(5) and s. 55(3)**; *R v Bellamy (1985)*; *R v McPherson* **[2005] EWCA Crim 3625.**
- Possibility of evidence being admitted as exception to hearsay rule—but see *R v Setz-Dempsey* **(1994)**.

James

- **YJCEA, s. 53.**
- Possibility also of submission by hearsay.

Special Measures Direction

- Janet and James eligible for SMD under 'primary rule' see **YJCEA, s. 21(1)(a)**.
- Hector eligible under **s. 16(1)(b) and s. 16(2)**.

Examiners' tip

Problem questions in Evidence examinations rarely cover just one area of the law. You will see in the following suggested answer that although the bulk of the answer covers the law on witness competence and compellability, it is also appropriate for you to demonstrate your knowledge of hearsay evidence.

Suggested answer

Janet

Janet is a competent witness (**Youth Justice and Criminal Evidence Act 1999 (YJCEA), s. 53**) and compellable for the prosecution or defence. The fact that a witness could not be imprisoned for failure to comply is not a good reason for refusing to issue a witness summons to compel her attendance: *R v Greenwich Justices, ex parte Carter* [1973] **Crim LR 444**. As a child under 14 Janet must give evidence unsworn: **YJCEA, ss. 55(2) and 56.** This provides that the evidence of children under 14 is to be given unsworn and that a child's evidence must be received unless it appears to the court that the child is incapable of understanding questions put to her and unable to give answers which can be understood: **YJCEA, s. 53(3).** The court must decide not whether she is competent on grounds of age but whether she is capable of giving intelligible evidence. It is submitted that a normal 12-year-old would be. The importance of giving truthful evidence must be explained to her by the tribunal as part of the process of putting her at her ease. If it is decided to receive her evidence it is a matter of fact for the tribunal as to how much weight to attach to it. The position of child witnesses was the subject of much controversy and research. The Pigot Committee on Video Evidence set up by the Home Office, reporting in 1989, condemned the existing position as being founded on an archaic belief that children could not be honest and coherent witnesses. The law was subsequently changed so that there is now no preliminary examination of the child's ability to give evidence. The present practice is that the child should give evidence and only be stopped if it becomes clear she could not give an intelligible account. The result is that there is now no minimum age below which a child cannot give evidence, although in practice judicial discretion may be exercised. In *R v N* (1992) 95 Cr App R 256, the Court of Appeal said that the fact that a child was too young to be prosecuted for perjury was not a reason for excluding her evidence. The present state of the law arguably brings it into line with psychological research on the veracity of children. The emphasis on judicial discretion rather than strict rule is a welcome development. It should be noted that under **ss. 54 and 55 of the YJCEA** the determination of the question of the competence of the witness should be carried out in the absence of the jury and that the court may question the child's competence of its own motion.

The changes in the law relating to children's evidence were the result particularly of the difficulty of achieving successful prosecutions in the case of child victims of sexual abusers. As Birch (1992, p. 269) argues, 'Children, contrary to what was once thought, are not necessarily unreliable at all, and are certainly no less dangerous as witnesses than those who abuse them.'

Hector

As regards Hector, the court will probably take a pragmatic view and allow him to testify if it considers he understands the nature of the proceedings and can speak the truth to the best of his ability. Under the rules set out in **ss. 53–57** persons suffering from a degree of mental difficulty are subject to the same tests as any other witness. The competence of witnesses may be raised by the parties or by the court of its own motion (s. 54(1)). It is for the party calling the witness to satisfy the court on the balance of probabilities that the witness is competent (s. 54(2)). In *R v Bellamy* (1985) 82 Cr App R 222, the Court of Appeal held that the cases then pertaining to the swearing of children applied in the case of an alleged victim in a rape case who was 33 years old but had a mental age of 10. It was not necessary for her to appreciate the divine sanction of the oath. This decision was welcomed as a break from earlier emphasis on the theological implications of understanding the oath. Under the **YJCEA 1999, ss. 53–57** witnesses who suffer from mental disorder, disability or mental illness do not form a separate category but are subject to the same test of competence as any other witness. This is that they must understand questions put to them as a witness and give answers to them which can be understood: s. 53(3). The Court of Appeal has set out a number of questions which should be addressed in deciding whether a witness is competent, see *R v McPherson* (2005). That case made it clear questions of credibility and reliability are not relevant to competence but are matters of weight which might be considered at the end of the prosecution case by way of a submission of no case to answer. Expert evidence may be admitted as to the witness's mental state (see s. 54(5)).

It is possible a party may raise that Hector has insufficient appreciation of the solemnity of the occasion and of the particular responsibility to tell the truth which is involved in taking an oath (s. 55(2)(b)). If he is able to give intelligible testimony he is presumed to have such appreciation unless evidence to the contrary is adduced. In that event then he may be able to give evidence unsworn provided he passes the basic test of competence (s. 56(1) and (2)).

If Hector is held incompetent as a witness it is unlikely that his evidence may be admitted under the statutory exceptions to the hearsay rule. The hearsay provisions of the **Criminal Justice Act (CJA) 1988** have now been repealed and replaced by **ss. 114–136 of the Criminal Justice Act 2003. Section 23 of the CJA 1988** made it a pre-condition of the admission of documentary hearsay evidence that there was no other objection to the admission of the evidence than the one based on hearsay. Under **s. 114 of the CJA 2003**, in deciding whether a hearsay statement is to be admitted the court must have regard, inter alia, to 'how reliable the maker of the statement appears to be' (s. 114(2)(e)).

The Court of Appeal held in *R v Setz-Dempsey* [1994] **Crim LR 123** that the admission of documentary statements from a mentally ill witness under s. 23(1)(a) **of the CJA 1988** was a material irregularity. The judge had erred in law in not exercising discretion under s. 26 and should have considered the psychiatrist's evidence about the likely quality of any evidence given by the witness and also that the statements could not fairly be admitted without the jury hearing the witness's evidence.

James

James, like Janet, is a competent and compellable witness under **s. 53 of the YJCEA**. His fear of testifying may make him eligible for Special Measures Directions, on which see the following section. Another possibility, since James fears bullying, is to use the exceptions to the rule against hearsay which were also brought in to deal with witness intimidation. Under **s. 116(2)(e)** one of the acceptable reasons for not calling the witness and allowing first-hand hearsay is that the witness does not give evidence through fear. Further information is needed to determine if James could claim this protection.

Special Measures Directions

1. Hector

Another possibility to be considered for all three witnesses is the use of Special Measures Directions under the **YJCEA**. It may be considered that Hector might encounter special difficulty in testifying. Under **ss. 16(1)(b) and 16(2)** witnesses other than the accused who suffer from a physical or mental disorder, or have a disability or impairment of intelligence and social functioning that is likely to diminish the quality of their evidence, may give evidence by means such as live video link or pre-recording. Since Hector is likely to be considered as eligible for SMD under **s. 16(1)(b)** the court in deciding whether to award them must consider his view (see **s. 19(3)(a)**). If the prosecution is allowed to use SMD for Hector's testimony then Dido will have difficulty in arguing that this is unfair. In *R (on the application of D) v Camberwell Green Youth Court* [2003] EWHC Admin 22, the Divisional Court held that special measures provisions, here involving children, were compatible with **art. 6(3)(a)**, which embodies the defendant's right 'to examine or have examined witnesses against him'. Although the specific provisions which were the subject of the action have since been amended the case is still of interest. As Choo (2012, p. 379) points out: 'it demonstrates a reluctance to find measures designed to ease the burden on witnesses to be a violation of human rights guarantees.'

2. James and Janet

As persons under 18 James and Janet may also be eligible for Special Measures Directions. Under **s. 21(1)(a) of the Youth Justice and Criminal Evidence Act 1999**, as amended by the **Coroners and Justice Act 2009**, the primary rule in requiring admission of a video interview as examination-in-chief and cross-examination through a live link at trial, applies presumptively to all witnesses under 18, regardless of the nature of the offence. However, under **s. 21(4)(c)** if the court determines that under the primary rule special measures would be unlikely to maximise the quality of the witness's evidence so far as is practicable optional measures such as a screen must be considered. It is open to James and Janet to elect to give oral evidence-in-chief and/or testify in the courtroom rather than using the live link (**s. 21(4)(ba)**). The court will have regard to the following factors in considering **s. 21(4)(c)**: (a) the child's age and maturity; (b) the child's ability to understand the consequences of giving evidence in a different way; (c) the relationship (if any) between the witness and the accused; (d) the child's social and cultural background and ethnic origins; and (e) the nature and alleged circumstances of the offence to which the proceedings relate. Although James if not Janet is arguably of an age where he might be expected to be able to give live testimony, the background factor of the alleged bullying would also be taken into account. If James or Janet elect to give evidence by live link they may be accompanied by an adult to provide support. The adult must be independent of the witness and his family, have no previous knowledge of or personal involvement in the case, and be trained in obligations imposed by national standards relating to witness support. Under **s. 27(5)(b)** if the prosecution wish to ask James or Janet supplementary questions in examination-in-chief they will require leave of the court if the matter had been dealt with in the video interview. The judge will decide if it is in the interests of justice to permit the additional questions.

 Question 3

Jane, aged 30, and her assistant Stacey, aged 40, are charged with physically assaulting Freda who is 20 years old. The prosecution case is that they struck her with the handle of a knife because she fell off her horse in the riding stables run by Jane. Freda is very frightened about appearing as a witness. Stacey has a mental age of ten but has been declared fit to plead. She is nervous about appearing in court and unhappy about testifying. She pleads not guilty. Jane has pleaded guilty.

In a separate civil action Jane is being sued for negligence since a pupil of the riding school, Grace, aged 11, has been injured.

Advise whether Stacey and Freda may be eligible for Special Measures Directions and what will be the consequence if Stacey elects not to testify. Advise also how Jane is likely to be treated as a witness in the criminal case. Advise how Grace is likely to be treated in the civil case.

 Commentary

This question requires you to be familiar with the statutory provisions on the competence and compellability of 'ex-defendants' as witnesses (you will see now how useful is **Table 4**), and of possible SMDs for defendants with low mental age and for victims. You are also asked about the separate provisions for witnesses in civil cases.

 Answer plan

Criminal case—Jane

- Competence and compellability of 'ex-co-defendants'; see **YJCEA, s. 53(5)**.

Criminal case—Stacey

- Consider SMD for vulnerable defendants, **YJCEA, ss. 33A, 33B, 33BA and 33BB**.

- If Stacey is competent what is the effect if she does not testify? See **CJPOA, s. 35** and *R v Friend* **(1997) (No 1) [1997] 1 WLR 1443** and *R v Friend* **(No 2) [2004] EWCA Crim 266**.

Criminal case—Freda

- Freda is a frightened alleged victim of an attack with a knife, this is a possible 'relevant offence' under **YJCEA, s. 17(5)** and SMD.

Civil case—Grace

- **Children Act 1989, s. 96**.
- **Civil Evidence Act 1972**.
- Special protective measures for children.
- Provisions for child witnesses.

Examiners' tip

Questions on competence and compellability may seem very straightforward but, bearing in mind that the point in an examination is to garner marks, do make sure that you do make use of all the legal points that are relevant. You will gain marks, for example, by demonstrating knowledge that SMD may be presumptively available in relation to specific offences such as knife crimes.

Suggested answer

Jane

By pleading guilty Jane is no longer a defendant. She is therefore competent and compellable as a witness for the prosecution or defence, according to **s. 53(5) of the Youth Justice and Criminal Evidence Act 1999 (YJCEA)**. She can thus give evidence for Stacey or the prosecution. Of course if she is compellable it is not necessarily the case that she will be called as a witness but if she is called and refuses she may be in contempt of court.

Stacey

Some limited protection was introduced for vulnerable defendants, now to be found in **ss. 33A, 33B, 33BA and 33BB of the YJCEA**. It is arguable that Stacey falls into the eligible category in that she is over 18 years and suffers from a significant impairment of intelligence and social function in that she is unable to participate effectively in the proceedings as a witness giving oral evidence in court (**s. 33A(5)(a) and (b)**). In that case she may be allowed a live link (**s. 33(5)(c)**) or be examined through an intermediary (**s. 33BA**) if these measures are judged likely to enable her to participate effectively in the proceedings. Stacey must be warned that she has quite a high hurdle to mount if she is to be offered these limited SMDs. Critics of the provisions for defendants contrast their requirements with those of ordinary witnesses. Hoyano (2010), for example, points out that according to the statutory provisions the mentally vulnerable defendant 'must be shown to be *unable* to participate effectively in the proceedings as a witness by reason of that incapacity, whereas for the ordinary witness it need only be shown that the quality of his or her evidence would be *diminished* by the incapacitating condition.'

Stacey is considering whether to testify. Presumably her decision will be influenced by whether she is granted a SMD or not. She should be warned that **s. 35 of the Criminal Justice and Public Order Act 1994 (CJPOA)** may apply if she chooses not to testify. Under this provision a defendant who chooses not to testify faces the possibility of adverse comment on his silence by the prosecution. *R v Cowan* **(1995)** sets out guidelines for how the judge should direct the jury to treat such evidence. He or she must remind them that the burden of proof lies on the prosecution, that the defendant was entitled to remain silent, that an inference from silence alone cannot prove guilt, that the jury must be satisfied that the prosecution have established a case to answer before drawing inferences from silence and that if the jury conclude that the silence can only be attributed to the defendant's having no real answer, or one that would stand up to cross–examination, they may then draw an adverse inference. In particular Stacey must be warned that her mental difficulty does not help her avoid an inference being drawn. In *R v Friend* **(1997) 1 WLR 1433** even though the defendant had a mental age of nine the Court of Appeal held that the judge had been correct to direct the jury that they could draw an adverse inference. The conviction was, however, quashed in *R v Friend* **(No 2) [2004] EWCA Crim 266**.

Freda

We are told that a knife handle was involved in the attack on Freda. It is possible therefore that Freda is now a vulnerable witness under **ss. 17 and 18**. These sections cover witnesses where the quality of evidence is likely to be diminished by reason of the witness's fear or distress about testifying. Under **Sch. 1A** to the Act such witnesses presumptively include witnesses where the offence is one in the **Offences Against the Person Act 1861** where it is alleged that a firearm or knife caused the wound or harm in question. Unless Freda has informed the court that she does not want to be eligible she will be entitled to SMDs listed in the statute. The court does not have to be first satisfied that the quality of the evidence will be diminished by her condition.

Finally Stacey's defence counsel should be aware that **s. 32 of the YJCEA** provides that where in a trial on indictment evidence has been given by an SMD the judge must give the jury such warning (if any) as the judge considers necessary to ensure that the fact that the direction was given in relation to the witness does not prejudice the accused.

Civil case—Grace

If the case goes to trial it may be that Grace will be called as a witness. Under **s. 96 of the Children Act 1989**, children are allowed to testify unsworn and the then existing common law test of competency was enacted to apply in civil proceedings. The test is that the child has sufficient understanding of the duty to tell the truth to justify the reception of her evidence. A 'child' is any person who has not reached the age of 18. The judge will question Grace before she gives any evidence to see if she shows sufficient understanding of the solemnity of the oath. Dennis (2010, p. 564) comments '. . . the first condition of **s. 96 of the Children Act** is certainly stricter than the criminal law, because it retains the requirement, now dropped by the criminal law, that the child understands the duty of truth-telling. Whether this strictness is justifiable is debatable. Its effect may be to exclude the testimony of very young children in civil cases.' The section reads:

(1) **Subsection (2)** applies where a child who is called as a witness in any civil proceedings does not, in the opinion of the court, understand the nature of an oath.

(2) The child's evidence may be heard by the court if, in its opinion, (a) he understands that it is his duty to speak the truth; and (b) he has sufficient understanding to justify his evidence being heard.

Keane (2008, p. 130) states 'it is submitted that the court should be guided by the common law authorities which governed in criminal as well as civil cases prior to parliamentary intervention'. He refers to *R v Hayes* [1977] 1 WLR 234 adding that the court adopted a 'secular approach' and appeared to have accepted a concession made by counsel for the defence that 'the watershed dividing children who are normally considered old enough to take the oath and children normally considered too young to take the oath, probably falls between the ages of eight and ten.'

 Grace may benefit from two further provisions. It is possible that some of her evidence may be heard as hearsay under the **Civil Evidence Act 1995. Section 5 of the 1995 Act** makes it clear that the child will be a competent witness if he or she satisfies the requirements of **s. 96 of the Children Act 1989**, thereby making any hearsay evidence by the child admissible. In *R v B, ex parte P* [1991] 2 All ER 65, 72 Butler-Sloss LJ referred to the need to treat such evidence 'anxiously and consider carefully the extent to which it can properly be relied on'. Secondly, **Civil Procedure Rules, r. 32.3** provides that the court may permit a witness to give evidence through a video link or other means. The court has a broad discretion to allow this.

? Question 4

Margaret, a partner in a hedge fund, is charged with conspiracy to defraud. It is alleged that at a meeting she and her partners agreed to send false VAT returns. At the trial, she refuses to testify but claims through her counsel that she left the meeting early before the matters alleged were discussed. She failed to submit an alibi notice. Gary, who was at the meeting wants to give evidence for the prosecution anonymously since Margaret is known to be violent and vindictive.

Advise the prosecution on how they can treat these facts.

Commentary

This question deals with a defendant's failure to submit an alibi notice and also failure to testify. This question does not require you to discuss pre-trial questioning by the police since it does not indicate whether Margaret gave an explanation to the police of her whereabouts. If she did not then this may permit adverse comment by the prosecution under **s. 34 of the CJPOA**. Pre-trial silence is covered in **Chapter 6**.

Answer plan

- Duty of disclosure—**Criminal Procedure and Investigations Act 1996**.
- Procedure on alibi notices.
- Permissible judicial comment on failure to testify, see **CJPOA s. 35**—see *Cowan* **(1995)**.
- Witness anonymity.

Suggested answer

The **Criminal Procedure and Investigations Act 1996** requires the prosecution and the defence to disclose evidence prior to the trial. It imposes a duty on the defence, which goes further than previously required. Prior to the **1996 Act**, the obligation on the defendant to disclose evidence pre-trial was limited including, for example, issuing an alibi notice under **s. 11 of the Criminal Justice Act 1967**. This has been superseded by **s. 5 of the 1996 Act**. This requires the defendant to disclose evidence of the defence that will be raised at trial, after the prosecution has made primary disclosure and the defence has been served with relevant documents, including copies of the indictment and the prosecution's evidence. Disclosure provisions are strengthened under **Part 5 of the Criminal Justice Act 2003** amending the **1996 Act**.

Under **s. 11 of the 1967 Act**, the defence could not without leave of the court adduce evidence of an alibi if they had not served an alibi notice on the prosecution. In practice leave was often given. However, **s. 5 of the 1996 Act** adopts a different approach. It is silent on whether the court can refuse to admit evidence for which particulars of the alibi had not been served on the prosecution in accordance with the section. **Section 11(2) of the 1996 Act** allows the court or any other party (with leave of the court) to make such comment on the defendant's failure to provide pre-trial particulars of alibi as appears appropriate. The court and jury may draw such inferences from such failure as appear proper in the circumstances of the case. Arguably, although **s. 5** is silent on the court's power to refuse to allow such evidence, the court retains its discretion under **s. 78 of the Police and Criminal Evidence Act 1984** to exclude evidence that would have an adverse impact on the fairness of the trial. Thus, even though Margaret may not have served particulars of alibi with her defence statement in accordance with **s. 5 of the 1996 Act,** she will be permitted to adduce evidence that she was not at the meeting at the time the agreement to send false VAT returns was made. However, the court and the prosecution, with leave of the court, may comment on this and the jury can draw such adverse inferences as are proper.

By **s. 35 of the Criminal Justice and Public Order Act 1994 (CJPOA),** adverse inferences can be drawn by the court from the refusal to give evidence at trial. It is not, however, contempt of court for Margaret to fail to testify at trial. Under **s. 35(4)** of the statute the common law principle is retained that the accused is not compellable to give evidence on his own behalf.

Before the **CJPOA** it was forbidden for the prosecution to comment on the accused's failure to testify, although comment was allowed by the judge. The law in this regard was restated by the Court of Appeal in *R v Martinez-Tobon* **[1994] 1 WLR 388.** The judge had to direct that the defendant was under no obligation to testify and that the jury should not assume he is guilty because he had not given evidence. The prosecution is now permitted by **s. 35 of the 1994 Act** to comment on Margaret's failure to testify but the section does not specify what kind of comment is appropriate and, unlike **s. 11(2) of the Criminal Procedure and Investigations Act 1996,** does not require leave of the court before such comment can be made. It may be some comfort to Margaret to rely on **s. 38(3) of the CJPOA:**

> A person shall not have the proceedings against him transferred to the Crown Court for trial, have a case to answer or be convicted solely on an inference drawn from such a failure as is mentioned in **section 34(2), section 35(3)** . . .

The procedure which must be followed by the court in relation to a defendant's refusal to testify is set out in **s. 35** and in addition a Judicial Studies Board Specimen Direction clarifies the process. In particular, before adverse comment may be considered the defendant must have pleaded not guilty, be physically and mentally fit to testify and be aware of the risks attached to silence. Margaret should be aware that the same risks apply if she did decide to testify but then refused to answer some questions put to her. Under **s. 35(5)** a failure to answer questions is presumed to be 'without good cause' unless the accused is either entitled under statute not to answer particular questions or has a legal privilege not to answer or 'the court in its general discretion excuses him from answering'. Guidance on judicial comment where the accused does not give evidence is to be found in the Court of Appeal's judgment in *R v Cowan* **[1996] QB 373.** In three separate cases, heard together on appeal, defendants who had not given evidence appealed against conviction on the grounds of non-compliance with **ss. 35 and 38(3) of the CJPOA.** The court held that **s. 35(4)** had expressly preserved the right to silence but that while the burden of proving guilt beyond reasonable doubt lay throughout on the prosecution the court or jury might draw the inference from a defendant's failure to testify to be a further evidential factor in support of the prosecution's case. A Specimen Direction from the Judicial Studies Board was a sound guide and before any inferences from silence could be drawn the jury had to be satisfied that a case to answer had been established by the prosecution. In G and C's case misdirections had been made and the convictions were quashed. In C's case the judge had failed to tell the jury that they could not infer guilt solely from silence or to warn them that they could not hold his silence against him unless the only sensible explanation was that he had no answer to the case against him which could have stood up to cross-examination. In G's case there were also shortcomings in the summing-up. In R's case the judge had directed the jury correctly. The guidance given in *Cowan* is amplified in Judicial Studies Board Specimen Direction No. 39. The direction is detailed and complex and underlines that jurors should take into account any evidence which might explain why the defendant elected not to testify. It is only if jurors are satisfied that the only sensible reason for Margaret not testifying is that she has no answer to the charge, or none that would stand up in cross-examination, can they draw an inference which will support the prosecution case. The prosecution may argue that Margaret may reveal incriminating details about the meeting if she takes the stand.

A key question is the extent of the prosecution case against Margaret. In *Doldur* [2000] **Crim LR 178**, Auld LJ set out the specific requirements of a **s. 35** direction which differ from those under **ss. 34, 36 and 37**. In the case of **s. 35** the jury should be directed to restrict its consideration to the prosecution case in deciding whether to draw adverse inferences. By contrast, in relation to **s. 34** the jury would have to consider both prosecution and defence cases since it was the contrast between the defendant's earlier silence and reliance on facts at trial that permitted the drawing of an adverse inference (see further **Chapter 6,** Suggested answer to Question 4). If the judge fails to give clear directions on the drawing of permissible inferences Margaret may have strong grounds of appeal under **art. 6** provisions (see *Condron v UK*).

The prosecution may benefit from the **Coroners and Justice Act 2009** (incorporating the temporary provisions of the **Criminal Evidence (Witness Anonymity) Act 2008**), reversing *R v Davis* [2008] AC 1128, HL. This may protect Gary's identity. There the Lords held that a murder trial was unfair and a violation of **art. 6(3)(d)** where an order preserved the anonymity of a witness. The new Act which applies to civilian and police witnesses allows various measures to be taken to protect the identity of a witness such as the use of a pseudonym, screening and voice modulation. The court must be satisfied that:

- The measures are necessary for example to protect the safety of the witness having regard to reasonable fear on his part if he were identified or to protect the carrying on of activities in the public interest.

- The taking of the measures is consistent with the defendant receiving a fair trial.

- The interests of justice require the order since it appears to the court that it is important the witness should testify and the witness would not testify if the order were not made.

The Act sets out in **ss. 88–99** matters the court must consider. These include whether evidence given by the witness might be the sole or decisive evidence implicating the defendant. **Section 90** provides that, 'the judge must give the jury such a warning as the judge considers appropriate to ensure that the fact that [a witness anonymity order] was made in relation to the witness does not prejudice the defendant.' The **2008 Act** was applied in a series of conjoined trials, see *R v Mayers* **[2009] 1 WLR 1915**. The appeal was allowed in *Mayers* since the court could not be sure that the non disclosure of the identity of the witness was fair to the defendant. In *Glasgow*, *Costelloe* and *Bahmanzahdeh* the convictions were safe since the true identities of undercover police officers were rarely important to the defendant. The court stated that evidence given by an anonymised witness could not include anonymous hearsay. In view of the reluctance of the courts to sanction witness anonymity it is unlikely on the facts given here that Gary's identity will be kept secret because it is arguable a fair trial requires that he be cross-examined.

Further reading

Birch, D., 'Criminal Justice Act 1991: Part 4: Children's Evidence' (1992) Crim LR 262, 8.

Birch, D., 'A Better Deal for Vulnerable Witnesses?' [2000] Crim LR 223.

Brabyn, J., 'A Criminal Defendant's Spouse as a Prosecution Witness' [2011] Crim LR 613.

Cooper, D., 'Pigot Unfulfilled: Video-recorded Cross-examination under S28' [2005] Crim LR 456.

Creighton, P., 'Spouse Competence and Compellability' [1990] Crim LR 34.

Durston, G., *Evidence Text and Materials*, 1st edn (Oxford: OUP, 2008).

Dwyer, D., 'Can a Marriage be Delayed in the Public Interest so as to Maintain the Compellability of a Prosecution Witness?' (2003) 7(3) E & P 1916.

Gillespie, A., 'Compellability of the Child Victim' (2000) 64 J Crim L 98.

Home Office Research Study, 'Are Special Measures Working?' (2004) www.homeoffice.gov.uk/rds/pdfs04/hors283.pdf.

Hoyano, L.C.H., 'Striking a Balance between the Rights of Defendants and Vulnerable Witnesses: Will Special Measures Directions Contravene Guarantees of a Fair Trial?' [2001] Crim LR 948.

Hoyano, L.C.H., 'Coroners and Justice Act 2009: Special Measures Directions Take 2: Entrenching Unequal Access to Justice' [2010] Crim LR 345.

Laudan, L., *Truth Error and the Criminal Law: An Essay on Legal Epistemology* (Cambridge: Cambridge University Press, 2008).

Ormerod, D., Choo, A. and Easter, R., '"The Witness Anonymity" and "Investigator Anonymity" Provisions' (2010) Crim LR 368.

Spencer, J.R. and Flin, R., *The Evidence of Children: The Law and the Psychology*, 2nd edn (London: Blackstone, 2003).

Character of defendant

Introduction

This chapter is concerned with one of the most complex questions in criminal evidence, namely, those situations in which the accused may adduce evidence of his good character to suggest lack of guilt and support credibility and those in which the prosecution counsel or the counsel for the co-defendant may cross-examine him on any previous discreditable behaviour. Before the **Criminal Justice Act (CJA) 2003** was in force, such cross-examination was for the purpose of eliciting evidence to show the defendant's lack of credibility. It was not for the purpose of suggesting he was guilty of the offence for which he was charged. Thus it was different from the purpose for which the common law rule on similar fact evidence was called, namely to suggest guilt. The exclusionary rule was fundamental to the English legal system and based on the principle that the defendant should have a fair trial based on the instant charge. As is the case with all exclusionary rules in evidence, there were exceptions to it. These occurred both at common law, which applied when the defendant did not give evidence, and in the **Criminal Evidence Act 1898**, which applied to cross-examination.

The 2003 Act made comprehensive changes to the rules relating to the *admissibility* of evidence of bad character of both the defendant and witnesses providing that 'the common law rules governing the admissibility of evidence of bad character in criminal proceedings are abolished' (**s. 99(1)**). Common law rules therefore arguably may apply to:

- the meaning of character, including good character;
- the admissibility of good character;
- rules relating to judicial directions on the meaning of good or bad character.

One further complication is that the **CJA 2003** has changed the law relating to the admissibility of bad character evidence of witnesses other than defendants: this is dealt with in **Chapter 10**.

With regard to the character of the defendant, you need to be familiar with the law on:

1. The definition of good character.

2. The admissibility of good character.

3. 'Putting character in issue'.

4. The evidential value of good character.

5. The definition of bad character.

6. The admissibility of bad character.

7. The evidential value of bad character.

You must appreciate that historically 'evidential value' refers to two possible impacts: that of issue, i.e. whether the defendant is more likely to be guilty or not, and that of credit, whether the defendant (or other witness) is more or less likely to be believed. In relation to the question of credit the assumption seems to have been that those who have previous criminal records are less likely to be honest, although this is of course a dubious assertion.

In answering questions on character you need to adopt a logical approach and ask a series of questions. It is a common mistake to concentrate on admissibility and ignore the issues of the evidential worth and judicial directions. The questions in **Diagrams 1** and **2** should help you to adopt a strategy for answering problem questions.

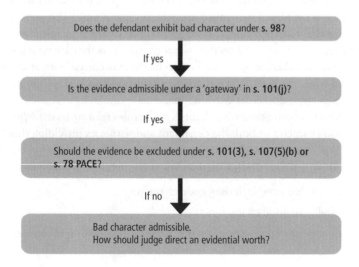

Diagram 1 Bad character of defendants

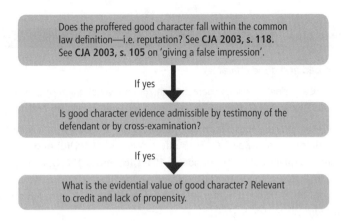

Does the proffered good character fall within the common law definition—i.e. reputation? See **CJA 2003, s. 118**. See **CJA 2003, s. 105** on 'giving a false impression'.

If yes

Is good character evidence admissible by testimony of the defendant or by cross-examination?

If yes

What is the evidential value of good character? Relevant to credit and lack of propensity.

Diagram 2 Good character of defendants

Question 1

Andy, Ben and Catherine are charged with theft of video machines brought to their shop for repairs by David. They all plead not guilty. Andy testifies in his own defence. He claims that Ben had asked him to help steal the machines but he had refused. Andy has several convictions for criminal damage. At the trial counsel for the prosecution and for Ben cross-examine Andy on these convictions. Ben gives evidence and claims he had nothing to do with the theft and that Andy had stolen the machines. He calls several witnesses to give evidence that he has done extensive charitable work for a local pensioners' club for many years. Catherine does not testify at trial but claims at interview that David was falsely implicating her out of resentment because she refused to have an affair with him. She also said at interview that Doris, David's girlfriend, had a grudge against her. David is a prosecution witness, Doris is not a witness. Catherine received a caution for shoplifting ten years ago. All the defendants' previous characters are admitted. In her summing-up, the judge tells the jury that they may take Ben's good character evidence as relevant to credibility and his propensity to commit offences and that Andy was more likely than Ben to have committed the offence. Ben is acquitted. Andy and Catherine are convicted.

Advise Andy and Catherine whether they have any grounds of appeal on the grounds that evidence has been wrongly treated at trial.

Commentary

This question requires you to be familiar with the complex provisions in **ss. 98–113 CJA 2003** and the relevant case law, particularly the cases of ***R v Hanson* [2005] EWCA Crim 824** and ***R v Highton* [2005] EWCA Crim 1985**. The issues to address are the specific gateways of the admissibility of previous convictions, whether the court exercised discretion reasonably, the use to which the evidence is put and how the judge directed on this. Errors in law could lead to the convictions being overturned.

Answer plan

Admissibility of bad and good character

- Did Andy and Catherine's previous character fall within the definition of bad character under **s. 98 CJA 2003**? Note that Catherine had a caution ten years previously and not a conviction.

- If Andy and Catherine's previous behaviours are considered to be bad character are they admissible under one of the gateways? (a) For Andy consider **s. 101(1)(e) and s. 104**, attack on co-defendant and (b) for Catherine consider **s. 101(1)(g) and s. 106**. Note that Catherine has arguably made an attack on a witness (David) and a non-witness (Doris) and that she made this at interview not at trial. Does it matter that she is not testifying? Is there judicial discretion to exclude any admissible evidence?

Judicial directions on character

- What is the relevance of the bad character of Andy and Catherine? How should the judge have directed on this bad character? Note that the common law still governs judicial directions. You need to bear in mind the point that even if the evidence is admitted under one gateway it may still be relevant under another.

- How should the judge have directed on Ben's good character and how far should she consider the impact of any direction on Andy and Catherine?

 Examiner's tip

In answering questions on bad character do not make the mistake of citing only the 'gateways' listed in the **CJA 2003, s. 101(1)(c)–(g)**. You should also cite the companion explanatory sections, **ss. 102–106, 109 and 112** and, where relevant, the Explanatory Note accompanying the Act.

 Suggested answer

Admissibility of Andy and Catherine's bad character

Andy has previous convictions for criminal damage. These convictions fall within the 'bad character' definition of **s. 98 CJA 2003** as 'evidence of, or of a disposition towards, misconduct on his part, other than evidence which (a) has to do with the alleged facts of the offence with which the defendant is charged, or (b) is evidence of misconduct in connection with the investigation or prosecution of that offence.' The Explanatory Note which accompanied the Act explained that previous convictions are included in the definition.

These convictions are admissible if, but only if, they are covered by one of the provisions in **s. 101**. Andy has given evidence against his co-defendant Ben in stating that Ben had asked him to help steal the machines. Ben denies this. **Section 101(1)(e)** permits bad character evidence to be admissible if 'it has substantial probative value in relation to an important matter in issue between the defendant and a co-defendant.' Note that under **s. 112** '"an important matter" means a matter of substantial importance in the context of the case as a whole.' **Section 109** provides that the relevance or probative value of evidence is a reference to its relevance or probative value on the assumption that it is true and that a court need not assume that the evidence is true if it appears that no court or jury could reasonably find it to be true. In other words, Andy will only trigger this gateway if his allegation against Ben that he set up the theft has some factual basis on which a jury could find it true. An allegation that has only marginal or trivial value would not be considered relevant. If this is the case here, **s. 101(1)(e)** allows evidence of Andy's propensity and credibility. Arguably, only credibility is at issue here, since the question in the trial is who is telling the truth, Andy or Ben. The question then arises whether the convictions for criminal damage do have substantial protective value in helping the jury decide whether Andy is untruthful. The criminal damage convictions may therefore be admissible if they are relevant to Andy's lack of credibility. In *R v Edwards (Stewart Dean)* [2006] 1 WLR 1524 the appellant claimed that a conviction for handling could not properly be regarded as evidence relevant to his propensity for telling the truth. The court acknowledged that a 13-year-old handling offence had marginal relevance to the question of whether the co-defendant was telling the truth. Relevant issues here will be how old the convictions are and whether Andy pleaded not guilty to them, thus suggesting lack of truthfulness. Andy's convictions for criminal damage arguably did not involve deceit but note that in *R v Lawson* [2006] EWCA Crim 2572 by contrast with *Edwards*, the court cited offences not involving dishonesty as potentially probative of the defendant's lack of credibility.

Here, from the facts we are given, it is very likely that Andy's evidence contradicts Ben's denial of involvement. There is no statutory discretion to prevent Ben's counsel questioning Andy on his previous offences but **s. 104** prevents the prosecution tendering such evidence. The statutory exclusionary discretion in **s. 101(3) CJA** does not cover **s. 101(1)(e)**. Furthermore, the right to cross-examine is arguably only limited on grounds of relevance. It is likely that Andy's bad character will be held to have been rightly admitted. The Court of Appeal is reluctant to interfere with the judge's discretion (see *R v Lawson* [2007] 1 WLR 1191).

Catherine has a previous caution for theft. The definition of bad character in **s. 98** refers to 'reprehensible behaviour'. This is broadly defined. The Explanatory Note refers to 'evidence where the charge is not prosecuted' and this arguably includes a caution. Her attack on David and Doris is arguably covered by **s. 101(1)(g)**: 'The defendant has made an attack on another person's character.' **Section 106** explains that 'evidence attacking the other person's character' includes evidence that the other person 'has behaved or is disposed to behave in a reprehensible way' so it does not only need to refer to criminal convictions. This appears to cover the allegations Catherine has made. The prosecution may therefore adduce evidence of her cautions although the court has discretion to exclude under **s. 101(3) and (4)**. **Section 101(4)** refers to the length of time which has passed since the bad character evidence was manifest so the fact that the cautions happened ten years previously would be a factor in exercising the discretion. There are three further issues to consider, namely that Catherine made the allegations at interview, does not give evidence at trial and Doris is not a witness. **Section 106(1)(c)(i)** specifies that the 'attack on another person's character includes those where a suspect is being questioned under caution'. The prosecution therefore will try to argue that Carol's comments at the interview have opened the gateway to admission of her caution. It will, however, on the authority of *R v Nelson (Ashley George)* **[2006] EWCA Crim 3412; [2007] Crim LR 709**, 709–711 have to convince the judge that a proper basis has been laid for putting Catherine's comments at interview in front of the jury. In *Nelson* the court considered that it would have been improper for the prosecution to seek to get such comments before a jury simply to provide a basis for satisfying gateway (g). However, in the event the requirements of gateway (g) were met by referring to the attack on the victim in cross-examination. David is being called as a witness and if the defence counsel had referred to Catherine's claims in cross-examination that would provide a stronger ground for admitting Catherine's conviction. In relation to the allegation against Doris who is not a witness, *R v Nelson* [2006] again gives some guidance. The defence argued that a victim and neighbour had conspired to fabricate allegations of violence. The defendant, in interview, had claimed that the neighbour was a liar who used illegal drugs. The neighbour was not a witness at trial. The judge ruled that there had been an attack on another person's character. Nelson was convicted and appealed on the ground that the comments in interview should not have been admitted. The Court of Appeal dismissed the appeal, holding that 'an attack on another person's character' did not confine that gateway to the situation where a defendant, personally or through his advocate, attacked the character of a prosecution witness. It had to be taken as Parliament's intention deliberately to widen the gateway in that fashion. The trial judge had a discretion, however, to exclude evidence of a defendant's bad character when he had merely made imputations about the character of a non-witness. That discretion could be exercised under **s. 78 of the Police and Criminal Evidence Act 1984 (PACE)** or **s. 101(3) of the 2003 Act**. The court stated that it would be a matter for the judge how he exercised that discretion but that it would be unusual for evidence of a defendant's bad character to be admitted when the only basis for so doing was an attack on the character of a non-witness who is also a non-victim. It is possible that the attack on Doris should not have triggered **s. 101(1)(g)** but that on David rightly did so. One further issue arises as to whether bad character evidence is admissible when the imputations made by the defendant are an integral part of the defence case. The comment on *Nelson* in the Criminal Law Review (2007, p. 711) states, 'the old law was criticised on the grounds that it made no exception to adduction of evidence of the defendant's bad character in cases in which the imputations that were cast were integral to the defence that was being run, e.g. that a confession had been fabricated. In this respect no change has been effected by the **2003 Act**.'

Judicial directions on character

Have Andy and Catherine grounds of appeal in that the judge may not have properly directed the jury on the evidential value of the cross-examination on previous bad character particularly since they are being tried alongside a person of good character? The defendant has long been entitled to adduce evidence of his good character with the aim of inducing the jury to conclude that a person with that character would not commit the alleged offence. The general common law rule is that evidence of character is confined to evidence of general reputation (*R v Rowton* (1865) Le & Ca 520; *R v Redgrave* (1982) 74 Cr App R 10), though as an indulgence, such evidence is often admitted for the defendant. After 1898, when the defendant became capable of giving evidence at his trial, his good character was said to go primarily to his credibility: *R v Bellis* [1966] 1 WLR 234. Where a defendant of good character has given evidence, the judge is required to direct the jury about the relevance of good character to the defendant's credibility, but also to refer to the likelihood that a person of good character would act as charged. Problems arise where, as here, a person without a blot on his record (Ben) is tried alongside a defendant of bad character (Andy). By drawing the jury's attention to the fact that a person of Ben's good character is less likely than a person of bad character to have committed the offence, the judge inevitably suggests that Andy is more likely to have committed it. However, there is authority that the judge should refer to the issue of whether a person of good character would commit the alleged offence, even where the co-defendant is of bad character: *R v Vye* [1993] 1 WLR 471. Andy is, however, entitled to a direction as to the limited relevance of his previous convictions. Without such a direction, the jury might assume that the previous convictions are relevant to the same issues as good character, and particularly to propensity to commit crime and, by extension, guilt. In *R v Cain* [1994] 1 WLR 1449, a case involving three defendants, one defendant had previous convictions, including an offence of dishonesty. The judge directed the jury as to the significance of one co-defendant's good character and said of another defendant only that he had 'had a spot of trouble with the police before'. However, the Court of Appeal dismissed the appeal of the latter on conviction. It accepted that the judge should have warned the jury to disregard the convictions as irrelevant to guilt but came to the conclusion that his dismissive language had reduced any adverse inferences which the jury might otherwise have drawn. Since a full direction would have reminded the jury that the convictions were relevant to credibility, the overall effect was not less favourable to the defendant than it would have been if a full direction had been given.

In relation to the directions on Catherine's bad character admitted under **s. 101(1)(g)**, it is well established that the jury should be directed that it is relevant to her lack of credibility since as Hughes LJ stated in *R v Singh* [2007] EWCA Crim 2140 in relation to defendants of bad character '. . . it is ordinary human experience that their word may be less than those who have led exemplary lives.'

Finally both Catherine and Andy should be warned that the Court of Appeal has indicated it will not readily interfere with the judge's discretion in this area (*Hanson* [2005] EWCA Crim 824).

Question 2

Thelma and Louise are jointly charged with murdering Harry. Both plead not guilty to the charge. Their explanation is that Harry had tried to rape Thelma and in the course of protecting her they both were obliged to push him and he fell down some stairs. Both had fled the scene but later gave themselves up to the police. Louise chooses not to give evidence but her counsel calls her local vicar to state that Louise had been a Bible School teacher and sang in the church choir. Louise has two previous convictions for theft. Thelma elects to testify and in the course of giving evidence explains her flight from the scene of the incident by saying she was afraid of the police because she had cannabis in her pocket. Thelma has several drug-related convictions and is awaiting trial on a charge of violent disorder. The police claim that Thelma had confessed to attempting to kill Harry but Thelma denies making such an admission.

Discuss the evidential issues involved.

Commentary

The provisions of the **CJA 2003** on character created, as Lord Phillips of Worth Matravers put it in *O'Brien v Chief Constable of South Wales* (2005) UKHL 26, 'rules of some complexity'. This problem question invites you to apply these complex rules by considering how the case law has interpreted the statute. It is important you consider the specific facts of the scenario and do not confine yourself to broad generalities about the law.

Answer plan

- Thelma and Louise appeared to attack Harry by claiming he tried to rape Thelma—consider **s. 101(1)(g) and s. 106**.

- Louise does not testify. Does the **CJA 2003** apply to testifying and non-testifying defendants?

- Bad character—meaning of, **CJA 2003, s. 98** does it include a pending charge?

- Louise called good character evidence—consider **s. 101(1)(f)**, see *R v Renda* [2006] 1 WLR 2948.

- Thelma—explanation of flight may inevitably include admission of misconduct; she denies police version of events.

Suggested answer

Louise as non-testifying defendant

The main issues in this case involve questions as to whether Thelma and Louise's character can be brought into the trial under the **Criminal Justice Act (CJA) 2003**. The **2003 Act** applies to both testifying and non-testifying defendants and so both Thelma and Louise are covered by its provisions.

With regard to Louise's failure to testify, the scope of permissible comment by the judge and counsel for the prosecution is covered by **s. 35(3) of the Criminal Justice and Public Order Act 1994,** whereby the court or jury in determining whether the accused is guilty of the offence charged may draw such inferences as appear proper from the failure of the accused to give evidence. The prosecution can therefore now comment on her failure to testify but under **s. 35(3)** no conviction can be made solely on the inferences drawn under **s. 35**. The Court of Appeal in *R v Cowan* **[1996] QB 373** laid down guidelines in this area. Provided an inference under this section is not the only evidence against the defendant, the section will usually operate.

Louise's good character

Under the common law the accused is entitled to adduce evidence of her own good character with the aim of persuading the jury that a person with that character is unlikely to have committed the alleged offence. The rule at common law, unaffected by the CJA 2003, is that evidence of character is confined to evidence of general reputation and not of specific creditable acts. The leading case on this is *R v Rowton* **(1865) Le & Ca 520,** which was followed in *R v Redgrave* **(1981) 74 Cr App R 10.** In the latter case the accused, who was charged with offences relating to homosexuality, was not allowed to prove his heterosexuality by evidence of past liaison with members of the opposite sex. The question that arises is whether the evidence of Louise's vicar is evidence of her general reputation, which is relevant to the case. It is likely that the court will accept that this evidence is admissible since the common law rule that it is, despite *Redgrave*, is not often strictly applied. The application of **s. 101(1)(f) of the CJA** must then be considered. The prosecution may be permitted to adduce evidence of bad character to correct any false impression that may have been created. The provision reads: 'In criminal proceedings evidence of the defendant's bad character is admissible if, but only if . . . it is evidence to correct a false impression given by the defendant.' In *R v Renda* **[2006] 1 WLR 2948** the defendant was held to be seeking to convey a misleading impression about his life and history by claiming that he had been a serving soldier in the Armed Forces, who had, while still employed, sustained serious head injuries, which had resulted in long-term brain damage. He said that at the date of his arrest he was in regular employment as a security guard. The court commented: 'For the purposes of **section 101(1)(f)** the question whether the defendant has given a false impression about himself and whether there is evidence which may properly serve to correct such a false impression under **section 105(1)(a) and (b)** is fact-specific.'

Louise's claim to be a Bible School teacher and sing in the church choir is likely to fall under **s. 101(1)(f)**. The question then arises what is permissible evidence to correct this impression. **Sections 98 and 112 of the CJA 2003** indicate what is meant by 'bad character'. The Explanatory Note to the Act (at para. 353) reads, 'the definition covers evidence of or a disposition towards misconduct. The term "misconduct" is further defined in **s. 112** as the commission of an offence or other reprehensible behaviour. This is intended to be a broad definition and recover evidence that shows that the person has committed an offence, or has acted in a reprehensible way (or is disposed to do so) as well as evidence from which this might be inferred.' Louise's two previous convictions for theft will be likely to qualify for admission under **s. 101(1)(f)**. Although this section is largely a reflection of **s. 1(3) of the Criminal Evidence Act 1898** the wording of the new section makes it clear that evidence is only now admissible if it goes no further than is necessary to correct the false impression, in contrast to the draconian common law position in *R v Winfield* [1939] 4 All ER 164 that character was indivisible. Louise may take advantage of **s. 105(3)** in withdrawing or dissociating herself from the false or misleading impression given by her counsel. There is no statutory discretion to exclude otherwise admissible evidence under **s. 101(1)(f)** except the general discretion under **s. 78 of the Police and Criminal Evidence Act**.

Allegation against Harry

Louise and Thelma claim that Harry tried to rape them. Their argument appears to be they acted in self-defence. This is likely to engage **s. 101(1)(g)**. In *Hanson* [2005] EWCA Crim 824 the Court of Appeal stated that 'pre-2003 authorities will continue to apply when assessing whether an attack has been made on another person's character, to the extent that they are compatible with the [new legislation].' In *R v Selvey* [1970] AC 304 the House of Lords stated 'cross-examination of the accused as to character [is permissible] both when imputations on the character of the prosecutor and his witness are cast to show their own reliability as witnesses independently of the evidence given by them and also when the casting of such imputations is necessary to enable the accused to establish his defence.' In *R v Lamaletie* (2008) the Court of Appeal applied similar reasoning.

Thus Louise's convictions may be admissible by the prosecution under this head also although here under **s. 101(3)** such evidence may be excluded 'if on application by the defendant to exclude it, it appears to the court that the admission of the evidence would have such an adverse effect on the fairness of the proceedings that the court ought not to admit it.' One factor is 'the length of time between matters to which that evidence relates and the matters which form the subject of the offence charged.' In *R v Bovell* (2005) 2 Cr App R 401 the Court of Appeal made it clear that the trial judge was not expected to conduct an investigation into why the defendant made the attack: 'the impact on the fairness of proceedings had to be assessed by reference to matters and other than what the defendant's particular intention may or may not have been.' Thus Louise runs the risk of her convictions being admitted under two gateways.

Thelma has also arguably 'made an attack on another person's character' under **s. 101(1)(g)** by claiming Harry had attempted rape and by denying the police version of her alleged confession. She has possible bad character within the meaning of **s. 98** in that she is awaiting trial on another charge. The Explanatory Notes which accompanied the Act specified that bad character included 'evidence relating to offences for which the accused has been charged'. However, Thelma is advised that the court will most likely protect her privilege against self-incrimination and not allow reference to the charge. In *R v Smith* **[1989] Crim LR 900** the Court of Appeal decided that the accused cannot be asked in cross-examination about pending charges since they may tend to undermine her privilege against self-incrimination.

Thelma's flight

Thelma's explanation of her flight from the scene of the alleged crime has introduced evidence of reprehensible behaviour, namely that she had cannabis in her pocket, which is unlawful. This is analogous to the position under the **1898 Act** of *DPP v Jones* **[1962] AC 635**, who had himself revealed his bad character to explain his change of alibis. Doak and McGourley (2012, p. 262) comment: 'The *Jones* case is likely to fall under **s. 101(1)(b)** in that "the evidence is adduced by the defendant himself or is given in answer to a question asked by him in cross-examination and intended to elicit it".' It follows therefore that the prosecution may cross-examine Thelma on her previous conviction. One question which arises is may the prosecution cross-examine on the details of previous offences where they are admitted? Since the bad character evidence is admitted in the case of Louise under **s. 101(1)(f)** and Thelma under **s. 101(1)(b)** rather than the propensity provisions under **s. 101(1)(d)**, it is arguable that the details should not be given; the fact of the conviction even for non-dishonesty offences is sufficient to raise questions about credibility. In *R v Clarke* **(2011)** the court noted (para. 29) 'all convictions are potentially relevant to assist the jury to assess the character of the accused and it is not necessary, or at least not generally so, for detailed facts about the nature and circumstances of those convictions to be put before the jury.'

Finally the judge should direct on the evidential value of the bad character. The Act is silent on the evidential value of evidence admitted through the 'gateways'. However, there is authority that evidence is likely to be admitted under (f) and (g) is relevant to credibility. That said, Thelma and Louise should both be warned that in *Highton* **[2005] EWCA Crim 1985** the Court of Appeal held that evidence which was admitted through one gateway, for example gateway (g), is nonetheless capable of being used according to the definition of another section. It stated (para. 10):

> In the case of gateway (g) for example admissibility depends on the defendant having made an attack on another person's character, but once the evidence is admitted, it may, depending on the particular facts, be relevant not only to credibility but also the propensity to commit offences of the kind with which the defendant is charged.

This approach also underlines the importance of the guidance that was given in the case of *Hanson* and others as to the care that the judge must exercise to give the jury appropriate warnings when summing-up. However, the Court of Appeal will not lightly interfere with the trial judge's decision.

In *Hanson* (para. 15) the court stated 'if a judge has directed himself or herself correctly this court will be very slow to interfere with the ruling either as to admissibility or as to the consequences of non-compliance with the regulations for giving notice of intention to rely on bad character evidence. It will not interfere unless the judge's judgment as to the capacity of prior events to establish propensity is plainly wrong, or a discretion has been exercised unreasonably in the *Wednesbury* sense.'

Question 3

'The law of evidence classically divides material into that which is admissible by virtue of its relevance to some issue in the case, and that admissible because of its relevance to the credibility of some witness or statement.'

(P. Mirfield. 'Character, Credibility and Truthfulness' (2008) 124 LQR 1.)

How far is this a satisfactory reflection of the law on character in the light of the **Criminal Justice Act 2003**.

Commentary

This is a very broad question which raises one of the most difficult questions in evidence, namely is it possible to direct the jury in a meaningful way so that they understand the difference between, on the one hand, bad character evidence assisting in deciding whether a defendant is guilty and, on the other, assisting in deciding whether he is telling the truth.

The question turns on the changes that were made to what was generally regarded as the unsatisfactory position under the **Criminal Evidence Act 1898** by the **CJA 2003**. It is important that you adopt an analytical approach to this essay question and do not simply give a narrative answer.

Answer plan

- Introduction on the criticisms made of the pre-2003 law. What is meant by satisfactory—consider fairness to defendant and clarity for the jury.
- Arguments to say that current position is satisfactory: (a) narrow interpretation of propensity to untruthfulness; (b) case law drawing a clear distinction between **ss. 101(1)(d) and 101(1)(e) and (g)**; (c) testifying and non-testifying defendant treated the same; (d) **s. 101(1)(f)** is applied so that character is divisible; and (e) better protection for non-defendant witness.

- Arguments to say current position is unsatisfactory: (a) evidence admitted under one gateway may be used under another and so non-dishonesty offences are still relevant to credibility; (b) difficulty of reconciling position on untruthfulness in relation to **s. 101(1)(e)**; (c) confusion in case law—e.g. compare ***R v Clarke* [2011] EWCA 939** and ***R v Chrisostomou* [2010] EWCA Crim 1403**; and (d) good character still relevant for lack of propensity and for credibility.

Examiner's tip

This question requires you to have a firm understanding of the various terms of art in this area, namely admissibility, evidential value, propensity, credibility, dishonesty and truthfulness. It is crucial that you use these terms in an exact way and try to convey their precise meaning.

Suggested answer

At the heart of the statutory structure of the now repealed sections of the **Criminal Evidence Act 1898** was the distinction between evidence going to propensity and evidence going to credibility. The statute only applied to the testifying defendant and, under certain conditions, allowed evidence of previous bad behaviour of the defendant to be admitted as evidence that the jury could draw the conclusion that the defendant might not be believed. A separate common law regime existed for evidence of propensity which was evidence of guilt, known as similar fact evidence. The problems with that structure will be identified and then, taking each one in turn, the essay will assess how far the **Criminal Justice Act (CJA) 2003** overcomes them.

The problems were identified as follows. First, the jury was directed that the evidence of the previous convictions could be taken as evidence of lack of credibility, which was arguably intellectually difficult when they were for offences of physical violence not involving dishonesty. Secondly, the non-defendant was entirely open to attacks on his or her credibility and had no statutory protection. Thirdly, the non-testifying defendants, avoiding cross-examination, did not risk having their convictions revealed. Finally, the directions on good character stated that lack of convictions was evidence of both lack of guilt and of credibility.

The **CJA 2003** was introduced in part to address such incoherences and partly to increase the extent to which previous convictions of the defendant were admitted at trial. Academic comment had been critical of the attempt to draw a distinction between evidence going to propensity and evidence going to credibility, let alone whether the judge could convey this to the jury. Munday (1985, p. 65), quoting Cross, refers to this as 'one of the distinctions without a difference'. Partly he drew on psychology to show the fallacy of the belief that there exists some unitary entity which can be called credibility and that dishonesty in one situation suggests dishonesty in all. In any case the jury was being asked to accept that there is a recognisable distinction between the statement that the accused is of bad character and is not telling the truth and that the accused is of bad character and is the sort of person who commits the instant offence. As the courts moved away from predominantly admitting cases which reflected dishonesty, the distinction between credit and propensity became more blurred. Thus in *R v Selvey* [1970] AC 304 previous character was admitted as a result of imputations against a prosecution witness but cross-examination, formally meant to be on lack of credibility, was actually directed to offences of a similar type to that charged, i.e. indecency, and the effect must have been to suggest an inference of guilt since the defendant had previous convictions for similar offences.

Ways in which 2003 Act has a more satisfactory approach to relevance to issue and credibility

The CJA to some extent has addressed this problem, although it will be also argued here that problems remain. The credibility of the defendant is referred to in **ss. 101(1)(d) and 103(1)(5)** and bad character is admissible if it is relevant to an important matter between the prosecution and the defence, and this includes 'the question whether the defendant has a propensity to be untruthful, except where it is not suggested that the defendant's case is untruthful in any respect.' In applying this section the courts have adopted what Mirfield calls (2009, p. 137) 'a restrictive view of credibility' which he argues started with *R v Hanson* [2005] EWCA Crim 824. In that case Rose LJ stated that propensity to untruthfulness was not the same as propensity to dishonesty. He added that 'previous convictions, whether for offences of dishonesty or otherwise, are therefore only likely to be capable of showing a propensity to be untruthful where, in the present case, truthfulness is an issue and, in the earlier case, either there was a plea of not guilty and the defendant gave an account, on arrest, in interview or in evidence, which the jury must have disbelieved, or the way in which the offence was committed shows a propensity for untruthfulness, for example, by the making of false representations.' In *R v Campbell* [2007] EWCA Crim 1472 the court went even further, stating that 'the only circumstances in which there is likely to be an important issue as to whether a defendant has a propensity to tell lies is where telling lies is an element of the offence charged.' The court observed that there would only be very rare cases of propensity to untruthfulness. This is arguably a satisfactory outcome since in relation to **s. 101(1)(d)** the court concentrates on the issue before the court.

The case law indicates that a clear distinction has been drawn between the application of **s. 101(1)(d)** and **s. 101(1)(g)**. In order to be admissible as evidence of lack of credibility under (d) there has to be a propensity for untruthfulness. This is not the case under **s. 101(1)(g)**. Thus in *R v Clarke* [2011] EWCA Crim 939 the Court of Appeal stated that under (g) the court could admit evidence which showed the general character of the defendant and the jury should be directed that they could bear these in mind when assessing who to believe. Judicial direction should be given that the offences did not show propensity. Again, in *R v Singh* [2007] EWCA Crim 2140, applying **s. 101(1)(g)**, Mirfield argues that 'the courts have stuck to the 1898 approach'. Hughes LJ pointed out that gateway (g) would be redundant if it did not allow of a wider concept of relevance to credibility than does gateway (d). Thus it is arguable that the **2003 Act** has drawn a clearer distinction between relevance to issue and relevance to credibility and to that extent it is more satisfactory than the earlier law.

Turning to another of the pre-2003 criticisms, the non-testifying defendant is now covered by the **CJA 2003**. *R v Butterwasser* **[1948] 1 KB 4** is overruled. It was seen as unfair to victims that a prosecution witness could be impugned by the defendant without means of redress. In the event there is scant authority on the operation of this provision. On one interpretation it seems to be a more consistent and therefore more satisfactory approach than that under the **1898 Act** since as Mirfield (2009, p. 143) points out in relation to the non-testifying defendant 'his credit is on the line in that he is offering a defence that may or may not be believed.' However, some problems remain. Mirfield also (2009) comments that the non-testifying defendant may be put at risk by evidence given by another witness. He cites *Lamaletie and Royce* **[2008] EWCA Crim 314** where the pre-2003 position on credibility was also under attack as being inadequately protective of the non-defendant witness. Parliament, anxious to protect victims, introduced **s. 100(1)(b)** providing the higher test than that for the defendant that the bad character evidence must have 'substantial probative value'. Arguably this puts the defendant at a disadvantage. It may therefore be satisfactory to a victim but unfair to the defendant. In the event there have been conflicting interpretations of the section, thus in *R v Stephenson* **[2006] EWCA Crim 2325** the complainant's convictions for dishonesty which did not involve fraud reached the threshold but those in *R v Garnham* **[2008] EWCA Crim 266** did not.

Ways in which 2003 Act is unsatisfactory

One application of the Act which is controversial is the sharp distinction between admissibility and evidential worth. As Lord Woolf (para. 14) put it in *R v Highton* **[2005] EWCA Crim 1985**, 'a distinction must be drawn between the *admissibility* of evidence of bad character, which depends upon it getting through one of the gateways and the use to which it may be put once it is admitted.' In that case it was permissible to invite the jury to use evidence admitted under **s. 101(1)(g)** as evidence of propensity. Another criticism is that as under the **1898 Act** it must be confusing for the jury to be told that offences not involving dishonesty are relevant to lack of credibility. Thus, in *R v Nelson* **[2006] EWCA Crim 3412** offences involving drugs amounted to such evidence. Hence, in applying **s. 101(1)(e)** non-dishonesty offences may be cited as evidence of lack of credibility when one defendant attacks another (see *R v Rosato* **[2008] EWCA Crim 1243**). More generally the position in relation to co-defendants is somewhat incoherent. **Section 103(1)(5)**, referring to **s. 101(1)(d)** is mirrored by **s. 103(1)(b)** which refers in restrictive terms to propensity to dishonesty. However, as Mirfield (2009) argues, the restrictive approach set out in *Campbell* in relation to (d) if applied to (e) is in contradiction to traditional policy on allowing a defendant to use all relevant evidence in conducting his defence.

Finally, in relation to good character directions, the *R v Vye* [1993] 1 WLR 471 provisions remain which it could be argued still present difficulties for jury comprehension of the differences between relevant to issue and relevant to credibility. In relation to s. 101(1)(f) the Explanatory Notes there provide that evidence of bad character will 'primarily go to the credit of the defendant'. The jury then has to be directed as to the evidential status of good and bad character. One pro-defendant change in the CJA 2003 is that the bad character evidence will only be admitted in so far as it counters the claim put by the defendant, so *R v Winfield* [1939] 4 All ER 164 is overruled, which is arguably a more satisfactory approach and more in tune with modern psychological theories of the divisibility of character. On the other hand, the defendant is more vulnerable under the provision in the 2003 Act which refers to conduct giving a false impression in the proceedings. Section 105(5) states that such conduct includes 'appearance or dress' so evidence of lack of credibility is more readily triggered than under the 1898 Act (see *R v Hamilton* [1969] Crim LR 486). Overall, the provisions of the CJA 2003 do go some way to make the distinction between propensity and credit more intellectually coherent. However, although s. 101(1)(d) has been restrictively operated in relation to propensity to untruthfulness it does appear that the 1898 approach on credibility still prevails in relation to s. 101(1)(e), (g) and to a limited extent (f). Overall, the Act has heralded an increase in the extent to which the defendant's convictions are admitted and the Court of Appeal only intervenes if the judge's decision is *Wednesbury* unreasonable. The emphasis on evidence to the issue rather than technically complex distinctions between credibility and propensity may be welcome but overall the Act appears to have brought great prosecutorial advantage.

 Question 4

'There can be no doubt that it was the intention of parliament to relax the strictness of the common law by dropping any requirement for enhanced relevance for similar fact evidence'

(I. Dennis, *The Law of Evidence* (London: Sweet & Maxwell, 2010), p. 839.)

Comment on this observation in the light of the provisions of **s. 101(1)(d) of the Criminal Justice Act 2003**.

 Commentary

A good answer will demonstrate a deep understanding of the intricacies of **s. 101(1)(d)** and of the leading cases. It is important that you do not simply give a factual account of the law in this area but develop an argument. Your answer should demonstrate in outline at least a critical awareness of the evolution of the law before 2003 and how the threshold of admissibility had been steadily lowered. You should then review the Law Commission's proposals for change and indicate your awareness of the extent to which the legislation departed from them. Again good answers will show some evidence of reading some of the leading academic commentators such as Cross and Tapper (2010) and Durston (2011).

Answer plan

- Common law background and gradual move towards greater admissibility.
- Law Commission proposals and leading to legislative changes in **CJA 2003**.
- Analysis of case law which suggests more propensity evidence is admitted, see *R v Highton* **[2005] EWCA Crim 1985**, *R v Hanson* **[2005] EWCA Crim 824**, *R v Freeman and Crawford* **[2008] 1 WLR 27**.
- Analysis of case law suggesting a more restrictive approach, see *R v Campbell* **[2007] EWCA Crim 1472**, *R v Tully* **(2006)** and see also **s. 103(3)** and exclusionary discretion.
- Evaluation, academic comment.

Suggested answer

Why propensity evidence is to be treated carefully

One of the most complex questions in the law of evidence is the extent to which the prosecution may present evidence of the defendant's previous bad behaviour to suggest his guilt. The Law Commission in its report in 1996 pointed out that evidence of previous misconduct or of discreditable propensity on the part of the defendant ran the risk of misleading a jury. First, it may be thought to be more relevant than it is and the jury then exhibits a 'reasoning prejudice'. Secondly, the actual relevance of the evidence to the facts in issue may be discounted and 'moral prejudice' may lead the jury to condemn the defendant as a disreputable person. Fairness therefore requires that such potentially powerful evidence should be admitted only after the court has considered an appropriate test to filter it. The history of the law in this area demonstrates, however, the continuing difficulties the courts faced in devising such tests. This essay will first briefly review the evolution of the common law tests and their replacement by the statutory regime in 2003. It will be argued that the **Criminal Justice Act (CJA)** continues the process previously demonstrated in the common law but that social and political considerations have led to a presumption of admissibility, of disposition evidence and the possibility of unfairness to defendants. The essay will conclude by reference to Zuckerman's recommendation of an alternative approach of free proof in this area.

Evolution of law on propensity

Overall, the development of law has shown the difficulty of putting flesh on what Lord Herschell in *Makin v Attorney-General of NSW* **[1894]** AC 57 identified as the key concept of relevance. Makin emphasised categories of admissibility, such as proof of identity, system or design or rebuttal of accident but this overly formulaic approach was replaced in *DPP v Boardman* **[1975]** AC 421 by the emphasis on probative force which arguably applied a more helpful structure for the admission of such evidence.

Two more House of Lords decisions accelerated the trend towards greater admissibility. In *DPP v P* [1991] 2 AC 447 the House stressed that there was no need for the evidence to be strikingly similar in order for evidence of similar fact to be admitted. The test was one of whether the evidence has sufficient probative value to outweigh the prejudicial effect which is a question of degree in each case. Then in *R v H* [1995] 2 AC 596 the House of Lords decided that where there is an application to exclude alleged similar fact evidence and there is a risk of collusion between the victims, the court had to approach the question of admissibility on the basis that the similar fact evidence was true and the test in *DPP v P* was applicable. It would be up to the jury to decide whether the evidence was contaminated by the risk of collusion.

Subsequently, the Law Commission in its Report argued that the rules on similar fact were difficult to apply and proposed a codification of the law. The tests of admissibility included that of 'substantial value' and 'the interests of justice'. However, the Government considered the Report too conservative. As Dennis (2010, p. 809) points out, 'None of the proposed requirements for leave, substantial probative value, or admission of the evidence in the interests of justice despite the risk of prejudice, were incorporated in gateway (d).' Under **s. 101(1)(d)** the defendant's bad character is admissible if 'it is relevant to an important matter in issue between the defendant and the prosecution'. There is no reference to the need for the relevance to be 'substantial'. **Section 103(1) and (3)** defines 'matter in issue between the defendant and the prosecution' as including '(a) the question whether the defendant has a propensity to commit offences of the kind with which he is charged, except where his having such a propensity makes it no more likely that he is guilty of the offence; (b) the question whether the defendant has a propensity to be untruthful except where it is not suggested that the defendant's case is untruthful in any respect.' **Section 112(1)** specifies that 'an important matter' means a matter of substantial importance in the context of the case as a whole. Further indication that the Government was determined, as Dennis points out, to increase the likelihood of admission of the defendant's prior bad character is that the statute specifies that where **s. 103(1)(a)** applies a defendant's propensity to commit offences of the kind with which he is charged should be established by evidence that he had been convicted of an offence of the same description as the one with which he is charged or an offence of the same category as the one with which he is charged. This approach appears automatically to allow admissibility of offences because they are of the same description rather than take into account more fully the surrounding circumstances. The increase in bureaucratic intervention is marked also by the provision that the Secretary of State may make orders for prescribing particular offences as offences of the same category.

Examples of an open approach to admissibility

The growing amount of case law on **s. 101(1)(d)** confirms the truth of the allegation made by Dennis. An example of the prosecutorial benefit the statute extended is evidenced in *R v Somanathan* [2006] 1 WLR 1885 where the Court of Appeal held that evidence of the defendant's sexual conduct from women members of his congregation was admissible even though it would not have been admissible under the old 'similar fact' rule, 'enhanced probative value' was not required. It is pertinent to note here the wide definition of bad character, **s. 98**, which includes 'the commission of an offence or other reprehensible behaviour'.

Another argument to support the Dennis analysis is that propensity evidence may be admitted under other 'gateways'. Thus in *R v Highton* the defendant's previous convictions had been admitted under **s. 101(1)(g)**. However, the court held that the judge had been right to give a direction on propensity. Conversely, the broader range of convictions admitted under **s. 101(1)(g)** means that even if not so directed the jury might well consider the behaviour exhibits propensity as much as credibility. Thus in *R v Clarke* **(2011)**, the defendant was charged with sexual offences and his previous record for violent offences was admitted through **s. 101(1)(g)**. The Court of Appeal stated that it was not unreasonable to admit the whole of C's character under **s. 101(1)(g)** and for the judge in summing-up to remind the jury that none of these offences were sexual offences and they did not show he had committed the offences with which he was charged.

The broad discretion available to the judge has meant that the Court of Appeal has been reluctant to overturn first instance decisions where it might be argued bad character evidence has been admitted too readily. Durston (2011, p. 196) cites *R v Awaritefe* **[2007] EWCA Crim 706** as 'indicative of the range of the trial judge's discretion'. The court was ready to admit previous offences as showing propensity although they were less serious than the current charge and took place some time previously. The Court of Appeal was of the opinion that some judges would not have admitted this evidence but it was within the range of discretionary action.

Finally, the propensity evidence may be admitted by joinder of similar charges; see *R v Chopra* [2007] where the court commented, 'The important change is that whereas previously evidence of the defendant's propensity to offend in the manner now charged was prima facie inadmissible, now it is prima facie admissible.' Again, in *Freeman* **(2009)** evidence in relation to one count in an indictment was capable of being admitted as bad character evidence in relation to the others. The common law more restrictive approach no longer applied.

Examples of a restrictive approach to admissibility

On the other hand, there are a number of indications that the courts may on occasion be more reluctant to admit propensity evidence. In the leading case, *R v Hanson*, the Court of Appeal set out the way in which propensity may be demonstrated. It stated: 'A simple previous conviction for an offence of the same description or category will often not show propensity. But it may do so where, for example, it shows a tendency to unusual behaviour or where its circumstances demonstrate probative force in relation to the offence charged.' Durston (2008, p. 200) commented, 'The approach adopted in *Hanson* is at variance to that originally anticipated (in October 2004) by David Blunkett, the then Home Secretary, who suggested that there would be "strong presumption" (albeit rebuttable) that previous convictions that were in the same category as that subsequently being tried should be admitted.' Further *Hanson* and *Campbell* both demonstrated a cautious approach to admitting evidence of propensity for untruthfulness under **s. 103(1(b)**. The court distinguished between dishonesty and untruthfulness and stated:

> . . . the only circumstances in which there is likely to be an *important* issue as to whether a defendant has a propensity to tell lies is where telling lies is an element of the offence charged. Even then, the propensity to tell lies is only likely to be significant if the lying is in the context of committing criminal offences, in which case the evidence is likely to be admissible under **s 103(1)(a)**.

The effect of specifying that a propensity for being untruthful will only be rarely found is, as Mirfield put it (2008, p. 5) 'to render **s 103(1)(b)** a dead letter'.

Finally, under **s. 101(3)** there is a test of fairness for admissibility and the court must not admit propensity evidence if, whether the defendant has made an application or not, it appears to the court that the admission of the evidence would have such an adverse effect on the fairness of the proceedings that the court ought not to admit it.

Before assessing the impact of the new law Tapper (2010, p. 378) reviewed criticisms of the earlier provisions. Noting that, 'The test eventually adopted for the admission of evidence of the accused's bad character in chief was roughly that it should be more probative then prejudicial', Tapper continued, 'It could indeed be argued that the test, as formulated in terms of weighing probative force against prejudicial effect, was incoherent. It was clear that "prejudicial effect" must mean more than that the admission of the evidence would tend to lead to an increased chance of conviction, and it was usually accepted that it meant that the trier of fact would attach more weight to the evidence than it deserved.'

It is questionable whether the new law has succeeded in removing this unfairness. There are some indications that the courts have adopted a more cautious approach to admitting evidence of propensity. Thus, in *Hanson* the court stated that even when offences were categorised as being of the same description, this was neither necessary, nor sufficient, to justify admission. The issue was still whether the convictions established propensity and if that propensity was relevant to the accused's guilt. But relevance again is a matter of degree and context. In *R v Edwards (Stewart Dean)* [2006] **1 WLR 1524** the trial judge regarded convictions of over 20 years ago as not admissible, however relevant the convictions were.

The comment by Dennis illustrates the continuing difficulty of establishing clear guidelines for the admissibility of disposition evidence. There is an inevitable conflict between fairness to the defendant, endorsed in **art. 6 of the European Convention on Human Rights,** and the public need to prosecute offenders successfully. As McEwan (1998, p. 52) points out, 'concepts of relevance or probative value are highly subjective'. The development of the case law shows the intractable problem of assessing the weight of the evidence. Waterman and Dempster see the current approach as a 'half way position between the old principles and the new' (2006, p. 627). They decry the absence of a 'logical analytical basis' in recent judgments. This is not, however, a matter of semantics. In part the development of the law has reflected different social values which have of course been reflected by the judiciary. Just as the notorious case of *Thompson* [1918] AC 221 reflects prejudice and ignorance, so the lowering of the threshold in *DPP v P* and then even further in the CJA 2003 reflects a growing awareness of the needs of victims and of the potential value of children's evidence. Perhaps too much attention has been directed to relevance as an aspect of admissibility. Just as important perhaps are clear judicial directions on matters of prejudice as well as logic on how the jury should view such evidence.

The complexity of the CJA 2003 and the sometimes contradictory decisions in the courts prompt reflection on the value of an alternative, open approach to admissibility of bad character evidence. Zuckerman (1989, p. 248) suggested that:

> [a] more effective way of combating prejudice would be to bring into the open the scope of prejudice created by evidence of past criminal record and strive to persuade jurors that the principles of criminal justice, which require resisting prejudice, reflect their own perception of justice.

This is an argument for saying that the criminal record should be routinely admitted as in continental jurisdictions. This perhaps would avoid highlighting the criminal record as a matter of importance. Zuckerman suggested that 'the question of admissibility [would be] less important because the tools will be in place for counteracting prejudice.' But this proposition arguably underestimates the amount of prejudice juries draw from prior bad character and also presupposes that the judiciary are able to convey such complex ethical messages to a jury of differing experiences and moral standpoints.

Question 5

Nicholas, a taxi driver, is charged with criminally damaging a small plantation of rare palm trees in a country park. His fingerprints are found on a note which was pinned to the gate of the plantation which called for 'British trees only to be planted in British parks'. Nicholas denies the offence and claims that he had picked up a passenger who asked to be dropped at the park. He claims that the customer asked him to put the note in the glove compartment of the car and took the note away at the end of the ride. Nicholas denies having entered the park and claims he drove away after dropping the customer off. He denies he has an obsessive interest in trees.

Advise the prosecution on the following matters:

(a) Whether they can adduce evidence of two previous acquittals of Nicholas on charges of criminal damage of tropical trees planted in country parks. On each occasion his defence had been that he had dropped a customer at the park.

(b) Whether evidence is admissible that Nicholas is a member of a group called 'Keep our Flora British' (KFB).

(c) Whether evidence from his wife is admissible that on their honeymoon 30 years previously Nicholas had insisted they visited a series of private woodlands of tropical plants and had been warned by landowners about trespassing.

Commentary

(a) The prosecution is likely to rely on **s. 101(1)(d) CJA 2003**. Bad character evidence is admissible if 'it is relevant to an important matter in issue between the defendant and the prosecution.' **Section 103** defines this as including (i) the question whether the defendant has a propensity to commit offences of the kind with which he is charged, except where his having such a propensity makes it no more likely that he is guilty of the offence; (ii) the question whether the defendant has a propensity to be untruthful, except where it is not suggested that the defendant's case is untruthful in any respect.

(b) The prosecution will try to argue that Nicholas's membership of this organisation increases the likelihood of his guilt and that **s. 101(1)(d)** applies. The issue here is whether non-criminal behaviour is admissible under **s. 101(1)(d)**.

(c) The question here is that of relevance.

Answer plan

(a) • Are previous acquittals admissible under the **CJA 2003, s. 101(1)(d)**?—see also *R v Z* **[2002] 2 AC 483**?

• What is the relevance of the number of acquittals?

• Does the Categories of Offences Order apply?

(b) • Does bad character evidence under **CJA 2003** include non-criminal behaviour?

• Applicability of common law cases, e.g. *R v Lewis* **(1982) 76 Cr App R 33**, *R v Barrington* **[1981] 1 WLR 419**.

• Post-**CJA 2003** cases: *R v Edwards* **[2005] EWCA Crim 3244**, *R v Hanson* **[2005] EWCA Crim 824**.

(c) Applicability to wife's testimony of **s. 101(1)(c)**, admitting relevant explanatory evidence. See *R v Davis* **(2008) EWCA Crim 1156**.

Suggested answer

(a) Here the prosecution will be helped by the Explanatory Notes on the statute and the decisions in *Hanson* **[2005] EWCA Crim 824** and *Highton* **[2005] EWCA Crim 1985**. The Explanatory Note reads 'evidence might be relevant to one of a number of issues in a case. For example, it might help the prosecution to prove the defendant's guilt of the offence by establishing their involvement or state of mind or by rebutting the defendant's explanation of his conduct.' In *Hanson* Rose LJ set out a three-stage test in relation to propensity.

1. Does the history of conviction(s) establish a propensity to commit offences of the kind charged?

2. Does that propensity make it more likely that the defendant committed the offence charged?

3. Is it unjust to rely on the conviction(s) of the same description or category; and in any event will the proceedings be unfair if they are admitted?

The **Criminal Justice Act 2003 (Categories of Offences) Order 2004 (SI 3346/2004)** lists two categories, namely, theft and sexual offences against a person under the age of 16, on which it is not unjust to rely. The prosecution will not therefore be aided by these categorisations in this case.

The other problem is that the previous behaviour of Nicholas is based on a record of acquittals not convictions. In the pre-**2003 Act** case of *R v Z* [2003] 3 All ER 385 the House of Lords admitted previous acquittals on a charge of rape since they had a direct bearing on the question of consent in the current charge. The Explanatory Note to the **2003 Act** makes it clear that the definition of bad character is broad. It reads:

> The definition is therefore intended to include evidence such as previous convictions as well as evidence on charges being tried concurrently, and evidence relating to offences for which a person has been charged, when the charge was not prosecuted or for which the person was subsequently acquitted. This reflects the state of the current law. On the latter point in the case of Z [2002] 2 AC 483, the House of Lords held that there was no special rule that required the exclusion of evidence that the person had been involved in earlier offences, even if they had been acquitted of those crimes, provided that the evidence was otherwise admissible. Thus if there were a series of attacks and the defendants were acquitted of involvement in them, evidence showing, or tending to show that he had committed those earlier attacks could be given in a later case if it were admissible to establish that he had committed the latest attack. The Act preserves the effect of this decision.

It continued: 'the scheme does not affect the admissibility of evidence of the facts of the offence. This is excluded from the definition, as is evidence of misconduct in connection with the offence.'

The approach taken in *R v Z* has been confirmed by *R v Mustapha (Mohammed Amadu)* [2007] EWCA Crim 1702, decided under the **CJA 2003**.

The court has discretion to exclude these acquittals under two sections. **Section 101(3)** reads: 'the court must not admit evidence under **subsection (1)(d)** if, on the application by the defendant to exclude, it appears to the court that the admission of the evidence would have such an adverse effect on the fairness of the proceedings that the court ought not to admit it.' On an application to exclude evidence under **subs. (3)** the court must have regard, in particular, to the length of time between the matters to which that evidence relates and the matters which form the subject of the offence charged. **Section 103(2) and (3)** read:

(2) . . . a defendant's propensity to commit offences of the kind with which he is charged may. . . . be established by evidence of (a) an offence of the same description as the one with which he is charged, or (b) an offence of the same category as the one with which he is charged.

(3) Subsection (2) does not apply in the case of a particular defendant if the court is satisfied by reason of the length of time since the conviction or for any other reason, that it would be unjust for it to apply in his case.

Arguably more information is needed as to how long ago the acquittals were. The fact that there were three, however, makes it more likely that they will be admitted. The prosecution will need to give notice in advance that they wish to put the acquittals in evidence and since they are likely to want to adduce similarities in the defence argument about dropping off customers they will need also to specify these surrounding details. In *Hanson* (para. 17) the Court of Appeal referred to the need to specify surrounding circumstances in the context of convictions but presumably the same point applies to acquittals with even more force, since it is the similarities of the defence which are at issue. The acquittals are likely to be admitted through the gateway of **s. 101(1)(d)**. It is uncertain whether the prosecution will also be able to rely on **s. 103(1)(b)** which refers to 'the question whether the defendant has a propensity to be untruthful, except where it is not suggested that the defendant's case is untruthful in any respect.' It is clearly the prosecution case that the defendant is putting forward a lying defence and the fact that he had put forward the defence several times before increases the likelihood that his defence is not to be believed. The acquittals in themselves, however, do not appear to fulfil the requirement for admissibility under **s. 101(1)(b)** in that they do not in themselves demonstrate a propensity to be untruthful (see *Hanson*). The judge may have to direct that the acquittals are relevant to his guilt but not to his propensity for untruthfulness.

(b) According to the Explanatory Note bad character can include 'evidence not related to criminal proceedings . . . might include, for example, evidence that a person has a sexual interest in children or is racist.' Nicholas is claiming no involvement with the offence of destroying the trees. The likelihood of his defence that he was in the area but did not engage in the offence would be undermined by evidence that he was a member of an organisation which probably only has a small number of members. It is not of the order of membership of a gardening club for example. Someone who is a member of the KFB is more likely to be involved in direct action on this issue than someone who is not. Bear in mind that evidence does not have to reach certainty but simply increase the likelihood of guilt sufficiently to overcome the obvious prejudice of admitting it. In *R v Lewis* (1982) 76 Cr App R 33, membership of the Paedophilia Society was admissible to rebut the defence of innocent association. Arguably here, membership of the KFB is likely to be admitted because it is relevant to the defence of non-involvement. It surely defies coincidence that a person who belonged to such an organisation and who was in the area at the time was not involved in the offence. In *R v Barrington* [1981] 1 WLR 419 evidence of prior disreputable but non-criminal actions were admissible since as the court stated (at p. 430) they were 'of positive probative value in assisting to determine the truth of the charges against the appellant.' The prosecution is likely to be allowed to put this evidence to the jury.

Some guidance on what is meant by bad character under the **CJA 2003** has been given in a number of cases. **Section 98** provides that 'References to . . . evidence of a person's "bad character" are to evidence of, or of a disposition towards, misconduct on his part . . .' Misconduct is defined in **s. 112(1)** as 'the commission of an offence or other reprehensible behaviour'. The Law Commission report (2002, paras 8.12–8.19) stated that, 'References in this Act to evidence of a person's bad character are references to evidence which shows or tends to show that (a) he has committed an offence, or (b) he has behaved, or is disposed to behave, in a way that, in the opinion of the court, might be viewed with disapproval by a reasonable person.'

It is arguable that Nicholas's membership of the KFB does not fall within the **s. 98(1)** definition. It might therefore be admitted on grounds of relevance and not under **CJA 2003**. Under *R v Kilbourne* [1973] AC 729 evidence is 'relevant' if 'it is logically probative or disprobative of some matter which requires proof'. On the other hand, if the court considers the statute applies it could be argued that **s. 101(1)(d)** applies and that the membership of KFB may be considered reprehensible. Arguments in favour of admissibility can be found in *R v Saleem* [2007] EWCA Crim 1923, which involved possessing disturbing rap lyrics; arguments against are found in *R v Edwards* [2006] 1 WLR 1524, where lawfully possessing an antique firearm was not reprehensible behaviour. The prosecution will seek to rely on *R v Weir* [2006] 1 WLR 1885. 'Reprehensible behaviour' short of a conviction was held to be admissible. The court stated that **s. 101(1)(d)** 'completely reverses the pre-existing general rule. The rule of exclusion subject to an inclusionary discretion is replaced by a presumption of inclusion with a discretion to exclude.' However, the defence should be aided by the warning that the Court of Appeal made in *Hanson* that bad character evidence must not be simply used to bolster a weak case.

The evidence will most likely, if adduced, be proffered by the prosecution as evidence of propensity. But, as Goudkamp (2008, p. 13) comments, reviewing these and other cases, 'it seems impossible to distil a common denominator from these authorities'.

(c) The evidence of the wife arguably is 'bad character evidence' in that trespassing could be regarded as 'other reprehensible behaviour'. It also seems to be a statement of contradiction of Nicholas's testimony that he is not interested in trees. In *R v Davis* (2008) the Court of Appeal made clear that such evidence could not be readily admitted. In that case, involving the murder of the defendant's long-term partner, evidence from the defendant's former girlfriend was wrongly admitted under **s. 101(1)(c)** as 'important explanatory evidence'. This is defined as admissible evidence if '(a) without it, the court or jury would find it impossible or difficult properly to understand other evidence in the case, and (b) its value for understanding the case as a whole is substantial.' It was not acceptable to admit propensity evidence which was not admissible under (d) because it was more prejudicial than probative. It is likely that the evidence would not pass the test set out in *Hanson* and so should not simply be admitted to contradict the defendant in relation to his obsessive interest in trees.

Further reading

Durston, G., 'Bad Character Evidence and Non-party Witnesses under the Criminal Justice Act 2003' (2004) 8 E & P 233.

Goudkamp, J., 'Bad Character Evidence and Reprehensible Behaviour' (2008) E & P 116.

Law Commission Consultation Paper, *Evidence in Criminal Proceedings: Previous Misconduct of a Defendant* (CP 141) (London: HMSO, 1996).

Law Commission Report No. 273, *Evidence of Bad Character in Criminal Proceedings* (Cm 5257) (London: HMSO, 2001).

Lloyd-Bostock, S., 'The Effects on Juries of Hearing about the Defendant's Previous Criminal Record: A Simulation Study' [2000] Crim LR 734.

McEwan, J., 'Previous Misconduct at the Crossroads: Which Way Ahead?' [2002] Crim LR 180.

Mirfield, P., 'Character, Credibility and Untruthfulness' (2008) 124 LQR 1.

Mirfield, P., 'Character and Credibility' [2009] Crim LR 135.

Munday, R., 'Reflections on the Criminal Evidence Act 1898' [1985] CLJ 62.

Munday, R., 'What Constitutes "Other Reprehensible Behaviour" under the Bad Character Provisions of the Criminal Justice Act 2003' [2005] Crim LR 24.

Munday, R., 'The Purposes of Gateway (g): Yet Another Problematic of the Criminal Justice Act 2003' [2006] Crim LR 300.

Redmayne, M., 'The Relevance of Bad Character' (2002) 61 CLJ 684.

Roberts, P., 'Acquitted Misconduct Evidence and Double Jeopardy Principles, From *Sambasivan* to *Z*' [2000] Crim LR 952.

Spencer, J.R., *Evidence of Bad Character* (Oxford: Hart, 2010).

Wasik, M., 'The Vital Importance of Certain Previous Convictions' [2001] Crim LR 363.

Waterman, A. and Dempster, T., 'Bad Character: Feeling Our Way One Year On' [2006] Crim LR 614.

Zuckerman, A.A.S., 'Similar Fact Evidence—The Unobservable Rule' (1987) 103 LQR 187.

5

Hearsay

Introduction

The rule against hearsay is historically one of the great exclusionary rules underlying the law of evidence. Little remains of the rule, however, in civil law, after the passage of the **Civil Evidence Acts 1968, 1972 and 1995.**

Hearsay in criminal proceedings is an area where piecemeal reform has been the order of the day. However, the pace of change has now accelerated. In 1997 the Law Commission recommended that hearsay evidence be admitted in criminal trials if the interests of justice require it (see *Evidence in Criminal Proceedings: Hearsay and Related Topics*, Law Commission Report No. 245 (Cm 3670, 1997)); this eventually led to wholesale reform in the **Criminal Justice Act (CJA) 2003.** The Act in essence preserves the rule but increases the number of exceptions and safeguards. It provides a comprehensive regime for hearsay, although some common law exceptions are preserved in **s. 118 CJA 2003.**

Table 7 gives an overview of the changes to hearsay introduced by the CJA 2003. The second column gives the earlier position under the common law and the **CJA 1988** and the third column the position under the **CJA 2003**, which repeals **Part 2 of the CJA 1988**. **Diagrams 3 and 4** give an outline of key sections of the **CJA 2003**.

Birch (2004, p. 573) had little comfort for long-suffering evidence students: 'As to the Royal Commission's criticism that the hearsay rule is "exceptionally complex and difficult to interpret", it is a fair bet that law students will continue to groan whenever the word "hearsay" is mentioned.' (See Chapter 10 for hearsay and previous inconsistent statements and other previous statements of witnesses.)

Table 7 Criminal hearsay rules: a brief history

Aspect of hearsay	Common law/CJA 1988	Criminal Justice Act 2003
Definition	'…an assertion other than one made by a person while giving oral evidence in the proceedings is inadmissible as evidence of any fact or opinion asserted' (*Cross on Evidence*)	Statement not made orally in the proceedings, tendered as evidence of any matter stated (**s. 114(1), s. 115, s. 121(2)**)
Admissibility	Inadmissible unless fell within common law or statutory exceptions.	Admissible under statute, or preserved common law exceptions or after court has considered provisions in **s. 114** including 'interests of justice'. See 'Inclusionary discretion'
Implied assertions	Inadmissible hearsay (***R v Kearley* [1992] 2 AC 228**)	Non-hearsay (**s. 115(3)**)
Common law exceptions	Included confessions, *res gestae*, dying declarations, common enterprise, public documents, statements against pecuniary interest by persons since deceased	Specifically preserved, **s. 118**, except dying declarations and statements against interest. Dying declarations however arguably now come under the *res gestae* exception
Expert evidence	Experts' reports were admissible with leave if witness not attending court (**s. 30**), section not repealed	Experts may rely on statements prepared by other persons, at trial judge's discretion (**s. 127**)
Oral hearsay statements	Only admissible under common law exceptions	May be admissible (**s. 116**) if witness unavailable for one of the statutory reasons
First-hand written hearsay	Were admissible (**s. 23**) if statutory reason for not calling witness with leave of court	May be admissible if statutory reason for not calling witness. Permissible reasons extended beyond those in **s. 23 CJA 1988** to include fear of death or injury to another person or financial loss (**s. 116**) admitted with leave of court
Multiple oral hearsay	Were not admissible (**s. 23**)	May be admissible under **s. 121(1)(c)**
Multiple written hearsay (non-business documents)	Were not admissible (**s. 23**)	May be admissible under **ss. 119, 120, or 121(1)(c)**
Multiple hearsay business documents	Were admissible (**s. 24**) with leave of the court (**ss. 25, 26**); supplier must have personal knowledge of fact	May be admissible (**s. 117**). No need for leave of court (**s. 121**). Documents do not have to form part of a record. Supplier must have personal knowledge of fact

Aspect of hearsay	Common law/CJA 1988	Criminal Justice Act 2003
Statements prepared for criminal proceedings	Were admissible under **s. 23** or (**s. 24**) if specified reason for not calling witness and with leave of court	May be admissible if statutory reason for not calling witness (**s. 117(4)**)
Exclusionary discretion	See **ss. 25, 26 CJA 1988**, **s. 78 PACE**	See **s. 101(3)** and **s. 114(2)**, **s. 126(1)**. Also **s. 125** provides judge must direct acquittal if case rests wholly or partly on hearsay and evidence provided by statement is so unconvincing that, considering its importance to the case against the defendant, a conviction could be unsafe
Inclusionary discretion	None	Introduced; see **ss. 114(1)(d) and 114(2)**
Credibility of absent witness	Evidence concerning credibility was admissible (**Sch. 2**)	Evidence concerning credibility is admissible **s. 124(4)**
Notice		Procedure under **s. 132(3)** (cf. civil hearsay); rules of court may specify.

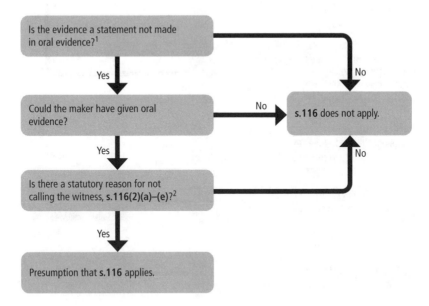

Diagram 3 Criminal hearsay—cases where a witness is unavailable, s. 116 CJA 2003

[1] The statement must be first-hand hearsay unless admissible under **s. 121(1)(a) or (b)**.

[2] If the statutory reason is **s. 116(2)(e)** ('that through fear &c') the statement is only admissible if the court has given leave.

Question 1

Harriet is charged with killing Ted. The prosecution alleges that Ted and Harriet, who were lovers, got into a heated argument whereupon Harriet, in a fit of rage, fatally stabbed him with a kitchen knife. She denies the charge and claims he killed himself.

Consider the admissibility of the following evidence:

(a) Evidence from Kit, a passer-by, who administered first aid to Ted when he staggered out of his house covered in blood. Ted gasped, 'Harriet knifed me. I've had it.' He died two hours later.

(b) Evidence from Ted's mother that Harriet told her on the day of the stabbing that she was going to confront Ted about his gambling.

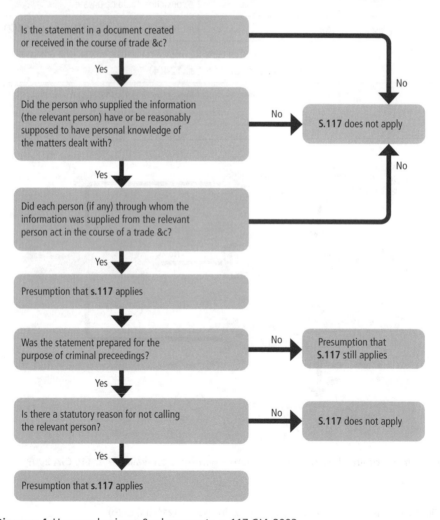

Diagram 4 Hearsay, business &c documents, s. 117 CJA 2003

Commentary

The first issue here is whether the statement made to Kit is admissible under **s. 116 CJA 2003** or, in the alternative, as part of the *res gestae*, in order for it to be admissible as an exception to the hearsay rule; it is also possible that the statement from Ted's mother infringes the rule against hearsay. What needs to be considered is whether a person's declaration of his or her intention is regarded as an exception to the hearsay rule.

Answer plan

(a) • Purpose of adducing statement to decide if it is hearsay.

   • If it is hearsay it may be admissible under the **CJA 2003** as first-hand oral hearsay or *res gestae*.

(b) • Ted's mother's statement of what Harriet told her is arguably hearsay if adduced to suggest motive.

   • If it is hearsay, the statement may fall within 'state of mind' exception in **CJA 2003, s. 118**.

   • Note the lack of clarity in case law whether court can infer from 'state of mind'.

Suggested answer

(a) Application of CJA 2003, s. 116

The statement made by Ted to Kit is a hearsay statement in that it is adduced for the purpose of establishing that what it says is true. The statutory definition of hearsay is to be found in **ss. 114(1), 115(2) and (3) and 121(2) of the Criminal Justice Act (CJA) 2003**. It is as stated (s. 114(1)). The statement by Ted fulfils this definition. It may, however, be given by Kit either under **s. 116 or s. 118 of the CJA 2003**. To take **s. 116** first, this section admits first-hand oral or documentary hearsay if there is a reason for not calling the witness, in this case Ted, who was the maker of the statement or the relevant person. **Section 116(2)(a)** gives the reason that 'the relevant person is dead'. Under **s. 116(1)(a)** that person who made the statement must be identified to the court's satisfaction. If Kit is a competent and compellable witness she can give evidence of the statement. Under **s. 124** Harriet may call relevant evidence on Ted's credibility to challenge the statement. If as a result of evidence admitted under this section an allegation is made against the maker of the statement the court may permit a party to lead additional evidence of such description as the court may specify for the purposes of denying or answering the allegation.

Under **s. 125** if the case against the defendant is based wholly or partly on a statement not made in oral evidence and the evidence provided by the statement is so unconvincing, considering its importance to the case against the defendant, that his conviction of the offence would be unsafe, the court must either direct the jury to acquit the defendant of the offence, or if it considers that there ought to be a retrial, discharge the jury. We are not told if there is any other evidence against Harriet such as forensic material. However, it is unlikely that **s. 125** will apply since recent case law confirms that a conviction may be based on hearsay alone, see *R v Horncastle* **[2009] UKSC 14** although the Supreme Court also acknowledged that this would not be commonplace. In *Al-Khawaja v UK* **(2011) 54 EHRR 23** the Grand Chamber of the European Court of Human Rights upheld this reasoning.

Part 34 of the Criminal Procedure Rules 2011 sets out the notice requirements for introducing certain hearsay evidence. A party who receives a notice of hearsay evidence may oppose it by giving notice to the court officer and all other parties.

Res gestae

Alternatively, the statement may be admissible under the common law exceptions preserved in **s. 118 CJA 2003**. The statement appears to be a dying declaration which is one common law exception to the rule against hearsay not preserved in the new statute. However, arguably the *res gestae* exception which is preserved is broad enough to include such a statement.

The test of admissibility of such statements depends on whether the statements were made in such circumstances as to make concoction or fabrication unlikely. This test was applied in later cases such as *R v Turnbull* **(1985) 80 Cr App R 104** and approved by the House of Lords in *R v Andrews* **[1987] AC 281**. In the latter case, the facts of which are similar to the facts of the case in hand, Lord Ackner stated that the judge had to consider all the circumstances of the case in order to satisfy himself that the event was so unusual as to dominate the thoughts of the victim, so that his utterance was an instinctive reaction to the event giving no opportunity for concoction or distortion. Where a possibility of malice on the part of the declarant is raised, the judge must be satisfied that there was no possibility of concoction or distortion. Further, the judge had to take into account the possibility of error, if only the ordinary fallibility of human recollection, but that this went to the weight of the evidence, not to its admissibility.

It could therefore be argued that Ted's statement falls within the test laid out in *Ratten* **[1971] 3 WLR 930** which was explained and approved in *Andrews*, in that the circumstances of the case are such that there is no possibility of concoction or distortion. In the absence of the court being satisfied that there was malice on the part of Ted, it is likely that this statement could be admitted as a *res gestae* statement under **s. 118(1), para. 4(a) CJA 2003**.

There are advantages in using the common law exception since the statutory exclusionary discretion does not apply.

(b) State of mind exception

It is arguable that what Harriet told Ted's mother on the morning of the stabbing is a hearsay statement. It indicates Harriet was angry with Ted which is relevant to the prosecution's case on motive. Thus it would be inadmissible unless it falls within one of the common law exceptions to the hearsay rule. Statements made by a person concerning his or her contemporaneous state of mind or emotion are admissible as evidence of his or her state of mind or emotion as an exception to the hearsay rule.

This common law principle is preserved in **s. 118(1), para. 4(c)**. The importance of this exception is seen in *Neill v North Antrim Magistrates' Court* **[1993] 97 Cr App R 121**. The House of Lords held that the statements by police officers recounting what the two witnesses who did not give evidence through fear had told the police officers could have been given as evidence of what the witnesses had said about their fear. This was based on the law that a person's declaration of his contemporaneous state of mind was admissible. Doak and McGourlay (2012, p. 313) point out that 'It was emphasised that the evidence must *not* be that the witnesses were afraid (that is an inference for the court to draw) but that the witnesses *said* they were afraid and that their demeanour was consistent with what they had said.' It is arguable that statements as to the person's intention fall under this exception, as evidence of his or her intention at the time when the statement is made. The difficulty that arises is whether, as in the case here, the court is able to infer from the statement that the intention was carried out.

There is a lack of agreement by the courts on this issue, and the court will doubtless draw on the common law authorities. In *R v Buckley* **(1873) 13 Cox CC 293**, the court admitted into evidence a statement made by the victim, a police officer, to his senior officer, that he was going to watch the movements of the accused the night that he was killed. Likewise, in *R v Moghal* **(1977) 65 Cr App R 56**, a tape-recording made six months earlier as to the intention of a third party, was admissible into evidence. However, the correctness of *Moghal* was doubted by the House of Lords in *R v Blastland* **[1986] AC 41**. In contrast, in *R v Wainwright* **(1875) 13 Cox CC 171**, the court refused to allow into evidence a statement made by the victim to a friend, on the afternoon of her murder, that she was on the way to the house of the accused. The court similarly refused to allow into evidence a statement as to where the victim was going just before her death, in *R v Pook* **(noted at (1875) 13 Cox CC 171)**. The reasons for the court's refusal to admit such evidence is on the basis that it was merely evidence of the victim's intention, which may or may not have been carried out. In *R v Callender* **[1998] Crim LR 337** a statement made by a defendant two weeks before his arrest about his intentions in relation to carrying explosive devices was not admitted. The defendant wanted to put as part of his defence that he intended to carry false explosives for publicity.

The rationale behind the admissibility of statements concerning contemporaneous state of mind was put in *R v Blastland* **[1986] AC 41**:

> It is of course elementary that statements made to a witness by a third party are not excluded by the hearsay rule when they are put in evidence solely to prove the state of mind either of the maker of the statement or of the person to whom it was made. What a person said or heard may well be the best and most direct evidence of that person's state of mind. This principle can only apply, however, when the state of mind

evidenced by the statement is either itself directly in issue at the trial, or of direct and immediate relevance to an issue which arises at the trial.

Choo comments (2012, p. 295) in relation to the conflicting authorities on whether evidence suggesting an intent to perform a particular act is admissible to establish that the intent was in fact carried out, that is, that the act in question was performed: 'The apparent conflict remains factually unresolved but a sensible approach may be to adopt the view of Mason CJ, expressed in the decision of the High Court of Australia in *Walton v R* that, "out-of-court statements which tend to prove a plan or intention of the author [should be admissible in evidence] subject to remoteness in time and indications of unreliability or lack of protective value"'. (See **(1989) 166 CLR 228, 290.**)

There is the possibility also of admissibility under **s. 114. Section 114(2)(a)–(d)** sets out the conditions for the exercise of the inclusionary discretion, namely that it is in the interests of justice to admit an otherwise inadmissible statement. *R v Xhabri* **[2005] EWCA Crim 3135** gives an illustration of the operation of the section which may be inadmissible by another section.

? Question 2

(a) David is charged with murdering his wife Heather. She had been found bound and naked hanging from the garden shed. The prosecution wish to adduce evidence of a text message sent to Heather and recorded by David two days before Heather's death on his mobile phone. 'Thanks for agreeing to pose for me.' David claims Heather's death must have occurred during a sado-masochistic experiment which Heather had frequently indulged in and in which he took no part. He produced a mobile phone photograph on Heather's phone of Heather bound and gagged on an earlier occasion. He claimed she had taken it of herself. However, Heather's sister Jean is willing to testify that Heather had told her that David had persuaded her to pose for the photograph against her will. He had claimed, she said, that he needed it as part of his plan to produce a book on erotic photography.

Advise whether any of the above statements may be held inadmissible because of the operation of the rule against hearsay.

(b) Anna, Freda and Monisha are charged with robbery from Hendfield Building Society. Tracker dogs were used to trace them. Freda was discovered walking alongside a railway line a few hours after the robbery. She denied involvement and said she had been picking blackberries.

At an identification parade held a short time after the robbery, Anna was picked out as one of the robbers by Paul, the manager of the branch. As a result of a concussion later received in a road traffic accident, Paul is now suffering from amnesia and is unable later to remember what happened at the identification parade. However, Detective Inspector Daniels was present at the identification parade and is able to testify that Paul picked out Anna during the parade. Monisha was identified by Edmund, the assistant manager, who recognised her when he viewed the video-recording of Monisha during the robbery. The recording was accidentally deleted by Edmund shortly afterwards.

A few months after the arrest of Anna, Freda and Monisha, just before she died, Gertrude spoke to her mother, and confessed to having been one of the two persons who committed the robbery.

Advise as to the admissibility of the evidence.

 Commentary

You need to consider the admissibility of the following possible 'statements'. First, the mobile phone diary entry raises the question of the status of implied assertions. You need to consider the admissibility of the photograph and whether it is real evidence or hearsay. The prosecution will wish to adduce Jean's statement to show Heather's state of mind as part of the *res gestae*. The question thus requires you to be familiar with the **CJA 2003** and the extent to which it has preserved the common law.

In the second part of the question you need to discuss whether the evidence of the tracker dogs is admissible. Another issue is whether Detective Inspector Daniels is able to testify to what occurred during the identification parade. The problem with his testimony is that it may be hearsay. A further issue relates to the video-recording and the identification of Monisha by Edmund and whether this infringes the rule against hearsay. The final point of the question requires a discussion as to whether an oral confession by a third party is admissible into evidence in view of the fact that it may infringe the hearsay rule and, if so, whether any of the exceptions apply. Here you need to consider the possibility of admissibility under **s. 116** and the inclusionary discretion under **s. 114**.

 Answer plan

(a) • The text message is possibly implied assertion and not hearsay.

  • Photography—real evidence or hearsay?

  • Jean's statement about what Heather told her arguably *res gestae* exception—***R v Gilfoyle* (2001) [1996] 3 All ER 883**.

(b) Tracker dogs evidence—***R v Pieterson* (1995)**.

  • Identification evidence avoids rule against hearsay—***R v McCay*, CJA 2003, s. 120**.

  • Video-tape as real evidence.

  • Admission by Gertrude inadmissible if ***Blastland*** followed—but see **CJA 2003, ss. 116 and 114**.

 Suggested answer

(a) The defence argument is that Heather caused her own death and so the photograph becomes relevant evidence to suggest that her death was consistent with her allegedly previous reckless behaviour.

The photograph

In *R v Maqsud Ali* [1966] 1 QB 688, where a tape-recording was admitted in evidence the Court of Criminal Appeal noted that the courts had long admitted photographs. The photograph here is thus a piece of real evidence and admissible. No statement is being relied on here. In the **Criminal Justice Act (CJA) 2003, s. 129** the common law presumption that a mechanical device has been properly set or calibrated is maintained.

The prosecution will want to undermine the defence by calling Jean to testify what Heather had told her. Statements made by a person concerning his or her contemporaneous state of mind or emotion are admissible as evidence of his or her state of mind or emotion. This common law rule is preserved in **s. 118 CJA 2003**. The exception was clearly acknowledged by the House of Lords in *R v Blastland* [1986] AC 41 accepting that 'statements made to a witness by a third party are not excluded by the hearsay rule when they are put in evidence solely to prove the state of mind of the maker of the statement or of the person to whom it was made.' The prosecution will argue that Heather's state of mind is of immediate relevance since it suggests that David had contrived to get her compromising photograph for his own purposes. In *R v Gilfoyle* [1996] 3 All ER 883 the accused on trial for murdering his wife produced what seemed to be suicide notes written by the wife. It was argued subsequently that the notes were manufactured by the accused. The Court of Appeal held that statements by friends of the wife in which she said the accused had asked her to write the notes as part of his study of suicide, should have been admitted at trial. They had been excluded as hearsay. The conversations with the friends were original evidence of the wife's state of mind in that they increased the likelihood that the 'suicide notes' were not written when she was suicidal. An alternative explanation was that the statements of the wife to the friends were hearsay if tendered to show she was prompted to write the notes by her husband. They were admissible, however, as a *res gestae* exception covering statements about contemporaneous states of mind or emotions. In *Gilfoyle* the *res gestae* exception extended in *R v Andrews* [1987] AC 281 was stretched even further to cover evidentiary facts as well as facts in issue. (Arguably now the statements would be admissible under **s. 116(2) CJA 2003**.) The court stated (per Beldam LJ at p. 323):

> In this case the statements themselves suggested that the events which prompted them were still dominating [the wife's] mind. The statements were made in the morning after the letters had been written as soon after as would ordinarily have been expected. The possibility of invention or unreliability could be discounted and there was little room for inaccuracy in the reporting of the statements.

The *res gestae* exception is preserved by **s. 118(1), para. 4(a)**. An alternative approach is that the statement by Heather may be admissible as oral hearsay under **s. 116(2)(a)**, the reason for the non-appearance of the maker being that she is dead. The common law approach may be preferred since the exclusionary discretion set out in **s. 125(1)** applies to the statutory exception.

In relation to the mobile phone text the prosecution may succeed in arguing that the messages are not hearsay and admissible as relevant evidence. Presumably they want to suggest that the phrase suggests that David had persuaded Heather to take part in the erotic games which led to her death. This contradicts his defence that she acted alone. The effect of the definition of hearsay in **s. 115(2) and (3)** is that implied assertions are not hearsay since a statement is only hearsay if the purpose, or one of the purposes, of the person making the statement appears to the court to have been to 'cause another person to believe the matter'. The appeal in *Singh* **[2006] 1 WLR 1564** turned on whether the prosecution should have been allowed to adduce evidence of entries in the memories of a mobile phone. The inference was that S had taken part in conspiracy. The court held that the evidence was an implied assertion and not hearsay. In the controversial case *R v Leonard* **[2009] EWCA Crim 1251**, phone text evidence was held to be hearsay and admissible under **s. 114(1)(d) of the CJA 2003**. *Singh* was distinguished. More recent cases, although not overruling *Leonard*, have established that text messages of this sort are not hearsay. In *R v Twist* **[2011] EWCA Crim 1143** the Court of Appeal considered four unrelated cases in which text messages were used as non-hearsay evidence. The two questions which had to be addressed in most cases were: (a) what was the matter which it was sought to prove and (b) did the maker of the communication have the purpose of causing the recipient to believe or to act upon that matter? To say that a communication was evidence of a fact (i.e. tended to prove it) was not the same as saying that the fact was the matter stated in the communication for the purposes of **s. 115**. On this reasoning David's text message is not making a statement of fact which is directed at causing another person to believe the matter and so is admissible.

(b) The tracker dogs will have picked up the scent of the robbers and presumably their barking led to Freda being discovered.

Tracker dogs

R v Pieterson **[1995] 1 WLR 293** established that an account of the behaviour of tracker dogs will be admissible provided there is evidence of its reliability, which doubtless those handling the dogs could give. The court stated:

> if a handler can establish that a dog has been properly trained over a period of time the dog's reactions indicate that it is a reliable pointer to the existence of a scent from a particular individual then that evidence should properly be admitted.
>
> However, it is important to emphasise two safeguards. First a proper foundation must be laid by detailed evidence establishing the reliability of the dog in question. Secondly the judge must, in giving his directions to the jury, alert them to the care that they need to take and to look with circumspection at the evidence of tracker dogs, having regard to the fact that the dog may not always be reliable and cannot be cross examined.

Identification

In *R v Sykes* **[1997] Crim LR 752** the court stressed the importance of the judge directing according to these guidelines. Detective Inspector Daniels may be able to testify that he saw Paul identify Anna, as one of the robbers during the identification parade. Prima facie, it could be argued that this would infringe the rule against hearsay. In *R v Osbourne; R v Virtue* [1973] QB 678, a witness could not recall what happened at an identification parade held some seven-and-a-half months earlier. A police officer who was present at the identification parade was permitted to testify that the witness picked out the accused. The Court of Appeal was of the view that the evidence was admissible as it sought to prove the fact of identification at the identification parade. The court did not deal satisfactorily with the point that the testimony of the police officer may be hearsay.

The decision in *Osbourne* has to be compared with *Jones v Metcalfe* [1967] 1 WLR 1286 and *R v McClean* (1967) 52 Cr App R 80. In these two cases, the issue revolved around whether a witness could refer to his conversation with another person as part of his testimony. It was held in both these cases that these were hearsay statements and therefore inadmissible. It is, however, likely that the court will be prepared to allow the testimony of Detective Inspector Daniels. If details of the identification parade had been written down, the position may be covered by the **CJA 2003, s. 117**. The common law provision on **para. 4(b)**. This is the principle which is applied in *R v McCay* [1990] 1 WLR 645.

As regards the evidence of Edmund who identified Monisha from the video-recording, it is clear that the video tape itself, if it was still available, would be admissible in evidence as original evidence: *Kajala v Noble* (1982) 75 Cr App R 149 and *R v Dodson* (1984) 79 Cr App R 220. However, in this case, it would appear that the video-recording has been accidentally erased by Edmund. In *Taylor v Chief Constable of Cheshire* [1986] 1 WLR 1479, a video-recording which was alleged to show the accused in the act of committing the offence was erased before the trial. The court decided that it was proper for the police officers who had seen the recording to give oral evidence of the contents of the tape. Thus, it would appear that on the facts of the case, Edmund could give evidence of what he saw on the tape.

Gertrude's admission

The final issue that has to be considered is whether the admission by Gertrude is admissible into evidence. Since she is unable to give evidence in court, her statement to her mother is clearly hearsay if adduced to suggest it is true. However, it could be argued that this evidence has probative value in that it may cast doubts on the prosecution's case that it was Anna and Monisha who committed the robbery. In *R v Blastland* [1986] AC 41, the House of Lords suggested that a confession by a third party that he committed the crime with which the accused was being tried, would be inadmissible because of the hearsay rule. The statement here fulfils the definition of hearsay in **s. 114(1), s. 115(2) and s. 121(2)**. On the assumption that Gertrude's confession is inadmissible because of the hearsay rule, the next question is whether it could be admitted under one of the exceptions to the hearsay rule.

One possible route to admissibility is under **s. 116 of the CJA 2003**. This admits first-hand oral hearsay if there is a reason for not calling the witness. One of the possible reasons is that the witness is dead (**s. 116(2)(a)**). This would apply in the case of Gertrude. Finally, this statement may be admissible under the 'interests of justice' inclusionary discretion in **s. 114**.

A statement not made in oral evidence in the proceedings is admissible as evidence of any matter stated if the court is satisfied that it is in the interests of justice first to be admissible. In deciding whether a statement is not made in oral evidence under this provision the court must have regard to the following factors (and to any others it considers relevant):

- how much probative value the statement has (assuming it is true) in relation to a matter in issue in the proceedings or how valuable it is for the understanding of other evidence in the case;
- what other evidence has been, or can be, given on the matter or evidence;
- how important the matter or evidence is in the context of the case as a whole;
- the circumstances in which the statement was made;
- how reliable the maker of the statement appears to be;
- how reliable the evidence of the maker of the statement appears to be;
- whether oral evidence of the matter stated can be given, and if not why it cannot;
- the amount of difficulty in challenging the statement;
- the extent to which the difficulty would be likely to prejudice the party facing it.

The court considered the application of the inclusionary discretion in *R v Xhabri* [2006] 1 All ER 776. Note should be taken of the procedural requirements in the **Criminal Procedure Rules 2011**.

 Question 3

'Rather than rely on precisely defined and technically complex, and at the same time, legally inconclusive exceptions, trial judges should have the power to admit hearsay whenever it is of sufficient probative value.'

(Zuckerman, *The Principles of Criminal Evidence* (Oxford: OUP, 1989), p. 216.)

Discuss in relation to criminal trials.

 Commentary

This is the type of general question on the hearsay rule that occurs frequently in evidence examinations. In answering this question, students must be clear as to the rationale for the hearsay rule. They must also recognise the criticisms of the rule, the main one being that credible and reliable evidence may be excluded as a result of the rule even though in some cases this may tend to prove the innocence of the accused. The answer should also cover the academic views on the rule and how the courts have found ways of avoiding its application.

Questions such as this, evaluating the justification for the rule against hearsay, demand you have at least an outline knowledge of the history of reform proposals in the Report of the Law Commission *Evidence in Criminal Proceedings: Hearsay and Related Topics*, No. 245 (Cm 3670, 1997), now largely enacted in the **Criminal Justice Act 2003**.

 Answer plan

- Outline reasons for exclusionary rule.
- Rule historically excluded apparently reliable evidence—***Myers v DPP* (1966)**.
- Devices adopted by court (hearsay fiddles) to admit hearsay.
- Particular difficulty over 'state of mind' exception and implied assertions.
- Law Commission proposals preserved rule but extend exceptions and allow discretion, now largely adopted in the **CJA 2003**.
- Dangers of Zuckerman's proposal and denial of 'right to confrontation', but contrast this with the complexity of the **CJA 2003**.
- Wider admissibility of hearsay may lead to unfairness to defendant. See ***Horncastle* (2009)** and ***Al-Khawaja and Tahery v UK* (2011)**.

 Suggested answer

Reasons for the rule

There are a number of reasons for the exclusionary rule on hearsay which is in principle still preserved in the **CJA 2003**. First, it has been argued that the person who made the statement may have wrongly perceived the events in question. Secondly, there is a risk that because of the fallibility of human nature, the memory of the person who heard the statement may be flawed. Thirdly, there is a risk of concoction or distortion of the events in question. Finally, the statement may have been misunderstood by the person who wrote down or heard the statement. Unlike a witness who is open to cross-examination, and the accuracy of his or her testimony can be tested, this is not normally possible with a hearsay statement. Zuckerman (1989, p. 178) argued that this is the central reason for the exclusion of hearsay statements. He goes on to suggest that there is a risk that the jury may attribute too much probative force to such evidence. Lord Bridge in *R v Blastland* [1986] **AC 41**, states that 'The danger against which this fundamental rule provides a safeguard is that untested hearsay evidence will be treated as having a probative force which it does not deserve.' In order to answer this question it is necessary first to briefly review the development of the law.

Whilst it is clear that the risk exists that such statements are unreliable because of concoction, distortion or fallibility of human nature, the extent to which the hearsay rule applied historically was much wider than is necessary. As a result of the rule, evidence which was both credible, reliable and of probative value was excluded if it did not fall strictly within one of the exceptions. An example of this can be seen in *R v Blastland* [1986] AC 41, where the House of Lords suggested that a confession by a third party that he committed the crime with which the accused was being tried, would be inadmissible because of the hearsay rule. Arguably, that evidence may have been credible but the rules of evidence would have prevented it from being admitted. Likewise in *Myers v DPP* [1965] AC 1001, credible evidence was held to be inadmissible because of the hearsay rule. It should be noted that the evidence in question is now admissible under the statutory exceptions but the point is that at the time of the decision it was inadmissible. The other criticism of the rule is that it excluded evidence which may prove the innocence of the accused: *Blastland* and *Sparks v R* [1964] 1 All ER 727 are examples of this.

Hearsay evasions

One criticism of the rule was that in order not to exclude potentially reliable and credible evidence, the courts have over the years used numerous devices in order to avoid excluding the evidence on the basis of hearsay. One illustration of the courts' evasion of the hearsay rule includes cases of hearsay conduct such as *R v Rice* [1963] 1 QB 857 (a case which is now subject to the **Criminal Justice Act (CJA) 2003** allowing documentary hearsay to be admissible). Other 'fiddles' such as the status of 'refreshing memory' documents have been largely rationalised by the **CJA 2003** (see **Chapter 10**).

Evasions of the rule have been described by Birch as 'hearsay fiddles' (1987). She writes (at p. 35), 'it is hard to avoid the conclusion that the courts fiddle the concepts of hearsay and relevance to admit only evidence which it is considered desirable to admit.' The tortuous reasoning and somewhat desperate reliance on the concept of relevance as a justification for exclusion evidenced in *Blastland* suggest that both Birch and Zuckerman may be right. It would arguably be better to concentrate on the probative value of the evidence rather than its form. This argument gets added weight from the controversial decision in *R v Kearley* [1992] 2 AC 228, where a majority of the House of Lords declared that implied assertions were hearsay. Such cases give further weight to Zuckerman's argument because as McEwan points out (1998, p. 236), 'It is sometimes difficult to disentangle that which merely indicates someone's state of mind from all manner of implied assertions which may simultaneously emerge from the statement.' An added complication is that the authorities have not agreed on whether evidence of state of mind or emotion is admissible as non-hearsay or as an exception to the rule against hearsay. There is indeed a significant lack of clarity in the current law in this area even after the implementation of the **CJA 2003**. Photofit pictures are admissible as non-hearsay, following *R v Cook* [1987] 1 All ER 1049, but as McEwan (p. 239) suggests the 'opportunities for error, suggestion and misunderstanding is almost endless'.

Thus the courts appeared before the **2003 Act** to be following somewhat contradictory paths, exclusionary one on the one hand, as in *Kearley*, but an inclusionary one on the other. Other examples of the latter approach are *Gilfoyle*, where the state of mind exception was extended to cover proof of facts which exist independently of the maker's state of mind, and *R v Myers* [1998] AC 124, where the exception for admissions by parties to litigation was extended to cover the use of a confession by a co-accused under certain circumstances.

In *R v Ward, Andrews and Broadley* [2001] **Crim LR 316** the Court of Appeal extended the admission of confessions to include a statement to the police by the defendant, W, identifying himself at the scene of the crime (the police officer could not identify W later). It was persuaded by the powerful quality of the evidence. Munday (2011, p. 493) points out that the case illustrates '. . . just how far removed the legal notion of "confession" can sometimes be from ordinary parlance'. Such a convoluted argument was necessary because of the strictures of the exclusionary rule before the CJA 2003.

Reform proposals

Thus it is clear that the hearsay rule was disliked by both jurists and courts and the latter have been prepared in some instances to avoid its application. However, there was little consistency to this approach and the reason is simply because of the fear of letting in unreliable evidence. Zuckerman (1989, p. 216) argued that there should be the legitimisation of the inclusionary principle in that trial judges should have the power to admit hearsay evidence which is of probative value. The effect of this, he argued, would be to get rid of the exception and its technical manifestations. There is much to be said for this approach, after all, the judges have been given discretionary powers in most instances, and there is no real reason why they cannot be given the discretion to rule whether the hearsay evidence is admissible because of its probative value. Further, the trend of legislative intervention in this area appears to be in favour of the admissibility of such evidence, the **CJA 2003** being the culmination of that approach.

The Law Commission had recognised the case for reform but its proposals did not go as far as some recommended by abolishing the rule. The approach taken in their Report *Evidence in Criminal Proceedings: Hearsay and Related Topics*, No. 245 (Cm 3670, 1997) was to preserve the rule but extend the range of exceptions alongside both an inclusionary and exclusionary discretion. One almost universally welcomed recommendation was that the decision in *Kearley* [1992] 2 AC 228 would be reversed. Implied assertions would not be hearsay. However, the overall cautious stance taken by the Law Commission which eventually led to legislation was criticised. Thus Jackson (1998, p. 187), commenting on the proposals, concluded that 'there are no functional reasons why the hearsay rule is needed in criminal proceedings any more than in civil proceedings.' He argued for an investigation code to govern police practice and for the defence to be given an opportunity to cross-examine an available witness on whom the prosecution depends by increased use of pre-trial procedures. He rightly stressed that in deciding admissibility 'the key issue is whether the police have discharged fair and accurate standards during the course of their investigation . . . rather than the technical question of whether out of court statements fall within the scope of the hearsay rule.'

Hearsay and fair trial rights

But erosion rather than abolition is the current approach. The **2003 Act** preserves the hearsay rule but increases the number of exceptions, particularly by the admissibility of oral statements, and also introduces an inclusionary discretion. The increased use of discretion creates more flexibility but also more uncertainty. Although often illogical in practice and at times defying common sense, the rule against hearsay has been long considered by many as contributing to the fairness of a trial. From this point of view current legislative changes allow oral first-hand hearsay, to extend the 'fear' exception to witnesses who are unavailable through fear of 'financial loss' and permit the, at least, theoretical possibility that a defendant could be convicted on hearsay evidence alone, which are some cause for concern. On the other hand it was unlikely that the application of the **Human Rights Act 1998** means that hearsay evidence necessarily breaches **art. 6(3)(a) of the European Convention on Human Rights** (see *R v Gokal* (1997) 2 Cr App R 266 and *Trivedi v UK* (1997) EHRLR 520. However, as Friedman (1998, p. 697) points out 'lurking within the rule against hearsay and often shrouded by its many excesses and oddities is a principle of magnificent importance, a principle first enunciated long before the development of the common law system but one that achieved its full development within that system. This is the principle that a person may not offer testimony against a criminal defendant unless it is given under oath face to face with the accused and subject to cross-examination.'

Zuckerman expresses in the quote in the question a common impatience and frustration with this ancient rule. However, an undue emphasis in this area on logic, even-handedness and flexibility may have the unfortunate result of further disadvantaging defendants at a time when, it is arguable, statutory changes are eroding long-standing principles such as the right to silence. After all, the biggest exception to the rule against hearsay, confessions, is clearly pro-prosecution. Reform of the rule against hearsay was long overdue but it is submitted that there is a case for accompanying any reform with a recognised right to confrontation, with the aim of assisting the innocent from wrongful conviction, ensuring procedural fairness and of improving the standards of police investigation.

However, it is arguable that in practice the statutory change may not in practice be overwhelming since the courts may continue their cautious approach to the admissibility of hearsay and be wary of abuse. In *R v Mills* [2003] 1 WLR 2931, the Court of Appeal quashed a conviction because, inter alia, a statement made to a police officer by a non-appearing witness had been wrongly admitted for the prosecution. It is of some interest to note that, under the **CJA 2003** provisions, if a non-appearing witness is put in fear by the parties, this may preclude admissibility of the statement the parties wish to tender. In *Mills* the allegation was that one police officer had warned the witness not to attend trial, illustrating that it is not only the defence who may carry out witness intimidation. Cross points out (2010, p. 609) one important difference from the old law is that under **s. 116** 'the statement need no longer be one made to those investigating offences, and hence can clearly be applied to defence witnesses who have become fearful, perhaps of the police, after providing an initial statement.'

The most important consideration, whatever the remaining technicalities of the law on hearsay, is that the question of fairness should be fully aired. This is explicitly reinforced by **art. 6** as well as the provisions of **CJA 2003**. Choo (2012, p. 302) comments 'the provisions of the **Criminal Justice Act 2003**, largely following the recommendations of the Law Commission, maintain a "rule and exceptions" approach to hearsay doctrine, albeit that the specific exceptions are brought and there is an interests-of-justice exception.' He points out that Lord Justice Auld was critical of any reform which continued the exclusionary rule and favoured 'making hearsay generally admissible subject to the principle of best evidence'. Choo convincingly suggests an alternative approach—that of maintaining a rule against hearsay but instead of recognising specific exceptions along with an interests of justice exception, simply to have recognised the interests of justice exception as the only exception. Birch (2004, p. 572) regrets that the Auld reforms 'were not taken as seriously as they should have been' and predicts that 'it is more likely that judges will over time resort to the safety valve as a flexible weapon of choice.' She points out that 'if we did not have a safety valve, the judges would have to invent one, if only by dint of the process of "reading down" under the **Human Rights Act 1998** in order to admit crucial defence evidence.' She also argues that 'some breaking down of the traditional barriers of the adversarial system may help with difficult cases such as those involving third-party confessions and complainants who have withdrawn their complaints.' Dennis also speculated on the possibility of the interests of justice exception assuming greater importance. He questioned whether it will be 'a marginal sweeping-up power operating outside the statutory and preserved common-law exceptions in **sections 116–118** or whether in practice it will be invoked in addition to, or even in substitution for, those exceptions' (2004, pp. 251, 252).

It appears under the **CJA 2003**, as before, that the hearsay rules are unlikely to fall foul of **art. 6**. In *R v Sellick* [2005] **EWCA Crim 651**, the Court of Appeal held that the safeguards under the **1988 Act** were sufficient to ensure compliance and there was 'still no absolute rule that, when a witness's statement was the sole or decisive evidence the admission in evidence of that statement would automatically lead to an infringement of the defendant's **article 6** rights.' In *Doorson v The Netherlands* (1990) the question was whether the proceedings as a whole were fair. In *R v Xhabri* [2006] **1 All ER 776** the court held that hearsay evidence adduced by the Crown satisfied the requirements of the **CJA 2003, s. 120** and was admissible under that provision, and alternatively the trial judge was entitled to exercise his discretion under **s. 114** of the Act to admit the evidence on the basis that it was in the interests of justice. **Article 6(3)(a)** did not provide a defendant with an absolute right to examine every witness whose testimony was used against him. In this case almost all the hearsay evidence derived directly or indirectly from the complainant, was available for examination. Thus although the current law is complex, it is arguably fair. This case illustrates that Zuckerman's scenario may almost be in place since the courts took a literal approach in holding that evidence may be admitted under **s. 114(1)(d)** where the conditions for admissibility under other sections are not met. Another welcome decision was *R v Singh* [2006] 1 WLR 1564 which affirmed that the common law definition of hearsay embracing implied assertions no longer applies. On the other hand, controversially, the Court of Appeal in *R v Leonard* [2009] EWCA Crim 1251 appeared to mistake an implied assertion for hearsay as Ormerod (2009, p. 802) has observed. The Court of Appeal appears to have been more concerned with analysing the form of the evidence than its reliability.

However, the pragmatic approach taken by the courts on definitional matters suggests that the question of relevance will be crucial. Emson (2010, p. 123) comments, 'so long as a relevance can be established, the tribunal of law is entitled to adopt a "belt and braces" strategy if there is any uncertainty over the admissibility of an inferable statement. If the judge is of the view that the evidence is relevant and ought to be admitted, he will be able to rule that the exclusionary rule does not apply, by virtue of **s. 115(3)** of the Act and also rule, in the alternative, that if the hearsay rules does apply the evidence ought nevertheless to be admitted under the new discretion to admit inadmissible hearsay evidence (**s. 114(1)(d)**).' He cited *R v Isichei* [2006] EWCA Crim 1815 in relation to an implied statement of identification during a telephone call as an example of this approach.

Subsequently, however, the approach of the English courts departed from that of the Strasbourg Court. In *R v Horncastle* [2009] UKSC 14 the Supreme Court rejected the reasoning in *Al-Khawaja v UK* (2009) 49 EHRR 1 and held that the **Human Rights Act 1998** does not compel English courts to apply the decisive or sole rule and that a conviction could fairly be founded on hearsay evidence alone. The Grand Chamber, disagreeing with the Court of Human Rights, has now accepted the Supreme Court's reasoning but with strong caveats, see *Al-Khawaja v UK* (2011) 54 EHRR 23.

The case thus suggests that the approach advocated by Zuckerman is being adopted by the courts in that hearsay is now more readily admitted, although within the context of the constraint of **CJA 2003**. The corollary, however, is that **art. 6** provisions may not be always complied with. As Dennis [2012] Crim LR 375 points out in his commentary on the Grand Chamber decision in *Al-Khawaja and Tahery v UK*, there is still a criticism of the approach of the English courts. As far as the Grand Chamber is concerned, where a conviction is based on hearsay evidence solely or decisively the court 'must subject the proceedings to the most searching scrutiny'. He suggests that the judgment 'will reinforce the current trend in English case law to approach **s. 114(1)(d)**, in particular, with caution.' The eventual rapprochement between the English and Strasbourg approaches suggests that the current hearsay framework now ensures the fairness and reliability that Zuckerman called for. Perhaps total abolition is not therefore needed. Indeed, it could be argued that the hearsay rule enshrines standards of fairness. As the Court of Appeal noted in *R v Y* [2008] 1 WLR 1683 (para. 56) the 'very real disadvantages of hearsay evidence, which underlay the common law rule generally excluding it, remain critical to the assessment of whether the interest of justice call for its admission.'

Zuckerman's comment seems to place much confidence in the judiciary to achieve fairness without the constraint of a rule against hearsay. However, some commentators cast doubt on this. Munday (2011, p. 459) points out for example that 'what is emerging in the reported case law is that **s. 114(1)(d)** appears to afford assistance to the prosecution more frequently than it does to the defence, and that the Court of Appeal shows itself ready to employ this provision as a second line of argument, buttressing rulings of which it is not otherwise entirely confident.' From the defence point of view perhaps a rule jainst hearsay would be safer.

 Question 4

Tom is charged with sexually assaulting Harriet at a residential university summer school. He denies the charge and claims that Harriet made it up because he had spurned her advances. She did not report the incident until some time after it allegedly happened. Tom claims that in fact he was away from the summer school on the day in question on a bicycle trip. However, the computer records which list the bicycle hirings have no record of his name and no one else can substantiate his alibi. The college bursar, Graham, has a note on file on the day in question, based on information from Carol, gardener at the school. She claims to have seen a couple she identified as Tom and Harriet struggling in the grounds. They had not seen her and she did not intervene but saw Harriet run off with her clothes dishevelled. Having thought about the incident she went later and reported it to Graham, who made a note of it on his tape-recorder and it was subsequently typed by his secretary, John. Carol is now working in Australia and has not been traced.

Discuss the admissibility of Carol's evidence and of the computer bicycle hire records.

 Commentary

In this question you are asked to consider whether the items in question are hearsay and then whether they may be admitted under any of the statutory or common law exceptions preserved by statute. Bear in mind that you must first characterise the statements as hearsay or not on the basis of the statutory definition. The bicycle records raise the preliminary matter of whether absence of a record is hearsay and you need not worry about acknowledging the uncertainty of the law in this area. In Carol's case you need to be familiar with the provisions of the **CJA 2003, s. 117** and what is meant by acting in the course of trade, etc. Bear in mind the need to discuss whether the document was prepared for the purposes of a pending or contemplated criminal investigation.

Answer plan

- Definition of hearsay.
- Graham's note and possible application of **s. 116 or s. 117 CJA 2003**.
- Application of **art. 6** to hearsay rule.
- Negative hearsay—computer printout.

 Suggested answer

The rule against hearsay provides that an assertion other than one made by a person while giving oral evidence in the proceedings is inadmissible as evidence of any fact charged (see **ss. 114, 115 and 121 of the Criminal Justice Act (CJA) 2003**). Carol could give direct oral evidence of what she had seen and this would clearly be relevant to the facts in issue since Tom's defence is alibi and fabrication. Since she is not available, the only evidence of this is what she has told Graham.

Section 117

The question then arises as to whether the evidence is admissible by virtue of the exceptions for documentary hearsay under the **CJA 2003**. Carol's statement may be admissible under **ss. 117 and 121**. Under **s. 117** in criminal proceedings a statement contained in a document is admissible as evidence of any matter stated if:

- oral evidence given in the proceedings would be admissible as evidence of that matter,
- the requirements of **subs. (2)** are satisfied.

Subsection (2) is satisfied if the document was created or received by a person in the course of a trade, business, profession or other occupation, the person who supplied the information (the relevant person) had or may reasonably be supposed to have had personal knowledge of the matters dealt with and each person (if any) through whom the information was supplied from the relevant person to the person mentioned in **para. (a)** received the information in the course of a trade, business, profession or other occupation. The creator of the document may be the person who supplied the information.

Carol was acting in the course of a trade and might reasonably be expected to have had personal knowledge of the matters dealt with.

The general common law rule is that a party who wishes to tender evidence must prove any necessary preconditions by admissible evidence. Proof must be to the appropriate standard, namely proof beyond reasonable doubt in the case of the prosecution and proof on the balance of probability in the case of the defence. Cross and Tapper point out (2010, p. 610) that it is far from clear why **CJA 2003, s. 133** cannot be employed for this purpose.

Some forms of documentary hearsay are admissible as an exception to the general hearsay rule. A 'document' by virtue of **s. 134 of the CJA 2003** is 'anything in which information of any description is recorded'. Graham's tape-recorded note of what Carol told him is thus to be treated as a statement in a document. The admissibility of evidence in this situation is governed by **s. 117 of the CJA 2003**. This provides that under certain specified circumstances a statement in a document can be admissible as evidence of any fact of which direct oral evidence would be admissible if the document was (a) created by a person in the course of a trade, business, profession or other occupation or as an office-holder, and (b) the information was supplied by a person (whether or not the maker of the statement) who had personal knowledge of the matters dealt with.

Whether or not the tape-recording is admissible, then, depends on Carol's and Graham's status. Carol had personal knowledge of the facts as she perceived them. Graham received the information in the course of his occupation as supervisor. The admission of the typed notes from Graham's recording is subject to the same principles as the tape-recording. They are admissible also under **s. 117 CJA 2003** because the typist, John, was acting in the course of business.

A statement prepared for the purposes of criminal proceedings or investigation, for example a witness statement, is not admissible under **s. 117** unless either one of the reasons for non-appearance of the witness in **s. 116** is met, or the maker of the statement (the 'relevant person') cannot reasonably be expected to have any recollection of the matters dealt with having regard to the time which has elapsed and all the circumstances (**s. 24(4)**). This here is Carol. It is also necessary to consider the purpose for which the tape-recording was made. In *R v Bedi* (1991) 95 Cr App R 21 the prosecution had been allowed to adduce evidence of bank reports concerning lost and stolen credit cards. The judge had not considered as he should have done the purpose for which the reports were prepared. Here, the Court of Appeal held they were business documents to which **s. 24(1) CJA 1988** applied but that **s. 24(4)** did not. This was a matter of fact to be determined by the judge in the light of the surrounding circumstances. On the facts, it does appear unlikely that Graham made the statement for the purpose of criminal proceedings. In any case even if he did, Carol's absence probably is one of the acceptable reasons for non-appearance, following the Court of Appeal in *R v French and Gowhar* (1993) 97 Cr App R 421. In this regard in examining whether it was 'not reasonably practicable' to secure the attendance of Carol the court will question whether the prosecution have done their best to produce her as a witness. In *R v Gyima* [2007] EWCA Crim 429 the Court of Appeal considered whether the prosecution should have employed a video link at the trial to enable a child witness to give evidence live from America. One of the factors was the expense. The court found 'the prosecution had proved that they had taken all reasonable steps to secure the witness' attendance.'

Credibility

Section 124 of the Act enables the opposing party to test the credibility of the absent 'maker' of the statement. The purpose is to put the absent maker in as close a position as possible to a witness who testifies in person. Thus for instance with leave of the court the other side may call evidence that could have been put to the 'maker' in cross-examination as relevant to his credibility, as if he had given oral evidence.

The party seeking to rely on **s. 117 CJA 2003** must satisfy the court that the requirements of the section have been met. Here it is the prosecution which wishes to use the statement and the criminal standard of proof will apply (see *R v Case* [1991] **Crim LR 192**). The judge must generally hear oral evidence in a voir dire. The court has a discretion to exclude the statement even if it is technically admissible under **ss. 117(7), 125, 126(1) of the CJA 2003** and **s. 78 of the Police and Criminal Evidence Act 1984 (PACE)** and at common law.

Under **s. 117(6) and (7)** the court has power to exclude otherwise admissible business and other documents.

Since Carol will not be available to be cross-examined on the identification, which is a fact in issue, it may be argued this would create unfairness to Tom. **Section 120** is not available to the prosecution because this only applies to prior statements of witnesses who are called to testify.

The defence may try to argue that particular care must be taken since the statement involves evidence of identification. It will not necessarily be excluded, however. Much depends on the strength of the evidence. Thus, in *R v Setz-Dempsey and Richardson* (1994) **98 Cr App R 23** the Court of Appeal held that statements ought not to have been admitted since medical evidence undermined the quality of the evidence and the evidence of identification might have been further undermined by cross-examination. However, in *R v Greer* [1998] **Crim LR 572** the evidence was admissible. It was held that the fact that there was other live identification evidence was not a reason for preventing the absent witness's evidence of identification from being read. Much will depend here then on whether the court is convinced that the defence is disadvantaged on the facts from being denied the opportunity to cross-examine Carol. It may be possible to take her evidence on commission. Thus in *R v Radak* (1999) **1 Cr App R 187**, where the prosecution failed to do this it was held that the statement should have been excluded under **s. 26 CJA 1988**.

Article 6

The defence will also argue that the court will have to take into account the provisions of **art. 6 of the European Convention on Human Rights** following the implementation of the **Human Rights Act 1998**. Article 6(3)(d) of the Convention states that a person charged with a criminal offence has the right 'to examine or have examined the witnesses against him and to obtain the attendance and examination of witnesses on his behalf under the same conditions as witnesses against him.' In *Trivedi v UK* (1997)

EHRLR 520 the Commission decided that the provisions of **ss. 23–26 of the 1988 Act** were not contrary to **art. 6**. In *Gokal* **(1997) 2 Cr App R 266** the Court of Appeal considered that the rights of defendants under this statute were safeguarded by **s. 26**. It drew on *Kostovski v The Netherlands* **(1989) 12 EHRR 434** to illustrate that the purpose of **art. 6** was not to regulate the domestic law of evidence but to ensure overall fairness of the trial. In *R v Horncastle* **[2009] UKSC 14** the Supreme Court held that hearsay alone could found a conviction, now upheld by the Grand Chamber in *Al-Khawaja and Tahery v UK* **(2011)**.

Negative hearsay

The prosecution may wish to show the computer printout from the bicycle hirings to suggest that Tom's alibi is false. The first issue is whether it is hearsay. There was a conflict of authority on whether absence of a record constituted hearsay. In *R v Patel* **[1981] 3 All ER 94**, the Court of Appeal, while accepting that the Home Office records which did not contain the name of the alleged illegal immigrant were hearsay, would have allowed the officer responsible for their compilation to give evidence. In the subsequent case of *R v Shone* **(1982) 76 Cr App R 72** the Court of Appeal took the view that the absence of a record was non-hearsay, circumstantial evidence. The 'non-statement' here is in documentary form generated by a computer. Tapper (2010, p. 568) considers that these cases may still apply under the new law. They point out that:

> Questions of implied assertion also arise when a negative is sought to be proved from failure to state a positive, in situations where one might be expected. In the old law the admissibility of such evidence was regarded as compatible with the exclusion of hearsay. It is envisaged that such evidence continues to be admissible under the new statutory regime, even without explicit general provision.

Under **s. 129** where a representation of any fact is made otherwise than by a person but depends for such accuracy on information supplied (directly or indirectly) by a person, the representation is not admissible in criminal proceedings as evidence of the fact unless it is proved that the information was accurate.

? **Question 5**

'Although the common law appears to regard some statements against interest as inherently more reliable than other hearsay statements, there appears to be no available exception in English common law to accommodate third party confessions.'

(Jenny McEwan, *Evidence and the Adversarial Process*,
2nd edn (Oxford: Hart, 1998), p. 243.)

Discuss.

Commentary

Hearsay is an area which lends itself to essay questions where you will be expected to discuss the rationale and alleged absurdities of the rule. To answer such questions well you need to show your knowledge of the law and also make some references to the academic debates. There are a number of controversial aspects of the rule against hearsay. Here you are just asked to deal with one, namely the exclusion of third-party confessions. Be careful you do not stray over into making a general diatribe against the rule. Focus as always on the specific question set. However, the exclusion of third-party confessions, of course, is one aspect of the general principle that the rule applies equally to the defence as to the prosecution. The difficulty with broad questions of this sort is in imposing your own plan on the material. A suitable one here would be to discuss first of all whether the extract describes an existing state of affairs. If so (and it will presumably be so to some extent at least!) give examples of exclusion of third-party confessions. Then go on to discuss why this is so. You should then discuss finally whether there is a case for reform. Your essay thus falls into three parts, not forgetting of course a well crafted conclusion.

 Answer plan

- Exclusion of third-party confessions one aspect of general principle that the hearsay rule applies to defence and prosecution.
- Does the quote accurately explain the current state of affairs?
- Examples of exclusion of third-party confessions—**R v Blastland**.
- Case for reform, particularly in light of operation of **CJA 1988, s. 23**, replaced by **CJA 2003, s. 116**, see **s. 116(2)**.
- Particular case of co-accused's confessions, **PACE, s. 76A(1)**.
- Effect of reforms under **CJA 2003**.

 Suggested answer

Here, McEwan is passing comment on the common law position in relation to hearsay evidence. This exclusionary rule operated to prevent admissions by third parties. That this is undoubtedly how the courts have interpreted the law is made clear in the House of Lords decision in *R v Blastland* [1986] AC 41. The Court of Appeal had refused to admit confessions made by M, whom the defendant B claimed had approached the victim after him; the court felt bound by the Court of Appeal decision in *R v Turner* (1975) 61 Cr App R 67, and also by *Myers v DPP* [1965] AC 1001, where the House of Lords held that it was for Parliament to create any new exceptions to the hearsay rule. This state of affairs raises the issues referred to in the question, namely is this an accurate assessment of the law, and if it is, is it desirable?

In *Turner*, the judge was held to have rightly refused to admit evidence that a third party, not called as a witness, had admitted that he had committed the robbery, with which the defendant was charged. The court rejected the view that any of the cases cited to it were authority for the proposition that hearsay evidence is admissible in a criminal case to show that a third party who has not been called as a witness in the case has admitted committing the offence charged. The principle applies even if the third party is dead. Thus, in *R v Thomson* [1912] 3 KB 19, the Court of Appeal upheld the trial judge's exclusion of statements by a deceased woman that she had intended to carry out an illegal abortion on herself and that she had in fact done so.

In *R v Blastland* [1986] AC 41 the exclusion of two sets of statements was upheld by the Court of Appeal. One was a confession by the third party to the police and the other a statement by him on the night of the murder and on the following day in which his state of mind was revealed, in particular his knowledge about the murder at a time when it was not generally known. Leave was given to apply to the House of Lords only on the second statement, and, although not clearly dissenting from the Court of Appeal who held it was hearsay, the ratio of their decision was that the statement should be excluded because it was irrelevant.

History of third party confessions

The case law suggests that the exclusion has primarily been applied to confessions made by third parties who are not called as witnesses, so arguably the evidence of their guilt is weak. However, as the above case law demonstrates, there is nothing in the rule to indicate it should be confined to those cases. The case law then does certainly affirm the existence of the rule to which McEwan refers. However, as she pointed out, it was at least theoretically possible for **ss. 23 and 24 of the Criminal Justice Act (CJA) 1988** to apply. This allowed documentary hearsay evidence to be admitted. A third-party confession could be admissible, if written or not oral. As regards first-hand documentary hearsay, it could have been admitted at the discretion of the court (under **s. 25 CJA**) provided the maker of the statement was unable to attend court as a witness for one of the reasons set out in **s. 23(2) and (3) CJA**, namely, that he was dead or unfit to attend as a witness, that he was outside the UK and it was not reasonably practicable to secure his attendance, that he cannot be found, or that having made a statement to a police officer or an investigating officer he does not give evidence through fear or because he is kept out of the way. Furthermore, under **s. 24 CJA**, which covered multiple hearsay, business documents may be admitted as long as each of the intermediaries was acting in the course of trade, business, etc. Thus, theoretically a confession by a third person made, for example, to a teacher could be admitted as long as it is made in the form of a statement.

Criminal Justice Act 2003

Under the CJA 2003 there are more possible statutory routes to admissible third-party confessions. First, **s. 116** covers oral or written statements where there is a statutory reason for not calling the witness. Second, the inclusionary discretion under **s. 114** may allow a statement to be admitted in the interests of justice. Finally the 'business' document exception under **s. 117** mirrors that in the **1988 Act**, so the arguments above apply.

The defence would probably try to argue that **s. 116** applied, since if one of the conditions listed in **s. 116(2)** was established the hearsay evidence is automatically admissible. The **CJA 2003** does not include an exclusionary discretion equivalent to **s. 25 or s. 26 of the 1988 Act**. The discretion under **s. 126(1)** sets a high test in that a hearsay statement may be excluded if the case for exclusion 'substantially outweighs' that of admitting it. The difficulty a defendant might have in admitting a third party confession is illustrated by *R v Finch* [2007] **1 WLR 1645**. The court refused to admit a statement under the **CJA** exonerating the accused, drawing a distinction between a witness who was unavailable and one who was unwilling. It stated (at para. 24): 'It is not, in short, the law that every reluctant witness's evidence automatically can be put before the jury under **s. 114 of the 2003 Act**.' By contrast in *R v Y* [2008] **1 WLR 1683** the prosecution had been allowed to admit a hearsay statement. Y was on trial for murder. X had previously pleaded guilty to the same offence. The court held that **s. 114(1)(d)** was available in law for all types of hearsay, and on application by any party to a criminal trial.

Co-defendants

One area of contention is whether a confession made by a co-defendant may be tendered by a defendant. Where there are two accused one defendant may want to make use of a confession by the other either because it supports his case or to cross-examine on any inconsistencies between the confession and the defendant's evidence at trial. If the confession is tendered by the prosecution this is possible but until recently there was conflict of authority in relation to confessions which either had not been used by the prosecution or had been excluded by the judge. **Section 76 of PACE** applies only where the confession is tendered by the prosecution. Clearly there is a potential conflict between the interests of the two defendants. The courts have gradually addressed this conflict. In *R v Rowson* [1986] **QB 174** the Court of Appeal held that the trial judge has no discretion to prevent counsel for the co-accused from cross-examining the maker of an inadmissible confession. Such questioning is for the purpose of attacking credibility by showing inconsistency. In *Lui-Mei Lin v R* (1989) **88 Cr App R 296** the Privy Council held that as long as the matter is relevant the right to cross-examine is unfettered. There was conflict of authority on whether the co-accused is able to use the confession as evidence of truth, for example where the confession exculpates him. In *R v Myers* [1998] **AC 124** the House of Lords resolved the conflict between *R v Beckford* [1991] **Crim LR 833** and *R v Campbell* [1993] **Crim LR 448**. Two defendants were jointly charged with murder. One made a statement which amounted to an admission that she had stabbed the victim but the statement was not preferred by the prosecution because of apparent breaches of the Code of Practice. The House of Lords held that the trial judge had rightly allowed the co-defendant to cross-examine about the statement and adduce it in evidence as relevant to his defence.

The case showed a welcome inroad into the practice of exclusion of third-party confessions. Under the **CJA 2003, s. 128** a new **s. 76A** is inserted into **PACE 1984** whereby a defendant may adduce a co-accused's confession if he can prove, on the balance of probabilities, that it was not obtained in violation of identical provisions as those in **s. 76 PACE**. *R v Johnson* [2007] **EWCA Crim 1651** shows the application of this provision. It applies where one defendant pleads guilty before the trial and is then permitted to change his plea. The co-defendant was allowed to adduce the earlier guilty plea, which had not been obtained by anything said or done which was likely to render any confession under these circumstances unreliable. This is thus a further inroad into the exclusion of third-party confessions.

Academic opinion generally has been critical of the exclusion of third-party confessions.

Third-party confessions are excluded primarily because of the risk of a spate of false confessions. McEwan points out that the Lindbergh kidnapping in the United States resulted in over 200 confessions. Obviously, many such cases can be eliminated early on because the maker has insufficient knowledge of the details of the offence. But McEwan suggests that the adversarial system is ill-equipped to test the untrustworthiness of third-party confessions, although an inquisitorial procedure, not relying on oral evidence, could do so more easily.

There is thus a strong argument on grounds of lack of reliability for excluding third-party confessions. The weakness of this type of evidence is that of hearsay evidence generally, summarised by Tribe (1977, p. 959) as faulty perception, erroneous memory, ambiguity and insincerity.

The question then arises, is there anything specifically at issue in third-party confessions which would argue for a new exception to be made to the hearsay rule? The major objection to the present state of affairs is that although it applies to prosecution and defence, obviously it most harms the defence (except in those cases where the third-party confessor is a co-defendant). Thus as Zuckerman (1989, p. 184) points out, the rule violates the principle of protecting the innocent. He also adds (p. 185) that it defies common sense. Arguably the non-admissibility of third-party confessions is all the more unfair to the defence since in *R v Hayter* [2005] **UKHL 6**, the House of Lords allowed a confession of one defendant to be considered by the jury as evidence against a co-defendant.

Under the **CJA 2003** the routes for the possible admissibility of third-party confessions have increased. First, the scope for admitting oral hearsay is now much broader (**s. 116**), and second, the existence of an inclusionary discretion (**s. 114**) means the court may, in the interests of justice, admit statements which do not fulfil the statutory requirements. However, the case law suggests that the courts will continue to be influenced by common law jurisprudence in exercising this discretion.

Question 6

Henry is charged with causing grievous bodily harm to James. The prosecution case is that he attacked James with a knife after a row in a public house. James has been disfigured as a result of the wounding. Henry denies the attack, claiming he was elsewhere at the time and that he has never met James. James was taken to hospital by ambulance. As he travelled there he gave an account of the incident to PC Green. PC Green read it back to James and he nodded his agreement, not being able to sign because of the drips in his arm. After an operation he has not regained consciousness. Tom and Gerry were eyewitnesses to the incident and both made statements to the police which they subsequently signed. However, Tom has told the police he is too afraid to tell the court about what he saw and Gerry's mother has told police he also is too scared to give evidence. Henry's alibi is that he was having dinner in his club with Freda, a Brazilian student, at the time of the attack. Freda subsequently wrote a letter to Henry thanking him for the dinner. Freda has now returned to Brazil. Henry also wants to submit in evidence a note he found on his car in the car park of the club when he left after the dinner. The note gave the number of a car whose driver had allegedly damaged Henry's wing mirror. Henry passed the note to the police in reporting the accident. He alleges this note is relevant to confirm his alibi.

Advise on evidence.

Commentary

You are presented in this question with several 'statements' and you are thus alerted that the **CJA 2003** may apply. You need to be aware of the recent case law on the application of this statute. It is not enough simply to summarise the sections. In this question you need also to be aware of how the courts have interpreted these somewhat overlapping provisions and how their requirements can be proved. Note that *Kamuhuza* **[2008] EWCA Crim 3060** suggests that first-hand documentary statements made to the police could in principle be admissible under **s. 116** if there is a statutory reason for not calling the witness. There is also some important case law on what is meant by 'fear' in **s. 23(3) CJA**, now included in **s. 116 CJA 2003**. This question is an illustration of how evidential issues are closely related to procedural ones. Evidence courses vary in their emphasis on this area.

Answer plan

- James's statement to police—**CJA 2003, s. 116**.
- *Kamuhuza* **(2008)**—documentary statements to police.
- Reason for non-appearance of Tom is fear—see **s. 116(2)(e)**.
- Freda's statement—not reasonably practicable to call her—see ***R v CT* [2011] EWCA Crim 2341**.
- Statutory discretion to exclude statements.

Examiner's tip

It is important to remember that the exclusionary discretion in **s. 126(1)(b)** applies to hearsay statements proffered by the defence as well as the prosecution, unlike **s. 78 PACE**. You should therefore refer to this when discussing statements which the defence want to submit. You might want to observe, however, that the court might in practice be reluctant to exclude defence evidence as the answer here suggests.

Suggested answer

First-hand hearsay

James makes a statement to a police officer but is not available as a witness at the trial because he is unconscious. **Section 116 of the Criminal Justice Act (CJA) 2003** provides that a statement by a person is admissible in criminal proceedings as evidence of any fact of which direct oral evidence would be admissible. Thus 'first-hand' hearsay evidence is admissible provided certain conditions are met (see *R v Kamuhuza* [2008] EWCA Crim 3060). The maker of the statement must be unable to attend court as a witness for one of the reasons set out in **s. 116(2)**.

Here, CJA 2003, **s. 116(2)(b)** will apply, since the witness is unfit to attend. Further conditions are that the statement must be first-hand hearsay and the person making it would be a competent witness. Thus, Green can testify about what James said to him.

'Fear' exception

With regard to Tom, the prosecution may seek to rely on **s. 116(2)(e)** that he does not give evidence through fear. **Section 116(3)** provides that 'fear' is to be 'widely construed' in line with the statute's objective of addressing the problem of witness intimidation. The prosecution may cite the pre-2003 case *R v Martin* **[1996] Crim LR 589** for the proposition that the fear does not have to be reasonable or be causally linked with the offence charged. Protection for the defendant is provided now by **s. 116(4)** which applies an 'interests of justice' test; see *R v Doherty* **[2006] EWCA Crim 2716**. In *R v Boulton* **[2007] EWCA Crim 942** the Court of Appeal considered the sort of evidence required to establish fear. The facts of the offence, although not sufficient reasons, could constitute the conditions in which to evaluate the evidence. It was not relevant that fear was not the only reason for not testifying if fear was a significant ingredient. The court has to give leave to allow such a statement.

It may be difficult to prove that a witness who is not present in court is fearful. If the witness attends the fear may be visible (*R v Ashford and Tenterden Justices, ex parte Hilden* **[1992] 96 Cr App R 93** and *R v James Greer* **[1998] Crim LR 572**). In *Neill v North Antrim Magistrates' Court* **[1993] 97 Cr App R 121** there was an inadmissible third-hand hearsay statement.

A problem may arise if the jury asks why a witness was not called. In *R v Churchill* [1993] Crim LR 285, where the judge told the jury he had decided circumstances applied in which a crucial witness who claimed to be in fear need not give evidence, the Court of Appeal said the judge should have discussed with counsel how to handle the question. The judge's 'explanation had amounted to something in the nature of a pat on the back for a witness whose testimony had been disputed but had not been tested in cross-examination.' The jury might wrongly have inferred that the failure to testify could be a matter to the discredit of the accused. In the circumstances the judge should simply have said he could not answer the question. In *Neill v North Antrim Magistrates' Court* [1992] 1 WLR 1220, a case arising under a similar Northern Ireland provision, namely **art. 3(3)(b) of the Criminal Justice (Evidence, etc.) Northern Ireland Order 1988**, the House of Lords held that the fact that a witness was absent through fear had to be proved by admissible evidence. There, the evidence of the police officer as to what he had been told by the mother of the two youths about their apprehensions had been hearsay and could not be admitted under the exception to the hearsay rule that enabled the court to receive first degree hearsay as to state of mind. The House held (at p. 1229) that:

> Whatever may be the intellectual justification of the exception to the hearsay rule which enables the court to receive first degree hearsay as to state of mind . . . it cannot be stretched to embrace what is essentially a third hand account of the witness' apprehensions.

Accordingly, the statements of the youths in that case should not have been admitted in evidence. *R v O'Loughlin* [1988] 3 All ER 431 was applied. The court held (obiter) that a statement by a witness who is afraid of appearing through fear would be admissible as a *res gestae* statement of present state of mind, the common law exception. Thus, the police officer may here give evidence of what Tom said directly to him but not what Gerry's mother told him, in explaining to the court why the witnesses will not give evidence. We are not told the reasons for Tom's fear. In *R v Sellick* [2005] 1 WLR 3257 the Court of Appeal held that a defendant's rights under **art. 6(3)(d)** of the Convention could not be infringed where he kept a witness away from a trial through fear as he was the author of his own inability to examine the witness and deprived himself of his only opportunity to do so. This principle is now enshrined in **s. 117(5)**.

Freda's letter

The defence will want to adduce Freda's statement in order to give the defendant an alibi. Her letter to Henry is first-hand documentary hearsay and may be admissible under **s. 116(2)(c)**. An earlier case under the **CJA 1988** may be cited. In *R v Case* [1991] Crim LR 192 the trial judge had admitted witness statements by two Portuguese tourists, including the victim. The Court of Appeal held that they had been wrongly admitted because the court should have been presented with other evidence on non-availability other than the contents of their statements. Thus, the defence may be required to produce additional evidence that Freda cannot attend. The court may take account of the costs of Freda's travel in deciding what is reasonably practicable. In **R v Gonzales [1992] Crim LR 180,** the Court of Appeal held that the trial judge had been wrong in concluding that it was not reasonably practicable to secure the attendance of two booking clerks from Bogota. Further steps could have been taken, such as offering to pay their fares. The prosecution in objecting to the admissibility of Freda's statement may cite **R v CT [2011] EWCA Crim 2341.** In that case the appeal against conviction was allowed since the prosecution's attempts to locate a complainant had fallen well below what was considered reasonable. Arguably, however, the court will be reluctant to exclude defence evidence.

Note passed to police

The question is raised whether the note left on Henry's car which he wants to submit to confirm his whereabouts is admissible. In *Maher v DPP* **[2006] EWHC 1271** a bystander left a note for the driver of an allegedly damaged car, and he passed it to the police, whose record was admitted at trial. This was a case of multiple hearsay, only admissible under **s. 121(1)(a)** if **s. 117, 119** or **120** were fulfilled. **Section 117** was not since neither the supplier of the information nor the first intermediary were acting under a duty. Here neither the writer of the note nor Henry are acting under a duty. The only routes to admissibility are **s. 121(1)(b),** if the parties agree, or **s. 121(1)(c)** 'the court is satisfied that the value of the evidence in question, taking into account how reliable the statement appears to be, is so high that the interests of justice require the later statement to be admissible for that purpose.' **Section 114(1)(d)** should also be considered. The defence might still find support in the decision in *Maher* however, where it was held that since the trial judge did not express any concerns about the statements' reliability under **s. 117,** the statement could be considered to be properly admitted.

For all of these statements, even if these preliminary requirements are met, the court will only admit in the light of the discretion afforded under **s. 126(1) CJA** which applies to defence as well as prosecution evidence. With regard to Tom and Gerry's statements, the fact that Henry may have to give evidence to controvert them is not in itself unfair, as the Court of Appeal held in **R v Moore [1992] Crim LR 882.** In each case, the court must conduct a balancing exercise between the interests of the public as represented by the prosecution and the interests of the particular defendant. It may thus be unfair to admit the evidence of Tom and Gerry and not Freda's letter because Henry requires this to back up his alibi. As Emson put it (2010, p. 412), 'Whatever the precise scope of **s 121(1),** as a matter of practical reality few trial judges are likely to feel confident about excluding defence evidence, even if the provision empowers them to do so, for the simple reason that the evidence might well be true. In practice the least dangerous course for any judge will be to allow the jury to consider the evidence and then guide them with a suitable direction so that in appropriate cases, it will be disregarded or afforded little weight.'

One final point of interest to note is that the Court of Appeal in **R v Montgomery [1995] 2 All ER 28** confirms that a witness who does not give evidence through fear and whose evidence is admitted in documentary form may still be sentenced for contempt of court. So Tom and Gerry may be punished on those grounds.

Question 7

Mike, Tony and John are charged with stealing cash from the safe of a restaurant. The prosecution case is that the three acted in concert to break into the cafe, Mike and Tony breaking and entering and John driving the getaway car. When the police conduct a (lawful) search of Mike's flat they discover a piece of paper in his writing which states: 'John to get £1,000 for the car job, Tony and me to split the rest.' John's library ticket is found in a stolen car abandoned a few streets from the burglary, and a quantity of cash is found in a shed on an allotment which is shared by Mike and Tony. Tom, a vagrant, who often slept on the allotments, tells PC Jones that he had been sitting near the shed till late on 19 June, the day of the burglary, and had seen the three defendants arrive together. He saw them put a bag in their shed and then leave. PC Jones makes a note of this information but does not ask Tom to sign it. Tom has now left the area and cannot be found. All three defendants deny the charges and say they have no idea how the cash came to be in the shed.

Advise them.

Commentary

A statement made in furtherance of a common purpose by one defendant may be admissible as evidence against the others. You need to consider this common law exception in relation to the note found in Mike's flat, or whether the **CJA 2003** should apply. The application of the statute should be considered in relation to Tom's evidence and in particular the implications of *R v Derodra* **[2000] 1 Cr App R 41**. The library ticket may be also classed as a document overcoming the controversial implications of the decision in *Patel v Comptroller of Customs* **[1966] AC 356**.

Answer plan

- Statement of common purpose may be admissible against defendants in conspiracy or common enterprise cases—**CJA 2003, s. 18**.
- Library ticket may be admissible under **CJA 2003, s. 118** or as real evidence.
- Application of **Criminal Procedure and Investigations Act 1996**.

Suggested answer

The prosecution are alleging that the three defendants acted together. The evidence of the note found in Mike's flat may be admissible as an exception to the rule against hearsay. The statement is in a document and therefore the question of **s. 116 of the**

Criminal Justice Act (CJA) 2003 may be raised. However, in order for this to apply there has to be a reason not to call the maker of the statement and this will hardly apply in Mike's case since he will be at the trial as a defendant. Recent developments in the case law have increased the likelihood of such statements being considered admissible under the common law and now included in s. 118 CJA 2003.

Common purpose

A long-standing principle allowed the acts and declarations of one conspirator to be admissible against another as long as these were in furtherance of the conspiracy. In *Tripodi v R* [1961] 104 CLR 1 the High Court of Australia observed 'the combination or pre-concert to commit the crime is considered as implying an authority to each to act or speak in furtherance of the common purpose on behalf of the others.' It now appears that this principle has been extended beyond conspiracy cases. Thus in *R v Gray, Liggins, Riding and Rowlands* [1995] 2 Cr App R 100 it was held that in cases where there is no charge of conspiracy against two or more defendants where they are engaged in a common enterprise to commit a substantive offence or series of offences, the acts and declarations of one defendant in relation to their common enterprise are admissible against the others if they constitute evidence which shows the involvement of each in the offences. The facts in this question are similar to *R v Devonport and Pirano* [1996] 1 Cr App R 221, where a document showing the proposed division of the proceeds of a conspiracy to defraud was admissible against both accused because, inter alia, there was further evidence beyond the document itself that the accused were all involved. Here there is other evidence, including the finding of the cash. An important aspect of the decision in *Devonport and Pirano* was that the document was a record of the planned distribution of the proceeds, not a record of what had happened. Therefore Mike's statement is likely to be admissible against all three defendants. If the statement is admitted the judge will have to warn the jury that they should be satisfied that the evidence was that of an intention to split the proceeds of a crime they were planning to commit with a common purpose.

Section 118 preserves 'any rule of law under which in criminal proceedings a statement made by a party to a common enterprise is admissible against another party to the enterprise as evidence of any matter stated.' The Explanatory Note on the statute gives an example: 'if it is independently proved that A and B are involved in a joint enterprise to rob a jewellers', any incriminating statements made by A will also be admissible against B'.

Real evidence

The library ticket may be relevant evidence if it links John to the getaway car. If he denies having been in the car the prosecution may want to adduce it to undermine his defence. If the ticket has his name on it the question whether it is hearsay arises in that it constitutes an implied assertion that John was there. In *Patel v Comptroller of Customs* [1966] AC 356 a label bearing the inscription 'Produce of Morocco' was hearsay evidence. Here, however, the library ticket is not making an express assertion. It could be treated as a mark of identification rather than an assertion. In *R v Rice* [1963] 1 QB 857 an issue in the case was whether Rice had been a passenger on a particular flight to Manchester. An airline representative was allowed to give evidence that a ticket found in the file of those used on the flight had Rice's name on it. Winn LJ explained: 'The relevance of that ticket in logic and its legal admissibility as a piece of real evidence both stem from the same root, viz, the balance of probability recognised by common sense and common knowledge that an air ticket which has been used on a flight and which has a name upon it has more likely than not been used by a man of that name.' The ticket could be taken as real evidence, from which an inference could be drawn that John was in the car.

The decision in *Rice* has been much criticised. An alternative approach would be to see if the library ticket was admissible by virtue of **s. 117 CJA 2003**. A 'document' under the statute has the widest possible application of 'anything in which any information of any description is recorded' (**s. 134**). The ticket with John's name on it was compiled presumably from information given by John, thus the information on his name was given by him, with personal knowledge of his identity to a person, the librarian, in the course of a trade, business, profession or other occupation. Finally, the prosecution may want to rely on PC Jones' statement of what Tom had told him. If the statement was admitted at committal proceedings it would be admissible at trial by virtue of the **Criminal Procedure and Investigations Act 1996** subject to the right of the opposing party to object. The court may override an objection if it thinks it is in the interests of justice so to order. If it was not a formal deposition but information given by Tom to PC Jones at an early stage of the investigation it may be admissible by **s. 116 CJA 2003** if Tom had endorsed the statement or in some other way adopted it as his own. Alternatively it may be admitted as a first-hand oral statement, as testified by Jones. There has to be a reason not to call Tom and on the facts we cannot tell whether an acceptable reason applies. Jones' statement may be admissible by virtue of **s. 117** but since it was part of evidence-gathering again there has to be a reason for not calling the maker. Again there may be difficulties in applying an acceptable reason to Tom's absence. There is judicial discretion to exclude the statement even if it is admissible. The continuing difficulty the courts have in distinguishing real evidence and hearsay is evidenced in *West Midlands Probation Board v French* [2008] EWHC 2631 which concerned the admissibility of a licence issued to a released prisoner under **s. 40A CJA 1991**. The court held the licence was admissible hearsay. Ormerod comments on the difficulties caused by the statutory definition of hearsay (2009(a), p. 287): 'Given the scheme we have been left with, advocates and trial judges face a very difficult task in deciding whether evidence is being adduced for the truth of the matter stated in the representation made by witnesses.'

Further reading

Birch, D., 'Hearsay-Logic and Hearsay-Fiddles: *Blastland* Revisited' in P. Smith (ed.), *Criminal Law: Essays in Honour of JC Smith* (London: Butterworths, 1987).

Birch, D., 'The Criminal Justice Act 2003. (4) Hearsay; Same Old Story, Same Old Song?' (2004) Crim LR 556.

Dennis, I., 'The Criminal Justice Act 2003, Part 2' (2004) Crim LR 251.

Friedman, R.D., 'Thoughts from Across the Water on Hearsay and Confrontation' [1998] Crim LR 697.

Hartshorne, J., 'Defensive Use of a Co-accused's Confession and the Criminal Justice Act 2003' (2004) 8 E & P 165.

Jackson, J.D., 'Hearsay: The Sacred Cow that Won't be Slaughtered' (1998) 2 E & P 166.

Law Commission Report No. 245, *Evidence in Criminal Proceedings: Hearsay and Relevant Topics* (London: TSO, 1997), http://lawcommission.justice.gov.uk/docs/lc245_evidence_in_criminal_proceedings_hearsay_and_related_topics.pdf.

Ormerod, D., '(a) Case Comment: *West Midlands Probation Board v French*' [2009] Crim LR 287.

Ormerod, D., '(b) Case Comment: *R v Leonard*' [2009] Crim LR 802.

Pattenden, P., 'Case Comment: *R v Horncastle* (2009)' [2010] E & P 176.

Tribe, L., 'Triangulating Hearsay' (1974) 87 Harv LR 957.

Worthen, T., 'The Hearsay Provisions of the CJA 2003: So Far Not So Good' [2008] Crim LR 431.

6

Confessions and the defendant's silence

Introduction

In many trials the most cogent evidence available to the prosecution, on occasion the only evidence, will be a pre-trial confession by the accused. This is most frequently obtained by the investigating authority, generally the police, since the state acts as chief investigator as well as prosecutor. But while confessions have long been accepted as authentic evidence of guilt, they also posed certain risks, those both of unreliability and of violation of individual autonomy. On the one hand, defendants may not be making a true confession and, on the other, even if the confession was likely to be true it may have been obtained in ways that were the result of unacceptable pressure on the suspect, thus arguably sapping his free will. At the most extreme level this could be by torture. The law on permissible inferences from a suspect's pre-trial failure to respond to questions by investigating officers has the crucial difference that, unlike the position with confessions, such failure alone cannot found a conviction.

Tables 8 and 9 give an overview of the relevant statutory framework in these two areas.

Table 8 Tests for admissibility of confessions—PACE 1984

s. 76(2)(a)	Oppression	Only applies to confessions
s. 76(2)(b)	Reliability	Only applies to confessions
s. 78	Fairness	Applies also to non-confession evidence
s. 82	Common law discretion	Applies also to non-confession evidence

Table 9 Defendant's silence

s. 34	s. 36	s. 37
Suspect must have been given general caution Code C para. 10.5		
Suspect or his counsel at trial must offer explanation which might reasonably have been given earlier (**s. 34(1)**)	Suspect must have been arrested and given the special warning (Code C para. 10.6)	
	Suspect must be interviewed at police station unless the special conditions of Code C para. 11.1 apply, e.g., danger of interference with evidence	
If arrested, suspect at interview should be given opportunity to confirm/deny earlier silence outside police station	Suspect should be given opportunity at start of interview to confirm/deny earlier failure to account outside police station	
	Suspect must fail to account for objects, substances or marks	Suspect must fail to account for presence
Silence cannot be used as part of primary case against suspect	His failure to so account can be used as part of the primary case against him	His failure to so account can be used as part of the primary case against him
Suspect shall not be committed for trial or be convicted solely on silence, failure or refusal to account (**s. 38(3)**)		

Note 1. Where the accused was at an authorised place of detention at the time of the silence, failure or refusal to account, the sections do not apply if he had not been allowed an opportunity to consult a solicitor prior to being questioned, charged or officially informed he might be prosecuted.

Note 2. The court may draw inferences from D's failure to explain under **s. 34** both after caution and before charge and on being charged.

? **Question 1**

'The curtailment of the right to silence in the police station is objectionable because of the risk of abuse of state power associated with custodial interrogation. Section 34 of the Criminal Justice and Public Order Act 1994 ought to be repealed as a matter of principle.'

(Dennis, *The Law of Evidence*, 4th edn (London: Sweet & Maxwell, 2010), p. 210.)

How far, in your view, does the provision in **s. 34**, specifying that the suspect must have been allowed an opportunity to consult a solicitor before the section applies, provide a safeguard against the risk of abuse of state power?

Commentary

The erosion of the right to silence remains a topical area for essay questions. Be careful here to answer the specific question set which requires you to assess whether the availability of legal advice to the suspect is a sufficient counterbalance to the extension of state power enshrined in **s. 34**. The question is about the relative advantages to the defendant in the interview situation rather than an invitation to recite all the arguments for and against the abolition of the right to silence. The area has generated much, often seemingly contradictory, case law and you will need to display your understanding of the evolution of the law in relation to the defendant's reliance on legal advice to remain silent. This has now been settled by *R v Beckles* **[2005] 1 WLR 2829** but you should show some understanding of the evolution of the law and criticisms made of it.

 Answer plan

- What is the effect of the suspect's claim to rely on legal advice?

- Does English law accord with **art. 6** provisions?

- Review the case law, in particular contrast the change in judicial approach. In *R v Betts and Hall* **(2001)** the court had held that genuine reliance on legal advice may preclude the permissible drawing of adverse inferences from silence but this was disapproved in *R v Howell* **(2005)** and *R v Beckles* **(2005)**.

- Does the availability of legal advice provide any counter-balance to the extension of state power in **s. 34**?

- Are there any other safeguards for the defendant?

 Suggested answer

The risk of abuse by state power referred to by Dennis is inherent in the very nature of police interrogation. Inevitably there is an imbalance of power between the suspect and the state actors who conduct the questioning. Historically, therefore, the common law provided that a refusal to give an explanation in the face of official questioning could not be proffered as prosecution evidence (apart from the special circumstances outlined in *R v Parkes* [1976] 1 WLR 1251). Pressure particularly from the police led to the changes effected in the **Criminal Justice and Public Order Act 1994 (CJPOA)**. The targets were said to be a small number of hardened criminals who persistently exercised their right to silence. Galligan (1988, p. 70) quotes the former Metropolitan Police Commissioner Peter Imbert as saying that the protection of silence had 'done more to obscure the truth and facilitate crime than anything else in this century.' The new provisions of course applied to all suspects and have generated considerable controversy and unease that they are disproportionately eroding defendants' rights.

Strasbourg decision

An early indication of the justification for the unease was the Strasbourg Court's decision in *John Murray v UK* (1996) 22 EHRR 29. There the court determined that the right to remain silent under police questioning and the privilege against self-incrimination were generally recognised international standards which lay at the heart of the notion of fair procedure. However, these immunities were not absolute. Whether the drawing of adverse inferences from an accused's silence infringed **art. 6** was a matter to be determined in the light of all the circumstances of the case, having particular regard to the situations where inferences might be drawn, the weight attached to them by the national courts in their assessment of the evidence and the degree of compulsion inherent in the situation. This judgment thus far then does not support Dennis's stance that **s. 34** exhibits excessive state power over the individual. The court held that it could not be said that the drawing of reasonable inferences from the applicant's behaviour had the effect of shifting the burden of proof from the prosecution to the defence so as to infringe the principle of the presumption of innocence. However, Dennis's analysis gains some support from one particular aspect of the judgment which was that denial of access to legal advice for 48 hours did infringe the article. In the light of this the UK amended the law. **Sections 34 and 36–38 of the CJPOA** are not operative if the defendant had not been allowed an opportunity to consult a solicitor prior to being questioned, charged, or officially informed he was to be prosecuted. Subsequent case law determined the nature of direction the judge should give the jury in order to maintain the fairness of the trial. In *Condron v UK* [2000] **Crim LR 679** the trial judge was held to have violated **art. 6(1)** by taking into account the fact that the accused had been advised by his solicitor to be silent and failed to direct the jury that only if, despite the evidence or lack of it, the jury concluded that the failure to answer questions at interview could *only* sensibly be attributed to the accused's having no answer, or none that would stand up to cross-examination, might they draw an adverse inference. The Court of Appeal had accepted that there had been a misdirection but nonetheless the guilty verdict should stand. They had addressed the question of legal advice in words that anticipated the current stance in *Beckles*. Lord Bingham stated, 'Under **s 34**, the jury is not concerned with the correctness of the solicitor's advice, nor with whether it complies with the Law Society's guidelines, but with the reasonableness of the [defendant's] conduct in all the circumstances which the jury have found to exist.'

Dennis's objections to **s. 34** are to that extent confirmed in that legal advice to remain silent in itself will not preclude the possibility of adverse inferences being drawn. The jury must be directed to consider if it was reasonable to rely on the advice and if the accused remained silent because it suited his purposes. The leading case is *R v Beckles (No. 2)* [2005] **1 WLR 2829** where the court held that even if the accused genuinely relied on his solicitor's advice to remain silent, it was nevertheless permissible for the jury to draw an adverse inference under **s. 34**, if it was not reasonable to rely on that advice. In *R v Hoare* **[2005] 1 WLR 1804**, Auld LJ stated (p. 1821): 'Legal entitlement is one thing. An accused's reason for exercising it is another. The belief in his entitlement may be genuine, but it does not follow that his reason for exercising it is.'

Suspect has to 'second-guess' jury

Thus the right of access to a solicitor may be devoid of content since the court will conduct an examination about the suspect's state of mind. As Dennis points out it seems that the Court of Appeal maintained that 'the purpose of **s. 34** is to flush out innocent explanations at the earliest opportunity' (p. 186). Malik (2005) argues that as a result of *Beckles* the suspect is having to 'second guess' the jury and calculate whether it will believe that reliance on legal advice was the true reason for his or her silence.

The approach of the courts in interpreting the legislation therefore appears to confirm Dennis's concern about **s. 34**. In particular, it means that in effect the trial is commencing at the interview stage which is where the suspect is expected to disclose his innocent explanation, if he has one. Further, it is clear that if the suspect gives his reasons at trial for his earlier silence he is thereby waiving his legal professional privilege and the solicitor can be cross-examined. In *Bowden* **[1999] 2 Cr App R 176** the Court of Appeal held that if the court is to examine the reasons for the legal advice there will be an implied waiver of the privilege. As Choo points out (2012, p. 135) 'the possible consequences of waiver would seem to place the accused in an unenviable "Catch-22" situation.' To prevent adverse inferences being drawn it may be necessary to provide reasons for the advice, yet this may be interpreted as a waiver of legal professional privilege, so the accused, or the legal adviser, may be cross-examined on whether there were additional, tactical reasons for the advice. He points out there was no assistance for the defendant on this point from the Strasbourg Court since giving reasons for the advice was regarded as problematic in *Condron v UK*. The courts have acted somewhat cautiously and in *R v Bresa* **[2005] EWCA Crim 1414** a conviction was overturned when the judge had failed to emphasise the importance of the defendant's right to privilege in relation to communications between him and his solicitors. The direction had contained nothing about the jury having to be sure that the offender remained silent not just because of the legal advice he received but because he had no answer to give in interview. On the other hand, there are difficulties for the defendant in giving reasons for deciding not to answer questions at interview because he is subject to the hearsay rule which might limit how he repeated what his solicitor had told him (*R v Davis* **[1998] Crim LR 659**).

Complex directions to jury

Dennis's concern is also supported by the resulting complexity of the directions the judge must give to the jury in relation to reliance on legal advice to remain silent. The Specimen Direction of the Judicial Studies Board is, as a result of these considerations, very complex. Roberts and Zuckerman (2010, p. 571) comment that Specimen Direction

No. 40 on **s. 34 of the CJPOA 1994** 'is easily one of the most lengthy and complicated sets of judicial instructions in the entire Crown Court Bench Book.'

There are nonetheless some reservations that could be expressed about the objections Dennis has put to **s. 34**. One such is the sometimes more anti-prosecutorial stance taken by the Court of Appeal. For example, Choo (2012, p. 130) cites the case law on the status of prepared statements read out by a solicitor at the beginning of the police interview and the failure of the suspect to answer consequential police questions. As long as the prepared statement is a full account of the defence later relied on the situation, as Choo puts it, 'as uncertainty . . . has now been resolved in favour of the defendant'. (See *R v Knight* [2004] **1 WLR 340** and *R v Turner* [2003] **EWCA Crim 3108**.) Another pro-defendant stance is that the court will take into account whether there had been insufficient disclosure by the police in directing whether it is reasonable for the suspect to rely on legal advice to remain silent (see *R v Argent* [1997] **2 Cr App R 27** and *R v Nickelson* (1999) **Crim LR 61**).

The question is raised therefore whether the stipulation that the suspect must have access to legal advice before any inferences from silence may be drawn is only cosmetic. The jury have to look at the context in which the advice was given. Doak and McGourlay comment (2012, p. 163), 'Logically, it would appear to follow that if a defendant kept silent on legal advice, and not because he had no story to give or none that would stand up to scrutiny, then it does not matter whether the advice was well-grounded or not. From a due process perspective, where defendants genuinely rely on the advice of their legal representatives, they should not be penalised for doing so. If this were the case, what would be given by way of concession with one hand would effectively be taken away by the other.' Indeed, since Parliament went to much trouble to amend the original statute to make provision for access to a solicitor it seems perverse for the courts to hold that it may be unreasonable to act on what he or she advises. As Munday concludes (2011, p. 549), 'It is difficult to suppress a wry smile.'

If Dennis is right and the current situation is an example of an excess of state power there are arguably two possible alternatives to the status quo. Zuckerman (1994, p. 117) argues that the principle of natural justice requires the suspect to have full notice of the evidence against him. In Zuckerman's view the right way to deal with an 'ambush' defence at trial is to institute a proper system of pre-trial pleading in which prosecution and defence set out in writing the essence of their cases. In those circumstances common sense might allow comment on silence. He adds, 'Once the courts have evolved parameters of fairness they would benefit not only the suspects who maintain silence but all suspects' questions by the police' (1994, p. 139). The other alternative, as Dennis says, is to repeal **s. 34**.

? **Question 2**

Darcy and Bingley are suspected of the murder of Mrs Bennett, Darcy's mother-in-law, who has disappeared in suspicious circumstances. They are both arrested, cautioned and taken separately into custody. On the way to the police station Bingley begins to sob and says, 'I'll miss the old bat, I should never have done it.' 'What do you mean? What have you done?' asked PC Collins. 'Everyone knew she was an old cow but I'll never forget her face when we put the plastic bag over her,' replied Bingley. At the police station Bingley asks for a solicitor but the police refuse on the grounds that since the body has not yet been found other family members may be alerted to help conceal it. Bingley is questioned continually for nine hours, with only one break for tea and biscuits. The police then produce a skeleton which they have borrowed from a local medical school and tell Bingley they found it buried on his estate. He mistakenly thinks it is Mrs Bennett and says, 'Oh my God. She has been moved.'

The police claim that Darcy said, when they called at his house to arrest him, 'I'm glad you've come. I did us all a favour by finishing her off.' Darcy has, unknown to the police, a rare medical condition which requires frequent rest periods. He is denied a solicitor at the police station because the police fear the solicitor might advise him to remain silent. Anxious to get some sleep because he knows he will black out otherwise, Darcy announces that he will cooperate with the questioning. He tells the investigating officer that he had killed Mrs Bennett and was proud of it. He says that 'Bingley had nothing to do with it'. At the trial both plead not guilty and want to retract their statements at the police station. Darcy denies making the initial statement to the police at his house.

Advise Darcy and Bingley on evidence.

 Commentary

You need to be careful to cover the rather specific issues in this question and not deal too generally with the law on confessions. Both Bingley and Darcy need to be advised whether their initial statements were made in the context of interviews as defined by the revised Code of Practice. Note that Darcy is in addition denying that he made the initial statement, not saying that it was improperly extracted from him. This is a question of fact not law and should arguably be tested by the jury. You need to discuss the possible breaches of the **Police and Criminal Evidence Act 1984 (PACE)** and the Code for each defendant and the implications of the trick played by the police on Bingley, as well as whether the earlier improperly conducted interview has tainted a subsequent one. With regard to Darcy you must consider whether his desire to end the interview and get some rest is self-induced and therefore since **s. 76(2)(b) PACE** has been interpreted in a restrictive way (see *R v Goldenberg* **(1988) 88 Cr App R 285**), whether it is applicable here. Finally there is the question of whether Darcy's claim that Bingley was not involved can be used by Bingley.

 Answer plan

Bingley

- Is initial statement admissible?
- Implications of possible breaches of **PACE** and Code and of trick played by police.

Darcy

- Whether initial statement was made is a question of fact for the jury not admissibility for the judge.
- Is Darcy's desire to end interview 'self-induced'—**s. 76(2)(b)** and **R v Goldenberg**?
- Does tainted first interview make even a properly conducted subsequent interview inadmissible?
- Status of exoneration of Bingley by Darcy, see **PACE, s. 76A**.

 Examiner's tip

A bad mistake sometimes made by students is to refer to **s. 78** as if it was available to exclude defence evidence. Note here how this point is dealt with in relation to **s. 76A PACE**. The statute clearly states it is only available for prosecution evidence as is the common law discretion. In fact exclusionary discretion is only rarely applied to defence evidence—see p. 86 (**Chapter 5**, Suggested answer to Question 3) on hearsay.

 Suggested answer

Initial statement by Bingley

Bingley's arrest and the administration of the caution suggest that his treatment by the police at this point is correct. In the van he makes what could be taken to be an implied confession of responsibility for Mrs Bennett's death, according to the definition of a confession in **s. 82(1) of the Police and Criminal Evidence Act 1984 (PACE)**. The question arises as to whether it is an entirely spontaneous statement outside the context of an interview. Paragraph 11.1A of Code C defined an interview as 'the questioning of the person regarding their involvement or suspected involvement in a criminal offence or offences which, by virtue of para. 10.1 of Code C is required to be carried out under caution.' Such interviews should normally be conducted at a police station. In **R v Matthews (1989) 91 Cr App R 43** the Court of Appeal adopted a broad approach to the definition of an interview but this has not always been followed. Bingley had volunteered to open the discussion. The issue is the intention of the police officer in making the response, whether to secure either an admission or an innocent explanation. In that case the suspect had requested that his conversation with the officer be 'off the record'. It was held that his confession was admissible even though the accused had not been shown a note of what had been said. On the facts, the former seems more likely. If so, there have been breaches of the Code; the questioning was conducted away from the police station and no offer of free legal advice was made. There do not appear to be any special conditions here as set in para. 11.1 of Code C. The question then arises as to whether the statement is admissible. This is clearly not an instance of oppression under

s. 76(2)(a) PACE. It is unlikely either that a submission under s. 76(2)(b) PACE would succeed since the courts appear to have confined its operation to those cases where something out of the ordinary has occurred, often in situations where the defendant is particularly vulnerable, for example in *R v Everett* [1988] Crim LR 826. Exclusion under s. 78 PACE is possible if the breaches are considered significant enough, as in *R v Canale* [1990] 2 All ER 187 or if the police acted with bad faith (see *R v Alladice* (1988) 87 Cr App R 380). However, there must be shown to be unfairness caused thereby to the proceedings to allow such a confession. If the defendant would have confessed anyway, as in *R v Alladice*, s. 78 PACE is not applicable. The judge is likely to take into account Bingley's mental state in deciding whether to exercise the discretion to exclude the confession. Even if it is admitted the weight to be attached to a confession in such circumstances would be light.

Interview at police station

At the police station the police are arguably acting correctly in the reason they give for delaying access to a solicitor. Murder is an indictable offence and the reason given for the delay appears to be within the scope of permissible reasons set out in s. 58(8) PACE and Annex B to Code C. However, in *R v Samuel* [1988] QB 615, the Court of Appeal stressed that the prosecution has a formidable task in satisfying the court that there are reasonable grounds for such a belief. The questioning without a proper meal break is unlikely to amount to a breach of the Code justifying exclusion under s. 76 or s. 78 PACE. The courts have held that in order to consider excluding a confession under s. 78, breaches must be 'significant and substantial' (*R v Absolam* (1989) 88 Cr App R 332). In *R v Canale* [1990] 2 All ER 187 two police officers failed to record interviews contemporaneously because they thought it best not to do so. The Court of Appeal had said that the officers had shown a cynical disregard of the Code, which they had flagrantly breached. However, although the breach here in itself may be minor it has to be seen in the context of other more serious police malpractice. On the facts it appears that the police acted with bad faith with regard to the trick over the skeleton. It may be significant that it was the defendant and not his legal adviser who was tricked. In *R v Mason* [1988] 1 WLR 139 deceiving the solicitor was described by the court as a 'vital factor' in leading to exclusion. Thus, a confession obtained as a result of deception will be in danger of being excluded, but the particular circumstances of the case are important. Lord Lane said in *R v Alladice* that if the police had acted in bad faith the court would have excluded the confession under s. 78, if not s. 76 PACE. In *R v Walsh* (1989) 91 Cr App R 161, the Court of Appeal looked at several breaches of the statute and Code and held that bad faith on the part of the police might make substantial or significant that which would not otherwise be so.

Tainting of second interview

It is submitted that Bingley's confession is likely to be excluded under s. 78 PACE. There is a further consideration in that the fact that there have been breaches of the statute and/or Code in an earlier, initial interview may so taint subsequent interviews that they may affect the reliability of even a properly conducted interview. Here, the earlier possible breaches may render the second interview unreliable, even if it is properly conducted. In *R v McGovern* (1990) 92 Cr App R 228, the Court of Appeal said that the question of whether a later interview should be excluded on these grounds is a question of fact and degree. However, in *R v Singleton* [2002] EWCA Crim 459 the Court of Appeal stated (at para. 10) '. . . where an early interview is excluded admission of a later interview must be a matter of fact and degree.'

In *McGovern* the accused, who had a very low IQ, confessed during two interviews. At the first interview her solicitor had not been present and there had also been breaches there of Code C. The solicitor was present at the second interview. It was held there was a direct line of causation so that the breaches in the first interview tainted the second. In *R v Neil* [1994] Crim LR 441 the court held that if there were a series of interviews the questions to ask in order to decide whether to exclude on grounds of unfairness a later unobjectionable interview were, first, the objections to the earlier tainted interviews of a fundamental and continuing nature and, second, if so, were arrangements made for the accused to have sufficient opportunity to exercise an informed and independent choice as to whether he should repeat or retract what he said in the excluded interview or remain silent? On the facts it is unlikely that either of Bingley's confessions will be admitted.

Whether confession made is a matter of fact

Darcy claims not to have made the initial statement at his house. This is a question of fact and arguably should be put to the jury as the Privy Council held in *Ajodha v the State* [1982] AC 204. In *Thongjai v R* [1998] AC 54 the Privy Council developed the position on this. If the defendant claims that he did not make an alleged oral confession and also that he was badly treated by police before or at the time of the alleged confession, the court held that the judge should first decide whether, on the assumption that the alleged confession was made, it was admissible or not as a matter of law or discretion. Only if the alleged statement is admissible, on issue decided in a voir dire, should it be put to the jury to decide if it had taken place or not.

Darcy as vulnerable interviewee

However, under para. 11.4 of Code C, at the beginning of an interview carried out in a police station, the interviewing officer should put to the suspect 'any significant statement or silence' which occurred before his arrival at the police station and ask him if he confirms it. Thus Darcy's alleged statement on the doorstep should have been recorded and put to him for confirmation. If these provisions have been breached there would be grounds to challenge the admissibility of the alleged confession on a voir dire (*R v Sat-Bhambra* (1988) 88 Cr App R 55). It is arguable that Darcy's police station confession is potentially unreliable under s. 76(2)(b) because he made it in order to get out of the interview so that he could get some rest because of his concern over his medical condition. In *R v Goldenberg* (1988) 88 Cr App R 285, however, the 'something said or done' limb of the test was held not to be satisfied by the conduct of the maker of the confession. Thus, the confession of a heroin addict who confessed in order to get drugs, could not be excluded under **s. 76(2)(b)**. The defendant had, like Darcy, requested the interview. However, Darcy appears to have been improperly denied access to a solicitor. The reason given is not one permitted under **s. 58**. Again the court will look for a causal connection between the lack of access to legal advice and the confession in deciding whether to exclude under **s. 78**.

Confessions exonerating co-defendant

If the statement made by Darcy is admissible as a confession then the reference to Bingley will be relevant to his defence. If, however, it is held to be inadmissible against Darcy, is it admissible for Bingley? In that case Darcy's defence should follow the process set out by **s. 76A PACE**. This was introduced to deal with this sort of situation. Since the contested statement by Darcy is a confession according to **s. 82 PACE**, Darcy remains an accused and the statement is relevant to Bingley's defence then it remains for Bingley to prove on the balance of probabilities that the statement was not obtained in violation of **s. 76A(2)**. Darcy cannot apply to have the statement excluded under **s. 78 PACE** since that only applies to prosecution evidence. If the statement is admitted his only protections are: judicial directions that the statement is not evidence against him, an application to sever the indictment or a stay of proceedings if the interests of justice are threatened. This section shows the difficulties of achieving fairness if there are co-defendants with different interests.

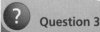 **Question 3**

Police are puzzled by a series of thefts of valuable greyhounds from kennels and suspect the perpetrators are involved in a gambling scam. They call on Gerry and Cliff, noted professional gamblers, as part of their routine inquiries. Gerry invites them in and agrees to answer any questions, although he is clearly upset because he has just heard his mother is dying in hospital with cancer. As they are talking, Gerry's 14-year-old son, Tom, comes in and says: 'I hope they arrest you for cruelty to animals. It's horrible leaving that greyhound tied up in the shed. Grandma will cry her heart out when I tell her.' Gerry breaks down in tears and says: 'What a fool I have been. I said I'd mind the brute but I didn't know it was stolen. Cliff made me take it in.' He is arrested and cautioned and taken to the police station for questioning. There the custody officer asks him if he has his own solicitor. Gerry replies that he has but since he owes him money for arranging the sale of his house he doesn't like to call him. The police do not offer a duty solicitor and proceed to question Gerry further. Gerry tells them that he doesn't know any details of the thefts but the police persist in questioning him. The police then produce photographs of Tom on animal rights demonstrations and say to Gerry, 'You know we could take this further if you don't play ball.' Gerry then confesses that he, Cliff and several others had organised the thefts. He tells them that they had been forced to kill some of the dogs and they are buried on Hackney Downs. The police visit Cliff and ask him to come down to the station to help with their inquiries. He agrees but at the station asks for a solicitor. They reply that there is no need for that at this stage. They then leave him alone for about two hours. Cliff, who is 18 years old, suffers from claustrophobia and when they return is in a very distressed state. Cliff is cautioned and told he is under arrest; he begins to sob violently and admits that he had stolen the greyhounds. At the trial he argues that he was forced to make the confession due to his mental distress.

Advise Gerry and Cliff.

Commentary

You must systematically list the circumstances relating to the admissibility of possible confessions by both defendants. In a question of this sort it is important not to miss any of the issues. The visit to Gerry is described as 'routine' initially, so you need to discuss if and when it becomes an 'interview', and thus whether the requirements of the statute and Codes of Practice apply. Is Gerry's 'mixed' statement a confession? It clearly is partly exculpatory and partly inculpatory. The information on legal advice given by the police to Gerry must be checked against the Code requirements. The confession in the police station is clearly obtained under some pressure and you must check whether **s. 76 or s. 78 PACE** can be applied to exclude it. Do not overlook the issue of the incriminating of a third party, namely Cliff and whether, even if the confession is inadmissible, the trial may still consider the discovery of real evidence which it prompted, the buried dogs. Cliff's treatment raises the question of whether the police should have treated it as an interview from the beginning since he was already under suspicion as a result of Gerry's statement. Consider finally his distressed state and the possible unreliability of the confession.

Answer plan

- Is the visit to Gerry an 'interview'?
- Status of Gerry's 'mixed' statement.
- Is information on legal advice given correctly?
- Application of **ss. 76–78** to confessions.
- Gerry's confession not evidence against Cliff, but see **R v Hayter (2005)**.
- 'Fruits of the poisoned tree'—discovery of real evidence as result of an inadmissible confession.

Suggested answer

Initial 'mixed' statement by Gerry

Gerry's initial statement in his house is clearly incriminating, although he is also trying to excuse himself. Since it is partly adverse to the maker it falls within the definition of 'confession' in **s. 82(1) of the Police and Criminal Evidence Act 1984 (PACE)**. If it is admitted the whole statement may be evidence of the truth of its contents, as the House of Lords held in *R v Sharp* **[1988] 1 WLR 7**. There is clearly no evidence of oppression here and therefore **s. 76(2)(a) PACE** is not applicable. However, it is necessary to consider the possible application of other sections of **PACE** and the Code of Practice. We are told the police are engaged in 'routine' inquiries, that is they are not conducting an interview, which is questioning of a person regarding his involvement in an offence, but rather questioning to obtain information. The state of mind of the police is the key question, but, on the facts as they are given, it seems the exchange was not an interview. The words uttered by Tom may amount to something said or done which was likely in the circumstances existing at the time to render unreliable any confession Gerry might have made. The Court of Appeal held that it is not necessary for the words or action to come from the police (*R v Harvey* **[1988] Crim LR 241**). There are two limbs to the test. First, circumstances existing at the time and here Gerry's emotional state concerning his mother's condition may be applicable; see also *R v McGovern* **(1990) 92 Cr App R 228**. Secondly, as regards anything said or done, can Tom's words be sufficient? The main question is to find a causal connection between the words and the confession such as to make any confession in such circumstances unreliable. On the facts, there does not appear to be anything in Tom's remark which would have made any confession unreliable, unless it could be argued that Gerry confessed in order to stop Tom's tirade and painful remarks about his dying mother.

Interview at police station

At the station, Gerry appears to have been properly cautioned but there may be inadequacies in the information given about access to legal advice which may, inter alia, render his confession inadmissible. Under **s. 58 PACE** and para. 11.2 of Code C, immediately prior to the commencement of any interview at a police station or other authorised place of detention, the interviewing officer must remind the suspect of his entitlement to free legal advice. It appears that, when Gerry is asked whether he has a solicitor and he replies that he is worried about owing him money, Gerry is not told of his entitlement to free legal advice. However, access to legal advice may be lawfully delayed for up to 36 hours in the case of indictable offences (**s. 58 PACE**). Thus, the failure in Gerry's case may well be permissible as long as the police can convince the court that they reasonably feared one of the contingencies referred to in **s. 58(8) PACE** would arise. In any case, a wrongly authorised delay in obtaining legal advice, does not render the confession automatically excluded under either **s. 76 or s. 78 PACE**. In *R v Alladice* **(1988) 87 Cr App R 380**, the court stressed that influential factors in excluding under **s. 78 PACE** were whether or not the police acted in bad faith and whether the presence of a solicitor would have made any difference, particularly to a seasoned offender.

Oppression test

However, there are arguably other pressing grounds to exclude the confession here under **s. 76 PACE**. Has this confession been obtained by oppression? Once the defence raises the issue and it is accepted by the judge as a possibility, the burden is on the prosecution to prove beyond reasonable doubt that it has not been so obtained. Does the implied threat to Tom amount to oppression of Gerry? Oppression is only partly defined in **s. 76(8) PACE** as including 'torture, inhuman or degrading treatment and the use or threat of violence whether or not amounting to torture.' Showing the photograph and the threat to 'take things further' probably does not fall within this partial statutory definition. However, in the leading case of *R v Fulling* **[1987] QB 426** the Court of Appeal adopted the dictionary definition of 'exercise of authority or power in a burdensome, harsh or wrongful manner; unjust or cruel treatment of subjects, inferiors, etc., or the imposition of unreasonable or unjust burdens.'

In the court's opinion, it was difficult to envisage any circumstances in which oppression would not entail some impropriety on the part of the police. It is clear that Gerry here is being placed under psychological pressure as a result of the threat. The main requirement is misuse of power or authority. Thus, in *R v Paris* **(1992) 97 Cr App R 99** the Court of Appeal held that it was oppressive within the meaning of **s. 76(2)(a) PACE** for police officers to shout at a suspect and tell him what they wanted to hear after he had denied the offence 300 times, so it is arguable that the treatment of Gerry amounts to oppression.

Reliability and fairness tests

Also **s. 76(2)(b) PACE** may be applicable in that in such circumstances any confession made by the defendant would be likely to be unreliable. This test is an objective one. **Section 78 PACE** is also widely applied to confession evidence (*R v Mason* **[1988] 1 WLR 139**) and the combination of factors, particularly police bad faith over the threat, could lead to exclusion here. Even if the confession is excluded the court may still allow evidence of finding the greyhounds, although clearly their evidential worth will be less considering that it may not be possible to admit its source (**s. 76(4) PACE**). One final point is that even if the confession is admitted it will not be evidence against Cliff and should be edited before the trial.

Confession evidence against maker

If the defence do not succeed in getting Gerry's confession excluded, the question then arises whether it is evidence against Cliff. It is a common law principle that a confession can only inculpate its maker (see *R v Hayter* [2005] **1 WLR 605**). One possibility is for it to be edited so that Cliff's name is excluded but the court will have to bear in mind fairness to Gerry. In *R v Silcott* [1987] **Crim LR 765** Hodgson J ruled that where the interviews of some of the defendants implicated others, names should be replaced by initials. This did not overcome the prejudicial effect since prosecutors were permitted to cross-examine over the meaning of the initials. Silcott was disapproved in *Lobban v R* [1995] **1 WLR 877** where the Privy Council upheld the importance of the legal principle that there is no discretion to exclude evidence sought to be relied on by a defendant. One possibility would be to order separate trials. If this is not ordered the judge must give very clear instructions that Gerry's statement is not evidence against Cliff. Cliff should be warned, however, it may be permissible for the jury to use Gerry's confession as the basis for establishing his guilt and then use that finding of guilt in determining whether Cliff is guilty (see *R v Hayter*).

Cliff's initial statement

With regard to Cliff's position, it is arguable that the police were wrong not to treat their initial exchange with him as an interview under the definition in Code of Practice C para. 11.1A. There were already reasonable grounds to suspect him because of Gerry's confession. He should therefore have been cautioned and told of his right to free legal advice, although it is arguable that this is an indictable offence and access to a solicitor could be delayed on appropriate grounds. There is perhaps, a breach of the Code also in leaving him for two hours, since under para. 1.1 of Code C, persons in custody should be dealt with expeditiously. As someone not under arrest Cliff was free to leave but clearly had not appreciated this. There are possible grounds for unreliability given that the 'something said or done' could be leaving him for two hours and the circumstances of his claustrophobia. For exclusion on grounds of **s. 76(2)(b)** PACE, there is no need for police impropriety. In *R v Crampton* (1990) **92 Cr App R 369** according to the court it was a matter for those present at the interview to decide whether a drug addict was fit to be questioned in the sense that his answers could be relied upon to be true. The series of breaches could also, especially if bad faith was found, amount to exclusion on grounds of unfairness under **s. 78 PACE**. Since *R v Ward* [1993] **1 WLR 619** the courts have taken an increasingly open stance on allowing expert evidence of a psychiatrist or psychologist on the reliability of a confession if the accused was suffering from a mental disorder that fell short of mental illness. In *R v O'Brien* [2000] **Crim LR 676** the Court of Appeal stated that admissibility of expert evidence depended on the satisfaction of three conditions: first, the disorder must be such that it would affect the reliability of the confession; second, the accused's condition must depart significantly from the norm, and, finally, there must be an earlier history of his mental disorder. In that case expert evidence should have been admitted, since the accused's mental disorder was associated with the making of false confessions. Cliff might be able to rely on the case of *R v Blackburn* [2005] **EWCA Crim 1349**. The suspect was a vulnerable teenager, aged 15 years, who did not have a mental disorder at the time of his interview when he made what was alleged to be a 'coerced compliant' confession. The Court of Appeal held that evidence of a forensic psychologist was admissible as relevant to the reliability of the confessions under s. 76(2)(b). The issue fell outside the jury's normal knowledge and experience. The court noted that the evidence of the expert was that 'the key feature giving rise to a coerced compliant confession is fatigue, which, together with an inability to control what is happening, may induce the individual to experience a growing desire to give up resisting suggestions put to him.' It added, 'normal people, not suffering from any personality disorder or abnormal disorder, could be rendered compliant by prolonged interrogation.'

The defence will therefore have to examine whether the circumstances of the defendant's interrogation, combined with his claustrophobia and mental vulnerability and his age, make it arguable that an expert witness should be called.

? Question 4

Arnold and Brenda are summonsed on charges of criminal damage of a wine shop in Boxfield High Street. The incident occurred at 3.00 a.m., when the window was smashed and the alarm sounded. Arnold was stopped shortly afterwards in the next street, where police suspicions are aroused because he is not wearing shoes. He is stopped and questioned in the street. He refuses to say why he was in the area at that time. He also refuses to explain why he is not wearing shoes. An abandoned pair of wine-covered sandals, which the police believe are Arnold's, are found in a bin near the scene of the burglary. Arnold is arrested and questioned about his whereabouts and the absence of shoes in the police station. He has, on his request, a solicitor present on this occasion. His solicitor, however, considers that he is under the influence of drink and advises him not to answer questions at this stage. At the trial Arnold puts forward the explanation for his failure to respond to questioning that his solicitors had so advised him. He explains that he had not volunteered why he was in the area because he had been drinking with his girlfriend and did not want his wife to find out. He also says he had passed by the wine shop and seen the damaged window. Some wine from a broken bottle had spilt on his sandals. When he heard the police car coming he took off the sandals and threw them away because he feared he would be implicated since he used to work at the shop. He denies involvement with the criminal damage. Brenda works at the wine shop and when she turns up for work the next day and sees the debris, she asks the manager, 'What happened here?' He replies, 'I think you know all about this don't you? Your friends and you smashed my window.' Brenda says nothing. She was interviewed by police with a solicitor present and again said nothing. At the trial Arnold and Brenda plead not guilty. She refuses to testify but her counsel cross-examines Arnold and puts it to him that it was Arnold who carried out the offence and that Brenda had nothing to do with it.

Advise on the evidence.

Commentary

The defendants here have acted in different ways in the face of questioning about their involvement in the offence. You will need to examine whether their reactions and behaviour amount to confessions; if so what is their evidential worth and if there are grounds to exclude them by rule of law or exercise of discretion. Arnold's behaviour raises several issues under the **Criminal Justice and Public Order Act 1994, ss. 34, 36, 37 and 38**. Brenda's situation involves a discussion of the law relating to silence in the face of questioning by the shop manager. You need therefore to discuss her behaviour in relation to common law provisions on silence. You are only given information about questioning outside the police station so do not speculate about other possible interviews.

Answer plan

- Admissibility of Arnold's silence when first questioned but not under arrest.
- Applicability of the **CJPOA, ss. 34, 36 and 37** to interview at police station—Code C Annex C.
- Directions to jury—see *Cowan* **(1996)**, *Condron* **(2001)**, JSB Specimen Directions.
- Legal advice to remain silent—***Bowden* (1999)**; effect on legal professional privilege.
- Admissibility of Brenda's failure to respond to manager's allegation—common law or **CJPOA**?
- Silence of Brenda at police interview—does **s. 34** apply if she does not testify?

Examiner's tip

In answering questions on silence as evidence students have a big task in applying the statutory provisions. It is important to remember, however, that you get marks for recognising all the issues as well as dealing with each issue thoroughly. In this question it is important not to overlook the common law position since you will probably lose about one-fifth of the marks if you do!

Suggested answer

Questioning in street

The question involves an examination of the overlapping provisions of the **Criminal Justice and Public Order Act 1994 (CJPOA)**, which cover circumstances where a court may invite the drawing of inferences from an accused's silence. **Section 34** applies after caution and up to charge, that is both before and after arrest. However, it only allows the court to draw inferences from silence if the defendant fails then to mention facts which he could reasonably have been expected to mention when questioned and which he relies on at trial for his defence.

The first question which arises is whether Arnold's silence when first questioned in the street is admissible. At this stage Arnold is not under arrest and **ss. 36 and 37** are not applicable. The prosecution may try to argue that **s. 34** does apply because Arnold gives an explanation at trial which he might reasonably have given when first questioned. It is unlikely that Arnold will be able to rely on **s. 34(2A)**, in that he has not had an opportunity to consult a solicitor; that provision only applies if he was at an authorised place of detention at the time of the failure. He does give an explanation at trial for his whereabouts and his lack of shoes, so **s. 34** may be engaged on those grounds. The prosecution will have difficulty, however, in successfully arguing that evidence from the interview 'at the scene of the crime' is admissible. A preliminary matter is that Arnold should have been cautioned (Code C, para. 10.4). Even if he had, it is doubtful that the failure to respond to police questions will be admitted.

Code of Practice C issued under the **Police and Criminal Evidence Act 1984 (PACE)** requires a police officer to caution the suspect before questioning him once there are grounds to suspect him of an offence. The caution now has been reworded and the suspect is warned of the possible consequences of his failure to mention relevant facts. It is unclear from the facts whether the police have reasonable suspicion of Arnold's involvement. His proximity to the scene of the crime and the lack of shoes do, however, appear to be significant. The issue is whether the questioning amounts to an interview. If it does then the statute and Code of Practice apply. The revised Code defines an interview as the questioning of a person regarding his involvement in an offence, but that questioning to obtain information or in the ordinary course of duty does not constitute an interview. This does leave some doubt, however, as to when questioning to obtain information turns into questioning about involvement in an offence. The case law is primarily based on the admissibility of confessions, but is arguably relevant also to the suspect's silence. *R v Park* [1994] **Crim LR 285** upholds the principle that 'at the scene' interviews are not admissible. In that case, it was held that exploratory questions at a roadside could give rise in due course to a well-founded suspicion that an offence had been committed. So what started out as an inquiry could become an interview. However, the Court of Appeal upheld the judge's decision not to apply **s. 78 PACE** to exclude that part of the evidence: 'even if the roadside conversation should now be regarded as an interview . . . it was, as prosecuting counsel said, only just an interview . . .'

In the instant case the police already know of the offence and so there might be more grounds for considering their questions to Arnold as an interview. Arnold will thus be advised that even if he has been cautioned it is possible that the prosecution cannot make use of his silence in the street, because he should not have been questioned away from the police station. It is, however, appropriate that 'emergency' provisions should be considered. He may be interviewed away from the police station if the consequent delay would be likely (a) to lead to interference with or harm to evidence connected with an offence or interference with or physical harm to other people; (b) to lead to the alerting of other people suspected of having committed an offence but not yet arrested for it; or (c) to hinder the recovery of property obtained in consequence of the commission of an offence. It does not appear on the facts that any of these do apply to Arnold and so it is unlikely his silence in the street will be admissible.

Interview at station

The prosecution may more successfully argue that **s. 34, 36 or 37 CJPOA** may apply in the circumstances arising from the interview in the police station. Arnold is allowed access to a solicitor, so **ss. 34(2A) and 36(4A) and 37(3A)** are satisfied. He should in addition have been given an opportunity to confirm or deny his earlier silence outside the police station, and for **ss. 36 and 37** to be operative he should have been given the special warning set out in Code C paras 10.10 and 10.11. The prosecution may seek to rely on **s. 34, 36 or 37**, although Arnold may argue that **s. 36** applied to the failure to account for the presence, not absence, of objects, namely his shoes. The plethora of case law which has been generated in this area is applicable to all three sections (as well as **s. 35**, see *R v Cowan* **[1996] QB 373**). In *Argent* **[1997] 2 Cr App R 27**, the Court of Appeal set out the conditions which have to be met before a jury can draw an adverse inference. In particular it will be a matter for the jury to determine whether in the circumstances existing at the time the defendant could reasonably be expected to mention a fact. Relevant factors to be considered include the particular circumstances of the defendant and the state of his knowledge, including information from the police. Arnold is only expected to account for or to mention facts he could reasonably have been expected to mention but it is certainly arguable that these included his absence of shoes and why he was in the area. The phrase 'in the circumstances' should not be construed restrictively, and references to 'the accused' must mean Arnold's actual qualities, knowledge, state of mind, etc. In *R v Kirk* **[2000] 1 WLR 567** insufficient information given to a suspect before questioning meant the confession should have been excluded under **s. 78**. It is not necessary, however, that Arnold should be told the precise details of the alleged offence. *R v Compton* **[2002] EWCA Crim 2835** also established that '**section 36**, unlike **section 34**, invites no comparison between the statement in interview and the evidence at trial since **section 36** contains no parallel to the question under **section 34(1)** of whether it was reasonable for the defendant to mention a particular fact: reasonableness usually being judged from the starting point of whether the fact was mentioned at trial.'

Judicial Directions on legal advice to suspect

The standard Judicial Studies Board Specimen Direction No. 40 should be given and the jury should be directed that only if, despite the evidence or lack of it, they concluded that the failure to mention a fact or to account could only sensibly be attributed to the accused's having no answer, or none that would stand up to cross-examination, might they draw an adverse inference. Arnold may plead that under the **Human Rights Act 1998** the absence of such a direction is a violation of **art. 6(1) of the European Convention on Human Rights** (*Condron v UK* **[2000] Crim LR 679**). However, each case depends on its own specific facts.

Arnold may argue that he had remained silent on legal advice. That in itself is not sufficient to preclude the operation of **s. 34, 36 or 37** but it would be one of the circumstances that the jury should take into account (*R v Beckles*). Arnold should be warned that if he goes beyond a bare assertion of the solicitor's advice he risks breaching legal professional privilege (*Bowden* **[1999] 1 WLR 823**). It may not be necessary for the judge to direct the jury that they must find a case to answer against Arnold before drawing any adverse inference under **s. 34, 36 or 37** (*R v Doldur* **[2000] Crim LR 178**).

What constitutes a proper inference for the court or jury in any particular case is a matter of fact. However, Arnold may gain some comfort from **s. 38(3) of the 1994 Act**, which provides that 'A person shall not have the proceedings against him transferred to the Crown Court for trial, have a case to answer or be convicted of an offence solely on an inference drawn from such a failure or refusal.' Here there does appear to be other circumstantial evidence, such as the finding of the sandals.

Silence and common law

Brenda faces the possibility of her silences being admitted by common law or statute. First of all, is her failure to respond to the manager's allegation admissible? Under **s. 82(1) PACE** a confession includes any statement wholly or partly adverse to the person who made it, whether made to a person in authority or not and whether made in words or otherwise. The first question then is whether her silence is a statement made otherwise than in words. It is by no means clear that silence would fit such a definition. The common law rule is that a statement made in the presence of the accused is not evidence against him except in so far as he accepts what has been said (*R v Christie* **[1914] AC 545**). It may be that a reply or indignant rejection of the accusation could reasonably be expected from Brenda and thus her failure to do that may be an implied acceptance of the truth of the accusation. Thus in *Parkes v R* **(1977) 64 Cr App R 25**, the defendant's silence when accused by a mother of stabbing her daughter was held by the Privy Council to have been properly admitted as evidence going to guilt. The courts have applied this principle to situations where the parties are on even terms. Brenda's accuser is her manager and she may have been quiet from considerations other than guilt. If her failure to reply is admitted, the jury should be directed to consider first whether the silence indicates acceptance of the accusation, and second whether guilt could reasonably be inferred from what she had accepted. A failure to leave both these issues to the jury led to the quashing of a conviction by the Court of Appeal in *R v Chandler* **[1976] 1 WLR 585**. **Section 34 of the CJPOA 1994** does not apply to Brenda because it is only relevant in relation to silence when being questioned by the police or others charged with investigating offences. The shop manager does appear not to fit this definition.

However, in relation to her silence at interview **s. 34** may well apply. She has a solicitor present, thus satisfying one of the statutory requirements. Is she at trial relying on a fact she could have referred to earlier? Arguably this is the case since the defence that it was Arnold and not her who committed the offence could have been known to her at the time of the police interview. It is no bar that the fact goes to the heart of her defence (*Milford* (2001)). Similarly, the fact that she presents the fact through her counsel does not per se preclude telling the jury that they may draw an adverse inference. In *R v Webber* [2004] UKHL 01 the House of Lords held that the word 'fact' should be given a broad meaning. A party relies on a fact, for example, when his counsel conducts questioning in such a way that he puts a positive case to the witness.

The judge in the case of both defendants will have to follow Judicial Studies Board guidelines in giving clear directions to the jury in the summing-up.

Further reading

Confessions

Ashworth, A. and Emmerson, B., 'Silence and Safety: The Impact of Human Rights Law' [2000] Crim LR 879.

Birch, D., 'The Sharp End of the Wedge: Use of Mixed Statements by the Defence' (1997) Crim LR 416.

Brooks, P., *Troubling Confessions* (University of Chicago Press: Chicago, 2001).

Choo, A., 'Confessions and Corroboration' [1991] Crim LR 867.

Choo, A., 'Corroboration of Disputed Confessions' (1991) 107 LQR 544.

Hartstone, J., 'Defensive Use of a Co-Accused's Confession and the Criminal Justice Act 2003' (2004) E & P 165.

Hirst, M., 'Confessions as Proof of Innocence' (1998) 57 CLJ 146.

Mirfield, P., *Confessions and Improperly Obtained Evidence* (Oxford: OUP, 1997).

Pattenden, R., 'Should Confessions be Corroborated?' (1991) 107 LQR 317.

Sharpe, S., *Judicial Discretion and Investigation* (London: Sweet & Maxwell, 1998).

Right to silence

Ashworth, A., *The Criminal Process*, 2nd edn (Oxford: OUP, 1998).

Birch, D.J., 'Suffering in Silence: A Cost–Benefit Analysis of s. 34 of the Criminal Justice and Public Order Act 1994' [1999] Crim LR 769.

Bucke, T., Street, R. and Brown, D., 'The Right of Silence: The Impact of the Criminal Justice and Public Order Act 1994', Home Office Research Study (London: Home Office, 2000).

Cape, E., *Advising on Silence*, Criminal Practitioners' Newsletter, Law Society, January 2006.

Dennis, I.H., 'Miscarriages of Justice and the Law of Confessions: Evidentiary Issues and Solutions' [1993] PL 291.

Dennis I.H., 'Silence at the Police Station: The Marginalisation of Section 34' [2002] Crim LR 25.

Easton, S., 'Bodily Samples and the Privilege Against Self-incrimination' [1991] Crim LR 18.

Galligan, D.J., 'The Right to Silence Reconsidered' [1988] CLP 69.

Greer, S., 'The Right to Silence: A Review of the Current Debate' (1990) 53 MLR 709.

Jackson, J.D., 'Silence and Proof: Extending the Boundaries of Criminal Proceedings in the United Kingdom' (2000) 5 E & P 145.

Jennings A., Ashworth A. and Emmerson, B., 'Silence and Safety: The Impact of Human Rights Law' [2000] Crim LR 879.

Keogh, A., 'The Right to Silence—Revisited Again' (2003) 153 NLJ 1352.

Leng, R., 'Silence Pre-trial, Reasonable Expectations and the Normative Distortion of Fact-finding' (2001) 5 E & P 204.

Malik, B., 'Silence on Legal Advice: Clarity But Not Justice, *R v Beckles*' (2005) E & P 211.

7 Improperly obtained evidence

Introduction

Confessions apart, English law has in the past been notoriously unwilling to acknowledge the case for excluding evidence which is obtained in a way which involves the police acting improperly or even illegally. However, there is now a growing body of case-law on a specific aspect of this, namely entrapment, whereby the police are arguably influencing the actual commission of the offence.

The common law test for exclusion requires the judge to consider whether the prejudicial effect of the evidence was more than its probative value. **Section 82(3) of the Police and Criminal Evidence Act 1984 (PACE)** preserves the common law discretion. It has been overtaken by **s. 78 PACE** which unlike **s. 76 PACE** applies to all prosecution evidence. Note that it applies to evidence on which 'the prosecution proposes to rely' and so unlike the common law discretion only applies *before* the evidence is admitted. **Section 78** applies a causal test for exclusion in that the disputed evidence must have 'such an adverse effect on the fairness of the proceedings that the court ought not to admit it'. The court must consider, inter alia, 'the circumstances in which the evidence was obtained' which can include impropriety on the part of the police.

However, in principle, though rarely in practice, the courts now appear willing to apply s. 78 to improperly obtained evidence other than confessions, specifically that obtained by undercover police operations involving entrapment.

With regard to other non-confessional evidence such as evidence obtained as a result of a breach of the law the courts are rarely inclined to exercise the discretion to exclude. This is in contrast to other jurisdictions, particularly the United States. English law applies the rule that illegality does not affect the admissibility of evidence, or the 'fruit of the poisoned tree', as a matter of law. This principle influences the rationale of the exclusion of evidence by discretion.

The cases here form into two groups. First, there are those where there is some impropriety in the investigation which may amount even to illegality. An example is surveillance without following the proper procedures. The other group of cases are on entrapment. These operations may involve breaches of **art. 6 and art. 8**.

Table 10 illustrates various stances the courts have taken to excluding evidence of secret police surveillance. **Table 11** gives examples of cases on entrapment.

This area overlaps considerably with that on confessions and silence (**Chapter 6**) since **s. 78** is frequently used to exclude such evidence.

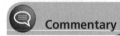

? Question 1

(a) The police are concerned about a spate of burglaries from clothes shops on the Che Guevara estate where the perpetrators have not been caught. Inspector Hilary, a plain clothes policewoman, strikes up a conversation with a group of women suspects in the estate's launderette but does not say who she is. She expresses an interest in the attractive silk shirts they are washing and says she is prepared to pay a great deal if they are what she wants. Alice, one of the women, agrees to get some for Hilary. They arrange to meet the next day and the shirts are exchanged for money. They turn out to have been stolen from Designer Modes, one of the shops on the estate. Alice is then arrested for dealing in stolen goods. Alice has a previous conviction for theft.

Advise on evidence.

(b) Ronan and Olaf are suspected of dealing in stolen cars but the police are finding it difficult to get evidence against them. Ronan has a 'for sale' notice on a car outside his house and PC Henry in plain clothes knocks to inquire about it. He chats to Ronan for a while and then asks, 'Has the car been nicked some time ago?' Ronan replies, 'Only a few weeks.' Ronan is arrested and taken into the police station for questioning. Olaf is unaware of this but is separately asked to go to the police station to help with an investigation over a missing child. While he is there he sees Ronan in a room and asks if he can have a few words. The police superintendent agrees. Unknown to Olaf and Ronan the police have set up video and sound recording in the room. Olaf and Ronan converse and are recorded as admitting they had dealt in stolen cars. Both are charged.

Advise on evidence.

Commentary

The police in these scenarios are engaged in undercover operations. The question turns therefore on the possibility of excluding evidence on the grounds that it has been obtained improperly. You must state the general rule of English law that the impropriety of the method of obtaining evidence generally bears no relevance to its admissibility, except in relation to confessions. However, although there is no rule of exclusion, there is a discretion to exclude if the admission of such evidence would be unfair. With regard to the common law discretion, the House of Lords in **R v Sang [1980] AC 402** seemed to suggest that discretion to exclude evidence because it was illegally or improperly obtained only applied to confession evidence (or evidence analogous to confessions), unless its probative value was less than its prejudicial effect. **Sang** also held that there was a substantive rule that entrapment is no defence and that this could not be undermined by the use of an evidential discretion. However, **s. 78 PACE** has, in theory at least, now been acknowledged as of possible application in entrapment cases, although the courts have been slow to identify actual agents provocateurs. With regard to the discussion between Ronan and Henry you need to consider whether **PACE** Code C is being deliberately evaded. The surveillance of Olaf and Ronan raises the question of police bad faith and obedience to the proper precedents.

Answer plan

(a) • Common law rule on improperly obtained evidence—*R v Sang* **(1988)**.

  • Fairness test applied by **s. 78 PACE** but no clear guidelines—see *R v Khan* **(1996)**.

  • Courts now accept that admitting evidence of entrapment MAY be unfair—see *R v Shannon* **(2001)**.

  • **Section 78** and **art. 6** arguably achieve same result—*Teixeira v Portugal*.

  • *R v Looseley; Attorney General's Reference (No. 3 of 2000)* **(2001)** shows more robust approach to exclusion under **s. 78** and to stay of proceedings.

(b) • Remarks by Ronan to PC Henry may be excluded if there was a deliberate attempt to circumvent Code—*R v Bryce* **(1992)**; **Regulation of Investigatory Powers Act 2000 (RIPA)** .

  • Secret surveillance: See *Allan v UK* **(2002)**.

Suggested answer

(a) Alice may try to argue that the evidence against her should be excluded because it has been obtained improperly.

Entrapment

Inspector Hilary did not reveal she was a police officer but appeared as a genuine purchaser. The test of admissibility is whether the evidence is relevant. Lord Fraser said in *Fox v Chief Constable of Gwent* [1985] 3 All ER 392, 397, 'the duty of the court is to decide whether the appellant has committed the offence with which he is charged and not to discipline the police for exceeding their powers.' However, although there is no rule of exclusion, it is open to the court as an exercise of discretion to exclude improperly obtained evidence if its admission would be unfair. In *R v Sang* [1980] AC 402 its exercise was limited to evidence obtained after the offence was committed. Thus the common law may apply to Tom because the questioning by the undercover officer relates to past events. In practice, however, the common law discretion has given way to the application of **s. 78** of the Police and Criminal Evidence Act 1984 (PACE), which gives a statutory discretion to exclude evidence which would adversely affect the fairness of the proceedings. Thus the court has to consider the interests of the prosecution as well as the defence.

Alice may possibly argue that she would not have committed the offence if she had not been asked for the shirts by Hilary. In *R v Smurthwaite* [1994] 1 All ER 898, the Court of Appeal accepted that **s. 78 PACE** had introduced some discretion to exclude evidence in such situations. It laid down guidelines to judges when exercising their discretion whether to admit the evidence of undercover police officers. The fact that the evidence had been obtained by entrapment does not of itself require the judge to exclude it unless it would have the adverse effect described in **s. 78 PACE**. However, factors to be taken into account were: was the officer enticing the defendant to commit a crime he would not otherwise have committed? What was the nature of the entrapment? Does the evidence consist of admissions to a completed offence or the actual commission of an offence? How active or passive was the officer's role in obtaining the evidence? Was there an unassailable record of what occurred or was it strongly corroborated? Reference was made to *R v Christou* [1992] QB 979, where the Court of Appeal said it was improper for police officers to adopt a disguise to enable them to ask questions without having to observe the Code, although they had not done so there in setting up a fake jewellery shop to take suspected stolen goods. The questions arose inevitably in the course of the exchange of goods. The **Human Rights Act** does not appear to have significantly changed the law in this area. In *R v Shannon* [2001] 1 WLR 51, the Court of Appeal considered that the approach of the Strasbourg Court in *Teixeira de Castro v Portugal* (1999) 28 EHRR 101 accorded with that in *Smurthwaite*.

The House of Lords decision in *Looseley; Attorney General's Reference (No. 3 of 2000)* may help Alice. This arose from two cases of 'entrapment' in one of which the undercover police officers had not abused their powers but in the other they had. The correct outcome was a stay of prosecution in the second case. As Lord Nicholls put it: 'Police conduct which brings out, to use the catch-phrase, state created crime, is unacceptable and improper. To prosecute in such circumstances would be an affront to the public conscience . . . Ultimately the overall consideration is always whether the conduct of the police or other law enforcement agency was so seriously improper as to bring the administration of justice into disrepute.' The judgment identified four factors to consider whether to apply a stay of prosecution or exclude the evidence: the nature of the offence, the reason for the particular police operation, the nature and extent of police participation in the crime and the defendant's criminal record. Criminal record is unlikely to be relevant unless, along with other factors, it leads to suspicion of current criminal activity. So Alice's conviction is not likely to be relevant on this issue.

Stay of prosecution

The House agreed that a stay of prosecution for abuse of process was the only appropriate outcome of extreme cases of entrapment but suggested **s. 78** could be brought into play where without the tainted evidence the trial could still proceed. In other words, in the wake of the enactment of the **Human Rights Act 1998** the courts take a more trenchant attitude to exclusion.

In Alice's case, the criteria set out in these cases are clearly relevant. In their light it would appear that evidence of the transaction of the shirts is probably admissible but not of any accompanying confession. Alice appears to have volunteered to get a shirt for Hilary without further prompting, so that the element of entrapment seems relatively minor. This appears to be one of those situations where the Inspector, Hilary, has been able to insert herself into a situation where the offence is already underway. In other words, she did no more than offer Alice an 'unexceptional' opportunity to participate in a crime. She appears as willing to accept goods which might reasonably be expected to be stolen. Alice is presumably already in possession of the goods, so it is not a situation where, but for Hilary's intervention, the offence might not have been committed. Thus the defence will be unlikely to rely on *R v Moon* [2004] **EWCA Crim 2872** where an appeal against conviction was allowed in an entrapment case. There was no evidence the defendant had previously acted as a drug dealer. Furthermore, the evidence against Alice relates to the actual commission of the offence, and not to an admission to an already completed offence.

RIPA 2000

It thus seems likely that Alice had a crime in mind or was already knowingly in possession of the stolen shirts before Hilary appeared. Alice's chances of having the evidence excluded are very slim. Despite the acceptance in principle in *Smurthwaite* that evidence obtained by undercover operations before the commission of an offence could be excluded, in recent cases, the courts have not so acted. Alice has been deceived into producing evidence against herself but as the Court of Appeal said in *R v Christou* 'The trick was not applied to the appellants; they voluntarily applied themselves to the trick.' The defence will want to check whether the Code of Practice under the **Regulation of Investigatory Powers Act 2000 (RIPA)** has been observed. Paragraph 1.9 of the Code states that the proper authorisation of the undercover operation 'should ensure the suitability of such evidence under the common law, **section 78 of the Police and Criminal Evidence Act 1984** and the **Human Rights Act 1998**.'

(b) The question here is how far Henry has adopted an undercover technique to circumvent the Code.

Confession obtained outside Code C

On the facts as given it appears that the situation is similar to that in *R v Bryce* (1992) **95 Cr App R 320**. However, it is not clear whether Ronan denies making the incriminating response to Henry. In *Bryce* the undercover police officer and the suspect had different versions of the offence. In that case the evidence of the effective confession was excluded on two grounds, the first of which may arguably apply here. The undercover officer in *Bryce* had asked two questions which were held to be a violation of Code C and had gone directly to the question of the suspect's guilt, unlike the position in *Christou* where the questions asked had been necessary to preserve the undercover officers' cover and had been indirect. In *Bryce* their questions were 'how warm' the car was and 'how long has it been nicked'. The second reason for exclusion, however, was that the suspect denied making the responses he was alleged to have made and since the Code was not followed there was no authentic, contemporaneous record of what had happened. It followed that there was a risk of concoction. Ronan is advised therefore that he has grounds for the exclusion of his alleged confession on the basis that the Code had been circumvented. If he has denied making the statements the case for exclusion is strengthened. The police undercover action in relation to Olaf and Ronan raises the questions of possible illegality and possible violation of **art. 8 and art. 6**. Article 8(1) ECHR provides that 'everyone has the right to respect for his private life'. However, Olaf and Ronan should be warned that even if a breach of **art. 8** is found this does not necessarily mean that the evidence should be excluded under **s. 78(1)**. Olaf and Ronan are entitled to challenge the use of the evidence and the trial judge should assess the effect of its admission on the fairness of the proceedings. More information is needed as to whether the secret recording was carried out according to the specifications of **RIPA**. In *R v Button* [2005] EWCA Crim 516 the police had approval for covert audio surveillance, but not video. However, acting in good faith they had recorded by video and audio a discussion of two suspects in a cell. There was a breach of **art. 8** but this was subsumed by the duty in **art. 6** to ensure a fair trial. Through its obligation to ensure a fair trial in accordance with **art. 6**, the court was acting compatibly with the Convention. The court played no part in the interference with private life occasioned by the covert surveillance. The court's obligation was confined to deciding whether having regard to the way in which the evidence was obtained it would be fair to admit it. The court regarded the proposition that evidence obtained in breach of **art. 8** should be excluded as a 'startling proposition, and one which we are pleased and relieved to be able to reject'. The defence are unlikely to rely on *R v Grant* [2005] 3 WLR 47 since there the secret recording involved the suspect and his solicitor. The trial was stayed because there had been a breach of legal professional privilege. However a Strasbourg decision may be more supportive of the defence. In *Allan v UK* (2002) 36 EHRR 12 the police had coached an informant (H) to question the suspect thus violating his privilege against self-incrimination. The court observed: 'In contrast to the position in the *Khan* case the admissions allegedly made by the applicant to H which formed the main or decisive evidence against him at trial were not spontaneous and unprompted statements volunteered by the applicant but were induced by the persistent questioning of H . . .' As Choo (2012, p. 179) suggests, it was the lack of reliability of the evidence which was decisive. Since Olaf and Ronan do not appear to have been prompted by interrogation it is more likely the evidence will be judged reliable.

Another argument for excluding the evidence is that this does not appear to be a serious offence, unlike the murder charge in *Button*. Lord Steyn stated in *R v Latif* [1996] 1 WLR 104, 'the judge must weigh in the balance the public interest in ensuring that those that are charged with grave crimes should be tried and the competing public interest in not conveying the impression that the court will adopt the approach that the end justifies the means.' On the other hand, in *Looseley* the House of Lords gave greater weight to the consideration of whether the integrity of the criminal justice system was being consciously undermined. It is likely, however, that Olaf and Ronan will not be able to resist the admission of the conversation.

Table 10 Cases involving covert police surveillance

Police secret recording operation	Authorised by regulation?	Police acting in bad faith?	Evasion of Code?	Outcome
R v Khan **[1997] AC 558** Listening device on flat, damaging property, drug dealing	There was then no statutory system to deal with covert listening devices	Police had trespassed and damaged property	No	Evidence admitted—gravity of offence outweighed possible breach of **art. 8**
Khan v UK **(2000) 31 EHRR 45 (ECtHR)**	Ditto	Ditto	No. Admissions were voluntary	Violation of **art. 8** not **art. 6**— national court had properly applied **s. 78**
R v Mason **[2002] 2 Cr App R 628** Robbers bugged in cell (CA)	Non-statutory guidelines not complied with	No	No	Breach of guidelines insignificant— evidence admitted, **art. 8** breached
Allan v UK **(2002) 36 EHRR (ECtHR)** Police coached informant to question A in cell and recorded conversation— murder charge	No	Yes	Yes	Breach of **art. 6** because of violation of suspect's privilege against self-incrimination— evidence should be excluded
R v Grant **[2005] [2006] QB 60** Secret recording conversation of suspect and solicitor (CA)	Not authorised	Yes	Yes	Trial stayed— breach of legal professional privilege
R v Button **[2005] EWCA Crim 516** Suspect recorded communicating in cell. Murder charge (CA)	Audio recording but not video authorised	No	No	Breach of **art. 8** but fair to admit evidence

Table 11 Cases involving entrapment

Case	Outcome
Teixeira de Castro v Portugal **(1999) 28 EHRR 101 (ECtHR)**	Suspect had not been known to police and officers had gone beyond acting as undercover agents, they had incited offence. Evidence should have been excluded
R v Smurthwaite **[1994] 1 All ER 898 (CA)**	The case set out the factors to be considered in excluding evidence. Evidence rightly admitted in this instance
R v Christou **[1992] 1 QB 979 (CA)**	Code C PACE inapplicable. Officers not acting as police officers. Evidence rightly admitted
R v Shannon **[2001] 1 WLR 51 (CA)**	Need to distinguish situation where credibility and reliability of evidence is at issue from that concerning complaint that it is in principle unfair as a matter of policy or wrong as a matter of law for a person to be prosecuted for a crime which he would not have committed without the incitement. The latter is not in itself sufficient for exclusion of evidence
R v Looseley; Attorney General's Reference (No. 3 of 2000) **[2000] 1 WLR 2060 (HL)**	Useful guide is did police do no more than present defendant with unexceptional opportunity to commit a crime. Proper approach is stay of proceedings, but evidence may be excluded if trial has commenced. Stay of proceedings correct where officers had instigated the offence

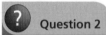

Question 2

'Evidence is the basis of justice: to exclude evidence is to exclude justice.' (Jeremy Bentham, *A Rationale of Judicial Evidence* (1827), bk. 9, ch. 3, p. 490.)

Discuss this statement in the light of the current approach of the courts to the use of illegally or improperly obtained evidence other than confessions and the defendant's silence.

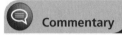

Commentary

You should not attempt a question such as this if you have not read some of the leading commentaries such as those by Ashworth (2000), Dennis (2010) and Laudan (2008). The question raises important issues of principle and asks you to discuss the proposition that factual accuracy is the most important requirement in considering admissibility and overshadows arguments about moral standing or legitimacy. Your answer should review the considerations which the courts bring to bear on exclusion of evidence obtained by police tricks such as entrapment or unauthorised undercover surveillance, or by breaches of primary or delegated legislation such as Codes C and D of **PACE**. You should demonstrate your understanding of the terms of **s. 78 PACE** which refers to 'the circumstances in which the evidence was obtained' as a ground for non-admissibility but only if the evidence would have 'such an adverse effect on the fairness of the proceedings that the court ought not to admit it.' In other words there has to be a causal connection between any impropriety and the trial proceedings. Note that the question refers to the 'use' of evidence obtained by improper means. You should distinguish between those situations in which a stay of prosecution is appropriate and those in which the prosecution may go ahead but the evidence may be excluded.

Answer plan

- What is meant by illegally or improperly obtained evidence?
- Outline of the current law, *Sang* **(1980)** replaced by **s. 78 PACE**.
- Arguments in favour of inclusion: see Laudan (2008) and Bentham.
- Need to distinguish exclusion of evidence and stay of prosecution, importance of *R v Sang*.
- Conclusion: constitutional arguments for dealing robustly with oppressive investigatory procedure.

Examiner's tip

Essay questions such as this one are more often the subject of coursework assessment than examination and the length of this answer reflects this. Although you need to refer to wide reading in your answer it is crucial that the examiners hear your voice also. It is expected, therefore, that candidates will engage critically with the academic comment and put their own views as the Conclusion here demonstrates. However, it is crucial your views are evidence-based!

Suggested answer

This question raises one of the most controversial questions in Evidence law, namely how should relevant and reliable evidence be excluded if there has been some impropriety in the way it was obtained? Bentham for one argued for a system of free proof, that is that all relevant evidence should be admitted. Others, however, maintain that the integrity of the trial is undermined if those gathering evidence, particularly if they are state actors, have acted illegally or improperly. The essence of this stance is expressed in **s. 76(2)(a) of the Police and Criminal Evidence Act 1984 (PACE)** which provides that confession evidence obtained by oppression, notwithstanding that it may be true should not be admitted. The case law demonstrates, however, that, confessions aside, the courts have traditionally been reluctant to exclude evidence because of some impropriety in the way it was obtained. Arguably, however, the **Human Rights Act 1998** has, as *R v Looseley; Attorney General's Reference (No. 3 of 2000)* [2000] 1 WLR 2060 demonstrates, brought about a significant change in recent years. The essay will first outline the evolution of the law in this area and then examine the arguments for and against a robust exclusionary doctrine.

Evolution of law on excluding improperly obtained evidence

At common law, courts have a general discretion to exclude evidence, albeit relevant, to ensure a fair trial. In *R v Sang* [1980] AC 402 the House of Lords acknowledged that this had two aspects, namely the exclusion of evidence if it would be likely to have a prejudicial effect outweighing its probative value, and a more limited discretion to exclude unfairly or illegally obtained evidence. This discretion took place in a context whereby the general rule of English law was that apart from confession evidence, impropriety in obtaining evidence has no relevance to admissibility. This is illustrated in cases such as *Kuruma v R* [1955] AC 197. Their Lordships in *Sang* limited the exercise of the discretion to exclude evidence obtained after the commission of the offence, likening the general exclusionary approach to that on unfairly obtained confessions based on the privilege against self-incrimination. A person should not be improperly led into giving evidence that could be used against him. In fact the courts rarely exercised the common law discretion to exclude. In *R v Christou* [1992] QB 979 Lord Diplock pointed out that the only case brought to their Lordships' attention in which the appellate court had actually excluded evidence on the ground that it had been unfairly obtained by a trick was *R v Payne* [1963] 1 WLR 637. Two 'strictures' therefore emerge from the pre-**PACE** position in *Sang*; first, that evidence obtained before the commission of the offence was not covered by the discretion and, second, that even with regard to evidence improperly obtained after the commission of the offence it would only rarely be appropriate to exercise discretion to exclude.

PACE, while preserving the common law discretion, introduced an additional statutory discretion, **s. 78**, which applies to non-confession as well as confession evidence, on which the prosecution proposed to rely if it appears that 'having regard to all the circumstances, including the circumstances in which the evidence was obtained, the admission of the evidence would have such an adverse effect on the fairness of the proceedings that the court ought not to admit it.' Two features of this provision are relevant to the question under discussion: first, that there is no automatic exclusion for impropriety, there has to be a causal connection between the impropriety and the fairness of the proceedings; secondly, the courts have to consider the interests of the prosecution and the defence when applying the discretion.

Cases concerned with impropriety at the investigative stage fall into two groups, namely those concerned with alleged entrapment by the police and secondly those involving some breach of procedure, such as unauthorised surveillance or an illegal search. It should, of course, be pointed out that it is getting increasingly difficult to argue that investigations are unlawful in the sense of not authorised by statute, see particularly the **Regulation of Investigatory Powers Act 2000 (RIPA)**. In *Re McE* [2009] **1AC 908** in a majority judgment the House of Lords held that RIPA permits covert police surveillance of a suspect's confidential interview with a lawyer. Of course any material gained may not necessarily be admissible at trial.

Arguments in favour of exclusion

Arguments in favour of maintaining an inclusionary approach to admissibility can be categorised as follows: first, the evidence exists and if it is relevant it should be admitted. This approach was adopted in *R v Chalkley* [1998] QB 848. There the trial judge had admitted evidence of secret tape-recordings obtained in breach of **PACE** and the civil law of trespass, and in violation of **art. 8 of the European Convention on Human Rights**. Auld LJ in the Court of Appeal held that the balancing exercise undertaken by the trial judge was unnecessary considering that 'save in the case of confessions and generally as to evidence obtained from the accused after the commission of the offence there is no discretion to exclude evidence unless its quality was or might have been affected by the way in which it was obtained.' The tape-recordings were highly probative of guilt and not affected by the unlawful police activity. This case thus supports the Benthamite argument about truth-seeking being the prime purpose of the trial. Similarly in *R v B (Attorney General's Reference (No. 3 of 1999))* [2001] 2 AC 91 the House of Lords held that retention of DNA samples which was then illegal meant that the sample could not be used in the subsequent trial of the same defendant on another charge. Lord Hutton stated that the key test was relevance and that the court was not concerned with how the evidence was obtained. Laudan, writing in the twenty-first century, also upholds this argument. He writes (2008, p. 190): 'it is perfectly clear that the exclusion of germane inculpatory evidence on account of the way in which it was obtained, significantly increases the likelihood of false acquittals.' The courts in the United States of course follow a more rigid and what Laudan calls 'a sweeping rule of inadmissibility' which he says 'gave the lie to the claim that the current system of criminal justice seeks, above all, to find the truth about a crime.' Laudan gives two further reasons for privileging truth seeking above other considerations. He points out (p. 191) the economic waste of time and energy 'currently going into wrangling about the admissibility of clearly relevant evidence could be profitably invested in a more thorough development of the evidential base that each side brings to the trial.' Laudan additionally argues that in cases of wrongful acquittals where the offences are serious the public would perceive an injustice.

It is also arguable that those in favour of exclusion in order to punish investigators fail to acknowledge that there are other ways to secure this disciplinary approach. Thus, in *Khan v UK* (2000) 31 EHRR 45, although there had been a breach of **art. 8**, the Strasbourg Court held that there was no breach of **art. 6**, there being no absolute rule of exclusion. However, in *Khan v UK* (2000) 31 EHRR 45 the Strasbourg Court found no violation as a result of illegal police bugging of a suspect. Policy considerations of crime control versus due process come into play. As Lord Nolan commented in the House of Lords judgment in *R v Khan* [1997] AC 558 at p. 573, 'It would be a strange reflection on our law if a man who has admitted his participation in the illegal importation of heroin should have his conviction set aside on the grounds that his privacy has been invaded.'

It is open to the defendant to pursue other means of redress against investigatory impropriety; however, it is acknowledged that such avenues are limited. Roberts (2004), writing in relation to breaches of Code D of **PACE**, points out: although **s. 67(8) PACE** originally provided that an officer would be liable to disciplinary proceedings for any breach of the codes of practice, this provision was repealed by **s. 37 of the Police and Magistrates' Court Act 1994.** As for the threat that breaches of the codes of practice might be admissible in evidence in subsequent criminal or civil proceedings, **s. 67(10) PACE** makes clear that a breach of the codes will not of itself render the officer who commits the breach liable to criminal or civil proceedings. Further, an absolutist exclusionary approach meets difficulty in establishing its application both in relation to minor breaches by investigators and minor offences. Thus, Roberts and Zuckerman (2010, p. 190) argue that a 'blanket rule of exclusion' would not be appropriate. They point out that it is short-sighted not to acknowledge that the evidence exists and that 'our knowledge of the world has changed forever and moral evaluation must take account of the realities of the situation' (p. 133). Thus, exclusion might not be appropriate if the breach by the police is minor and the crime is a minor one.

Counter-arguments

There are, however, powerful counter-arguments to those outlined earlier. The shift in the approach of the courts away from the pragmatic approach taken in *Chalkley* will be examined followed by a review of supportive academic arguments. The leading case in the area is *R v Looseley*. There, an undercover police officer who had been given the defendant's name as a potential source of drugs arranged with him to exchange heroin for money. The defendant was charged with supplying or being concerned in supplying to another a class A controlled drug. The trial judge refused a preliminary request to exclude evidence or stay proceedings. The defendant pleaded guilty. In another case two undercover police officers, offered contraband cigarettes for sale at a housing estate, were introduced to the accused as a potential buyer. They sold him cigarettes and asked also if he could get heroin—at first the defendant hesitated and then agreed. He was also charged. The judge stayed the proceedings on the grounds that the police had incited the commission of the offence and that otherwise the accused would be denied his right to a fair hearing under **art. 6(1)**. The stay was lifted, the prosecution offered no evidence and the accused was acquitted. The Attorney General referred to the Court of Appeal the question whether in cases of entrapment the judicial discretion conferred by **s. 78 PACE** and the power to stay proceedings as an abuse of process had been modified by **art. 6(1) of the ECHR.** The Court of Appeal held that it had not and that the trial judge had been wrong to stay the proceedings. The defendant in the first case appealed and reference was made from the Court of Appeal in the second. The House of Lords stated that the court must ask the central question which was whether the actions of the police were so seriously improper as to bring the administration of justice into disrepute. If there was an abuse of state power than the appropriate remedy was a stay of the indictment, rather than exclusion of evidence. The appeal of the defendant in the first case was dismissed since the undercover officer did no more than present himself as an ordinary customer to a drug dealer. The judge had been correct in the second case to stay the proceedings. The decision of the Court of Appeal was reversed in part. This judgment demonstrates strong judicial recognition of the dangers of excessive police behaviour in cases of entrapment. Lord Nicholls stated that *R v Sang* [1980] AC 402 had been 'overtaken' by statute and case law. In terms of criminal procedure it is notable that the decision paid more attention to stay of prosecution than it did to exclusion of evidence. Choo (2012, p. 201) notes: 'It is arguable that, while not encapsulated in a statute, a reasonably coherent doctrine of entrapment that recognises non-conviction of the defendant as the appropriate remedy is now in the light of *Looseley; A-G's Reference* recognised in English law.'

The House of Lords stated that it was following the approach of the Strasbourg Court in *Teixeira de Castro v Portugal* (1999) 28 EHRR 101 which had stated that the use of entrapment was a violation of **art. 6**: 'The use of undercover agents must be restricted and safeguards put in place the right to a fair administration of justice nevertheless holds such a prominent place that it cannot be sacrificed for the sake of expediency.'

Academic opinion on integrity of trial process

Dennis (2010) is one of a number of academics who argue for a principled approach to exclusion. He sees the overriding reason to be that of protecting the moral legitimacy of the verdict. That is more important than the deterrent effect on the police or the need to protect defendants' rights. Ashworth (2000) argues for an underlying principle of fidelity to legal values which should guide the exercise of the exclusionary discretion. He stresses that the principle of integrity means that those who enforce the law should obey the law. This might mean that prosecutions should be dropped. He writes (at p. 659): 'where government officials have played a part in creating an offence it seems appropriate to consider a procedural response that prevents a trial from taking pace—notably a stay of the prosecution on grounds of abuse of process.' He identifies particularly the importance of compliance with Convention rights under the **Human Rights Act**. He lists (2002, p. 35) 'the right to trial on evidence not obtained in violation of a fundamental right' as one of the procedural rights for persons accused of potentially serious crime. He points out (p. 36) that 'whereas a breach of **art. 3** [ECHR] will make it unfair to rely on a resulting confession, it seems that a breach of a defendant's **art. 8** rights (for example by listening in to his conversation without authorisation to do so) will not necessarily render it unfair to rely on the resulting evidence' (p. 26).

There are indications that this principled approach is being increasingly embraced by Strasbourg as well as the English courts. Examples are *Allan v UK* (2002) 36 EHRR 12 and the landmark judgment *A v Secretary of State for the Home Department (No. 2)* **[2006] 2 AC 221**. Evidence obtained by torture abroad, including that by non-state actors, may be contaminated and should not be admitted. However, it is arguable that the Benthamite inclusionary approach is more the norm than exclusion on grounds of impropriety. As Choo (2012, p. 201) concludes: 'Evidence obtained by torture aside, there appears to be marked judicial reluctance to sanction the exclusion of improperly obtained evidence the reliability of which is not disputed. In criminal proceedings giving consideration to the possibility of excluding the evidence under **s. 78 of the Police and Criminal Evidence Act 1984** is regarded as sufficient to secure compliance with the **European Convention on Human Rights**.' On the other hand, the abuse of process doctrine in relation to entrapment seems to be gaining some ground as recent cases illustrate. In *R v Maxwell* **[2010] UKSC 48** the trial had been based on a confession obtained by misconduct by the prosecutors and a stay was ordered. By contrast, in *Warren v Attorney-General of Jersey* **[2011] UKPC 10** the misconduct (illegal surveillance) had not influenced the defendants' behaviour and a stay was not ordered. In *Warren* Lord Dyson observed that a stay was correct in cases of abduction and entrapment but not illicitly intercepting privileged conversations (disapproving of the judgment in *R v Grant* (2005)). Stays are also apparently now appropriate in cases where the 'trick' is perpetrated by a non-state actor. The development is illustrated by comparing *R v Shannon* with more recent cases. The abuse of process argument was held not to be available in *Shannon* since the entrapment was conducted by the prosecuting authority. But in the more recent *Council for the Regulation of Health Professionals v GMC* **[2007] 1 WLR 3091** sufficiently gross misconduct by a non-state agent was potentially an instance where the use of evidence could be a breach of **art. 6**. Such instances would, however, be rare. Goldring J stated that where there had been 'sufficiently gross misconduct by the non-state agent it would be an abuse of the court's process and a breach of **Article 6** for the state to seek to rely on the resulting evidence.' These developments are significant in view of the increased involvement of lay people and individuals in forensic activity through social networking and the growth of what O'Floinn and Ormerod (2012, p. 506) call 'private entrapment'.

Of course, it should be pointed out that not all exclusions of evidence arising from secret surveillance arise from defence demands. Exclusion on grounds of security is ordered for 'intercept' evidence. **Section 17 of RIPA** provides that 'no evidence shall be adduced, question asked, assertion or disclosure made or other thing done, for the purposes of or in connection with any legal proceedings which (in any manner) (a) discloses, in circumstances from which its origin in anything falling within **subsection (2)** may be inferred, any of the contents of an intercepted communications or any related communications data.' In its essence the purpose is to prevent the admission of a communication intercepted in the course of its transmission by means of a postal service or telecommunications system if the evidence might reveal the existence of a warrant. For policy reasons, not the integrity of criminal justice, it is regarded as necessary to keep surveillance operations secret.

In conclusion, it is acknowledged that there are powerful moral arguments, particularly those involved in safeguarding the public, in favour of excluding improperly obtained evidence and that Bentham's utilitarian stance is ethically unattractive. Against the view that reliability of evidence should be the overriding consideration is what Dworkin (2003) has called a need 'to keep faith with our humanity'. He argues that, 'the government says that only our own safety matters. That is a counsel of shame: we are braver than that, and have self-respect.' Bronitt and Roche (2000) similarly argue that the consequence of tolerating abuse of the criminal justice process is the erosion of the rights of citizenship. Doubtless there is a need for undercover policing but there are dangers in upholding the view that secrecy and lack of accountability are paramount objectives, or ends justify means in policing and in investigating alleged criminal activity as recent scandals concerning police infiltration of protest groups have shown. A more critical approach to the way evidence is gathered encourages public participation in the criminal justice process, a necessary ingredient of a healthy democracy. Bentham too lightly dismisses both abuse of power and inequalities of its distribution.

Further reading

Ashworth, A., 'Excluding Evidence as Protecting Rights' [1977] Crim LR 723.

Ashworth, A., 'Should the Police be Allowed to Use Deceptive Practices?' (1998) 114 LQR 108.

Ashworth, A., 'Testing Fidelity to Legal Values: Official Involvement and Criminal Justice' (2000) 63 MLR 633.

Ashworth, A., 'Redrawing the Boundaries of Entrapment' [2002] Crim LR 159.

Bronitt, S. and Roche, D., 'Between Rhetoric and Reality: Sociolegal and Republican Perspectives on Entrapment' (2000) 4 E & P 77.

Choo, A.L.-T., *Abuse of Process and Judicial Stays of Criminal Proceedings* (Oxford: OUP, 2008).

Dworkin, R., 'Terror and the Attack on Civil Liberties' (2003) *New York Review of Books*, vol. 50, no. 17, 6 November.

Ho, H.L., 'State Entrapment' (2011) 31 LS 71.

Laudan, L., *Truth, Error and Criminal Law* (Cambridge: Cambridge University Press, 2008).

Mirfield, P., 'Regulation of Investigatory Powers Act 2000. Evidential Aspects' [2001] Crim LR 91.

O'Floinn, M. and Ormerod, D., 'Social Networking Material as Criminal Evidence' [2012] Crim LR 486.

Ormerod, D. and Birch, D., 'Evolution of the Discretionary Exclusions of Evidence' [2004] Crim LR 138.

Ormerod, D. and Roberts, A., 'The Trouble with *Teixeira*: Developing a Principled Approach to Entrapment' (2002) 6 E & P 38.

Roberts, A., 'The Problem of Mistaken Identification: Some Observations on Process' (2004) 8 E & P 100.

Sharpe, S., 'Covert Police Operations and Discretionary Exclusions of Evidence' [1994] Crim LR 793.

Sharpe, S., *Judicial Discretion and Criminal Investigation* (London: Sweet & Maxwell, 1997).

Squires, D., 'The Problem with Entrapment' (2006) 26 OJLS 351.

8 Supporting evidence: lies, identification evidence and suspect witnesses

Introduction

This area is variously referred to in textbooks as hazardous evidence, supporting evidence or safeguards against unreliability and error. Thus it covers types of evidence which might intrinsically be of questionable reliability and therefore require supportive evidence. Key areas are disputed identification and lies told by the defendant.

As regards identification evidence, students will have to be familiar with the *Turnbull* [1977] **QB 224** guidelines. Note also the provisions on identification evidence in the **Criminal Justice Act (CJA) 2003**. Further, students may be expected to be familiar with Code D of the Codes of Practice of the **Police and Criminal Evidence Act 1984 (PACE)** (revised 2011). It is clear now that as a general, but not absolute, rule a suspect who disputes an identification has a right to a parade.

If the very detailed specifications of Code D are breached then **s. 78 PACE** may be applied to exclude the evidence. Code D para. 3.12 states that a parade is to be held when 'the suspect disputes being the person the witness claims to have seen'. The leading case of *R v Forbes* [2001] **1 AC 473** makes it clear that this is to be strictly applied. In short, therefore, you should familiarise yourself with the two distinct ways that the reliability of identification evidence is enhanced: first, the judge should issue the *Turnbull* guidelines and, secondly, Code D should be followed in relation to identification procedures.

Diagram 5 should help you understand the procedure where a *Lucas* warning is required when lies told by the defendant are used as evidence of guilt.

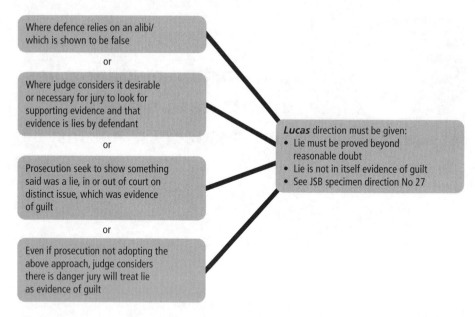

Where defence relies on an alibi/ which is shown to be false

or

Where judge considers it desirable or necessary for jury to look for supporting evidence and that evidence is lies by defendant

or

Prosecution seek to show something said was a lie, in or out of court on distinct issue, which was evidence of guilt

or

Even if prosecution not adopting the above approach, judge considers there is danger jury will treat lie as evidence of guilt

Lucas direction must be given:
• Lie must be proved beyond reasonable doubt
• Lie is not in itself evidence of guilt
• See JSB specimen direction No 27

Diagram 5 Lies (non-hearsay) by defendant—*R v Burge* (1996)

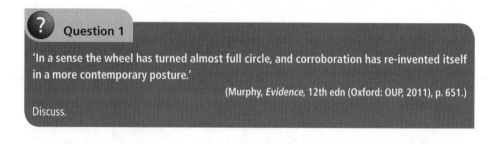

? Question 1

'In a sense the wheel has turned almost full circle, and corroboration has re-invented itself in a more contemporary posture.'

(Murphy, *Evidence*, 12th edn (Oxford: OUP, 2011), p. 651.)

Discuss.

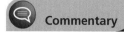

Commentary

You are required here to demonstrate an understanding of how and why the former corroboration rules have been replaced by the system of care warnings. You will need to demonstrate knowledge of the statutory changes made in 1988 and 1994 and the developing case law which has prompted Murphy's comment, suggesting new practices are becoming systematised. Again, as in all essay questions, you will be expected to have read some of the leading texts, such as those by Pattenden and Dennis and also show familiarity with the theoretical arguments about the concept of corroboration put by Roberts and Zuckerman. Your answer should address the following questions:

• What if any are the differences between the former corroboration regime and the current practice?

• What does Murphy mean by 'contemporary posture'?

• Is the circle complete and are further changes likely or necessary?

By deconstructing the question into smaller propositions you will develop a framework for your answer. As always it is important to realise that the examiner in essay questions is not only requiring you to demonstrate up-to-date knowledge but also skilled legal analysis.

Answer plan

- Meaning and development of the concept of corroboration and how it was transformed into care warnings.
- Difference between former and current systems, examining what Murphy means by 'contemporary posture'.
- Review of case law demonstrating some perceived inadequacies in the current system, especially in relation to identification evidence and confessions.
- Possible future reform strategies.

Suggested answer

The Law Commission report, *Corroboration in Criminal Trials* (Cmnd 1620, 1991) (adopted by the Royal Commission on Criminal Justice, see Cm 2263, 1993) had described the law as it existed then as 'arcane, technical and difficult to convey'. It had led to unnecessary formalism and unjustified categorisation of witnesses. A major weakness was the mandatory requirement of a corroboration warning for certain groups of witnesses, irrespective of their specific individual characteristics. Historically, the three categories of witnesses were first child witnesses, the need for a formal warning having been abolished by **s. 34(2) of the Criminal Justice Act (CJA) 1988**. Particular criticism was directed at the mandatory requirement of a corroboration warning for the second category, complainants in sexual cases, who were predominantly women. The third category was accomplices testifying for the prosecution. The latter two categories were removed in **s. 32 Criminal Justice and Public Order Act 1994 (CJPOA)**. The Law Commission report was itself the latest in a series of expressions of judicial unease about the formal system of corroboration. In *R v Spencer* **[1987] AC 128** the House of Lords, overturning earlier authority held that where the prosecution relied on the evidence of a witness who because of his mental condition and criminal background may give suspect evidence, the judge should warn the jury that it is dangerous to convict on the uncorroborated evidence of the witness. However, the House of Lords stressed that the judge need not give the full corroboration warning required in the established categories. Another example of judicial acceptance of the need to temper the technical rules was *R v Chance* **[1988] QB 932** where the Court of Appeal decided that where the only issue was one of identity in a rape case, only a *Turnbull* warning was required. Of course, *R v Turnbull* **[1977] QB 224** had set, albeit lengthy, 'guidelines' for identification cases rather than setting a requirement for a formal corroboration warning. Murphy's comment suggests that the courts here eschewed an absolutist stance on corroboration. While recommendations were made to abolition of formal categorisation of witnesses there was a parallel argument that there should be acknowledgement of the need to maintain a residual class of cases where some form of warning should be given because the testimony of the witness may be suspect or tainted for some reason. This could be because he or she may have a grudge against the defendant, or is malicious, or has some other purpose of his or her own to serve. Thus the approach in *Spencer* outlined earlier, was followed in subsequent cases.

Apart from the categorisation of a witness, another major criticism of the corroboration rules had been the complex definition of corroboration, as set out by the Court of Appeal in *R v Baskerville* [1916] 2 KB 658. As Bronitt (1991) pointed out, the definition articulated in this case concentrated on the quantity of testimony rather than its quality. By requiring 'independent evidence implicating the accused' rather than independent evidence that confirms the suspect witness is telling the truth, the definition concentrated on guilt rather than witness's credibility. The move away from formalism indicated by Murphy, is further illustrated in *R v Hills* (1987) 86 Cr App R 26 where the Court of Appeal held that cumulative corroboration was possible as a matter of principle, even though individually no one piece of evidence might fit the technical definition. Thus once again the court took a pragmatic stance which was generally welcomed.

This trend was confirmed in the 1990s. The Law Commission in its Report considered that where the courts exercised discretion in calling for the need for caution, they did not need to rely on the technical definition of corroboration. Then in *R v Makanjoula* [1995] 1 WLR 1348 the Court of Appeal rejected the need for a 'full old style direction' in cases where the trial judge decided that some form of warning may be necessary. Lord Taylor CJ said (p. 1351) '[it] was in our judgment, partly to escape from the tortuous exercise which juries must have found more bewildering than illuminating, that parliament enacted s 32.'

Murphy's 'contemporary posture' means therefore that discretion has replaced rule, arguably a welcome development. Since the warnings are discretionary, the Court of Appeal will only overturn the trial judge's decision if it is *Wednesbury* unreasonable. The value of introducing discretionary warnings was illustrated in the case of *Pringle v R* [2003] UKPC 9. Lord Hope's speech referred to the need to consider a discretionary warning 'where an untried prisoner claims that a fellow untried prisoner confessed to him that he was guilty of the crime for which he was then being held in custody.' Cell confessions in particular have proved a fertile area for the development of the type of case where discretionary warnings are more or less expected. Guidance on these are given in *R v Stone* [2005] EWCA 105. In *Benedetto and Labrador v R* [2003] 1 WLR 1545 the prosecution case rested largely on a cell confession. The Privy Council stated that in these circumstances the prisoner would normally have an interest in providing information to the authorities and there should be safeguards in place. A judicial warning as to possible dangers in relying on the confession was normally required.

Murphy's analysis of an element of continuity in this area of law is also evidenced in the use of discretionary warnings in the case of accomplices. Thus in *R v Jones and Jenkins* [2002] EWCA Crim 1966 the Court of Appeal required a discretionary care warning in a case where co-defendants operated a 'cut-throat defence'.

Some commentators have expressed concern about what they identify as too close an affinity with the earlier practice. Thus Choo (2012, p. 363) writes, 'There is a danger that trial judges may in fact be continuing to give strong warnings in relation to alleged accomplices testifying for the prosecution and complainants in sexual cases, even if a warning is not warranted in the circumstances of the particular case.' He points out that particularly in sexual assault cases there may be a danger of wrongful acquittals.

Implicit also in Murphy's comment is the suggestion that the courts may be slow to recognise new areas where it would be wise to look for supportive evidence. One area of some controversy is that of confessions. As the earlier discussion indicated in the case of cell confessions, discretionary warnings are frequently required. There is some pressure to make them compulsory. As Leake and Ormerod (2005, p. 571) comment on *R v Stone* [2005] EWCA Crim 105, 'the especially damning nature of the evidence' together with other dangers renders cell confessions 'a qualitatively more dangerous category of evidence in all cases'. Pattenden (1991) reviewed the arguments for extending corroboration requirements to all confessions. Dennis (2010, p. 664) writes, 'there remains a good case for the introduction of such a warning but to date no legislation has implemented the recommendation and the courts have shown no inclination to give effect to it.' The tendency thus, or the 'contemporary posture', is to favour warnings which are, as Dennis puts it, 'less formal and less technical'.

An indication of the reluctance to return to the earlier state of affairs is the current controversy over flawed expert scientific testimony. In *R v Cannings* [2004] 1 WLR 2607 the Court of Appeal called for 'additional cogent evidence, extraneous to the expert evidence' where there was a dispute between experts over the cause of sudden infant deaths. This was not, however, applied in *R v Kai-Whitewind* [2005] EWCA Crim 1092 where there was a previously admitted urge on the part of a parent to kill the infant.

In two particular areas Murphy's statement may be taken to suggest an unwelcome reappearance of the earlier rigidity, which is arguably the case in two areas, namely identification evidence and to a lesser extent lies as evidence. With regard to the latter, Kennedy LJ in *Burge and Pegg* [1996] Cr App R 163 stressed the danger of overuse of *Lucas* directions: 'if a **Lucas** direction is given where there is no need for such a direction (as in the normal case where there is a straightforward conflict of evidence) it will add complexity and do more harm than good.' The risk is the jury might be confused (see also *R v Middleton* (2001) Crim LR 251).

Identification evidence is a more complex matter. Here the risk perhaps is that the emphasis on discretionary warnings detracts from other means of treating this area of evidence which is a notorious cause of miscarriages of justice. Roberts and Zuckerman (2010, p. 689), although acknowledging that *Turnbull* can hardly be said to have eliminated the risk of mistaken eyewitness identification leading to wrongful conviction, argue that the guidelines have probably achieved all that can be achieved in this regard without fundamentally rethinking the basic adversarial structure of English criminal procedure and trial practice. Roberts (2004) sees a less revolutionary path to reform which, following Twining, sees safeguards beyond the rules of evidence in areas such as cognitive psychology which would aid understanding of how a witness's memory is open to distortion.

Murphy perceptively illustrates how the concept of corroboration has been given a new lease of life in the case law on discretionary warnings. It should not be forgotten that it is open to Parliament to prescribe corroboration practices as for example **ss. 34–37 CJPOA 1994.** Finally, one further point could be made to amplify Murphy's analysis. Overall, English law remains wedded to the doctrine that one piece of evidence is sufficient to convict as *R v Horncastle* **[2009] UKSC 14** has recently demonstrated in the case of hearsay. In the face of this somewhat intransigent aspect of the common law, it is surely helpful that there should be an acknowledgement that at times other safeguards should be put in place. Although care warnings are discretionary and the flexibility of the current approach is more seductive than the former rigidity, it is important that the concept of corroboration as a theoretical device should be kept alive. As Roberts and Zuckerman point out (2010, p. 663) 'Abolishing the law of corroboration no more dispenses with epistemic standards assessing evidential support than abolishing the law of hearsay would curb the inherent infirmities of second-hand evidence.'

? Question 2

Sam and Alan are charged with the attempted rape of Amy. The case against them is that Amy met Sam and Alan in the local wine bar and they started chatting. She had not known them before. After a short while Amy, who was feeling drunk, went outside to an alleyway for some fresh air. The alleyway was very dark at the time. Two men approached her and attempted to rape her. She thought she recognised them as the men in the wine bar but she is unsure. As a result of her screams the two men stopped and ran away. A passer-by, Mandy, saw two men running away. She saw the face of one of them under a street lamp and the police made a photofit to her description. Giles, a police constable, recognised the photofit picture as being that of Alan whom he had previously arrested on suspicion of criminal damage. Amy is taken to the wine bar the next day by police and picks out Sam, a customer, as one of the men who tried to rape her. The police had failed to take a description of the attackers from Amy before they took her to the wine bar. At first Sam claimed he was at work on the night of the alleged attempted rape but later admitted this was a lie and that he was in the wine bar with a girlfriend. He claims he lied to protect the girlfriend because she was married. Mandy was killed in a road traffic accident shortly after the alleged attempted rape. Alan denies he was at the wine bar on the night in question. Both Sam and Alan deny any involvement in the attempted rape and demand that identification parades are held.

Evaluate the difficulties which the prosecution may face with the evidence.

Commentary

This question requires a discussion of the rules relating to the treatment of identification evidence in court and also the use of lies told by the defendant as prosecution evidence. As regards the victim's evidence, it is clear that because of her state of intoxication and the bad lighting conditions, a *Turnbull* direction will have to be given. The other issue revolves around the photofit picture and how the court should treat this evidence. Another difficulty that will be encountered is with regards to the identification of Alan by Giles. The basis of Giles's recognition of Alan and whether that is admissible in evidence will have to be considered. There is also the point in relation to corroboration in this case in that it needs to be made clear that no corroboration warning is required as a result of the **CJPOA 1994**. And the controversial area of voice recognition is also in issue.

Answer plan

- Identification evidence and *Turnbull* direction—**s. 78 PACE**.
- Revised Code D **PACE**—identification and video identification parades—see **R v Forbes (2001)**.
- Sam's lie—consider **Lucas (1981)**; Sam accepts he was at scene but denies involvement in offence—arguably Code D should apply and identification procedure held.
- Giles's identification of Alan—not permitted to say why he knew Alan.
- No need for corroboration warning.
- Admissibility of voice identification.

Examiner's tip

It is important in these procedural questions that you keep up to date with the statutory instruments which update the Codes of Practice. The latest version of Code D was issued in 2011 and made a number of changes.

Suggested answer

The problems faced by the prosecution counsel start with the identification of Sam by the victim, Amy. In effect, her identification evidence is weak both because of her intoxicated condition and the bad lighting conditions. In *R v Turnbull* [1977] QB 224, the Court of Appeal laid down guidelines for the treatment of identification evidence where the case depends wholly or substantially on the correctness of the identifications. The guidelines state, inter alia, that the judge should warn the jury of the special need for caution, before convicting the accused in reliance on the correctness of the identification evidence which the defence alleges to be mistaken. The judge should draw the jury's attention to the possibility that an error was made and should invite them to examine closely the circumstances in which the observation took place. The guidelines go on to provide that the jury should also examine closely the conditions under which, and the length of time for which, the observation took place. Factors such as whether the witness knew the accused, or whether there was any particular reason for the witness to remember the accused, or how soon after the event did the witness give a description to the police should also be considered. The guidelines make it clear that the judge should remind the jury of any weaknesses in the identification evidence and that where the identification evidence is weak, the judge should withdraw the case from the jury unless there is any other evidence which will support the identification evidence.

It has been made clear by the Court of Appeal in *R v Oakwell* [1978] **1 WLR 32**, that the *Turnbull* guidelines are not to be interpreted inflexibly. It is thus clear that on the facts of the present case, the judge will need to draw the jury's attention to the weaknesses present in Amy's identification evidence, namely that it was dark, that she was intoxicated, and the fact that she may have remembered him because of the time spent talking to him in the wine bar. If the judge considers that the quality of the identification is good then he may allow the case to proceed in the absence of any other evidence supporting the identification, as long as he delivers the *Turnbull* warning in the summing-up. On the other hand, if the judge is of the opinion that the quality of Mandy's or Amy's identification is poor but sees there is other evidence which could support the two identifications then he should point this out to the jury. It is for the jury to decide whether the evidence does support it. He should also warn the jury about any evidence which, it is felt, they might wrongly believe is supportive. The possible supporting evidence is Sam's admitted lie (on which, see later).

The defence may suggest that the police should have held a video identification rather than take Amy to the wine bar for the identification. However, it may be argued that they had no information whereby they could make an arrest of Sam. Code D of **PACE** including Annex B governs the procedure for obtaining identification evidence. Code D 3.2 and Annex C provides that where the identity of a suspect is not known a police officer may take a witness to a particular neighbourhood or place to see whether he or she can identify the person allegedly seen on the relevant occasion. Before doing so however, and, where practical, the police should take a record of any description given by the witness of the suspect (Annex D 3.2(a)). Here the police have failed to do this. They should also have made a video of the general scene if practicable, to give a general impression of the scene and the numbers present. One question is whether a video identification should have been held. In *R v Forbes* [2001] **1 AC 473** the appeal turned on whether the street identification of the defendant could be admitted. It was held that the breach of Code D did not require the evidence to be excluded under **s. 78**. However, Lord Bingham stated that a parade should be held if the suspect consented and unless the specified exceptions applied whenever a suspect disputes an identification. The facts are similar here to *Forbes* and it is arguable that the judge will not exclude the evidence of the identification in public, directions should be given, however, that the jury should be aware that a breach of Code D had occurred. If Amy cannot recall at the trial who she identified, the accompanying police officer may give details of her identification evidence (*R v McCay* [1990] 1 WLR 645). The common law exception to the rule against previous consistent statements allowed evidence of out-of-court identification to be given by the witness or a third party who had witnessed the identification. The **Criminal Justice Act 2003** extends this exception. **Section 120(4) and (5)** allow a witness's previous statement which 'identifies or describes a person, object or place to be admissible of any matter stated if the witness indicates that to the best of his belief he made the statement, and that to the best of his belief it states the truth.'

The identification evidence against Sam is arguably weak and the prosecution may seek to rely on his admitted lie as supportive evidence of his guilt. If they do so the judge will have to warn the jury about the dangers of relying on this evidence. In *R v Goodway* (1994) 98 Cr App R 11 Lord Taylor CJ stated that 'where lies told by the defendant are relied on . . . as support for identification evidence, the judge should give a direction along the lines indicated in *Lucas* [1981] QB 720.' In *R v Burge and Pegg* [1996] 1 Cr App R 364 the Court of Appeal summarised the circumstances in which a *Lucas* direction should be given. Sam has admitted the lie so it is therefore unnecessary for the judge to direct that the jury must find it proved beyond reasonable doubt. The lie can support the prosecution case only if the jury is sure Sam did not lie for an innocent reason. There is thus a significant amount of case law. The jury must be satisfied that there is no innocent motive for the lie, as here there may be. It may be that Sam lied to protect his girlfriend. On the facts as given this does not appear to be the sort of case where a direction would be otiose, in that to reject Sam's account would all but leave the jury with no logical alternative but to convict.

Sam accepts he was present at the scene but denies involvement in the offence. There is disputed authority as to whether the police are required to conduct a video parade when a suspect accepts he was present but denies involvement. In *K v DPP* [2003] EWHC 351 it was held that the judge was wrong not to hold a procedure but in *Chen* [2001] EWCA Crim 885 it was held that this was not necessary. It is arguable that *K* is the better decision and that a video identification or parade should be held. The procedure should follow that in Code D revised in 2011. Part 3 of the Code has two parts, A and B: A covers identification by eyewitnesses and B identification from films, photographs and images by persons who are not eyewitnesses.

Mandy does not appear to have seen Sam but only Alan. Since the evidence against Alan is so weak and in view of the *Turnbull* guidelines, it is possible that the judge will withdraw the case against him and direct the jury to acquit him. If, however, there was another eye witness who saw Alan running away, albeit in a fleeting glimpse-type situation, whilst the judge may leave the evidence to the jury, he would need to give the *Turnbull* warning and direct them specifically that even a number of honest persons can be wrong: *R v Weeder* (1980) 71 Cr App R 228 and *R v Breslin* (1984) 80 Cr App R 226.

The other difficulty that the prosecution may have with the evidence is Mandy's testimony. If Mandy was still alive and gave testimony in court, her testimony would be subject to the *Turnbull* direction, as it could be argued that her evidence falls within the situation which the *Turnbull* guidelines were intended to cover. Again, arguably an identification parade should have been held, although clearly Mandy's death was unforeseen. However, now that she is dead the question is whether the photofit is admissible into evidence. In *R v Smith* [1976] **Crim LR 511**, a photofit picture was held not to offend the rule against hearsay. However, the Court of Appeal in *R v Cook* [1987] **1 All ER 1049** went a step further. The Court of Appeal decided that photofit pictures were in a class of evidence of their own. Neither the rule against hearsay nor the rule against previous consistent statements had any application to such evidence. The photofit pictures are, according to the Court of Appeal, manifestations of the seeing eye, translations of vision onto paper through the medium of a police officer's skill of drawing or composing which a witness does not possess. The Court of Appeal's approach in drawing an analogy between a photofit or sketch and a photograph is arguably surprising in view of the acknowledged differences between them. Nonetheless, the decision in **Cook** has been followed by the Court of Appeal in *R v Constantinou* (1989) **91 Cr App R 74**. Thus, on the facts of this case, it is clear that the photofit picture would be admissible in evidence notwithstanding that Mandy is not able to give evidence.

However, in view of the fact that Mandy's identification originally was as a result of a fleeting glance situation, it seems probable that the judge will have to give the *Turnbull* direction with respect to this evidence and may have to withdraw the case from the jury unless there is some other evidence to support it.

The third problem with the evidence is with regards to Giles's identification of Alan. Whilst it is likely that he can say that he identified Alan from the photofit picture, he is not allowed to say why he knew Alan. It is not permissible to tell the jury that the reason why Giles recognised Alan was because he had previously arrested Alan for criminal damage. Tony may also be called as a witness. He may be able to identify the voice of one of the two suspects. It is now accepted that a *Turnbull* warning should be given in the case of voice recognition, see *R v Hershey* [1998] **Crim LR 281**. The police should have given Tony an opportunity to hear recordings of the voices of the suspects before the trial but this is an area which is as yet subject to scant regulation leading to possible mistaken identification. Since then guidance has now been given in *R v Flynn and St John* [2008] **2 Cr App R 266**. In that case the evidence against the defendants had included covert police recordings from a probe placed in the van used in a robbery. Police officers claimed the voices on the recording matched those of the defendants which they had heard following arrest. The defendants successfully appealed to the Court of Appeal. The court held that it was desirable but not mandatory for voice recognition to be carried out by experts. The prosecution should try and establish if the text message is available on the mobile phone. If it is, it may be admissible as non-hearsay evidence, see **s. 76(4)(b) PACE** and *R v Voisin* [1918] **1 KB 531**. Thus, the judge will need to give strong directions in relation to the danger of misidentification in relation to voice recognition.

Thus, on the facts of the present case, it is likely that the case against Sam will be withdrawn from the jury and the *Turnbull* direction will, at the very least, have to be given with respect to the identification of Alan. It is not altogether clear whether the case against Alan will be withdrawn or not. This would depend on whether there was any other evidence available to support it.

Further reading

Birch, D., 'Corroboration in Criminal Trials. A Review of the Law Commission's Working Paper' [1990] Crim LR 667.

Birch, D., 'Corroboration: Goodbye to All That?' [1995] Crim LR 524.

Bronitt, S., '*Baskerville* Revisited: The Definition of Corroboration Reconsidered' [1991] Crim LR 30–37.

Choo, A., 'Confessions and Corroboration: A Comparative Perspective' [1991] Crim LR 867.

Cutler, B.L. and Penrod, S.D., *Mistaken Identification—The Eyewitness, Psychology and the Law* (Cambridge: Cambridge University Press, 1995).

Law Commission, Law Com No. 202, *Corroboration of Evidence in Criminal Trials* (London: HMSO, 1991).

Leake, S. and Ormerod D., 'Case Comment. *R v Stone*' [2005] Crim LR 569.

Mirfield, P., 'Corroboration After the 1994 Act' [1995] Crim LR 448.

Ormerod, D., 'Sounds Familiar—Voice Identification Evidence' [2001] Crim LR 595.

Pattenden, R., 'Should Confessions be Corroborated?' (1991) 107 LQR 317.

Roberts, A., 'Does Code D Impose an Unrealistic Burden on the System of Summary Justice?' (2001) 165 JP 756.

Roberts, A., 'The Problem of Mistaken Identification' (2004) 8 E & P 100.

Tinsley, Y., 'Even Better than the Real Thing? The Case for Reform in Identification Parades' (2001) 5 E & P 99.

Twining, W., *Rethinking Evidence* (Oxford: OUP, 1990).

Opinion evidence

Introduction

This area of Evidence law is dominated by the question of expert witness evidence and the extent to which flawed testimony has led to miscarriages of justice. When experts are mistaken the consequences can be very serious—as illustrated, for example, by Professor Frank Scuse and Home Office forensic scientists in relation to the Birmingham Six, Maguire Seven and Judith Ward miscarriages of justice. It should be stressed, however, that expert evidence is now commonplace in both criminal and civil trials and the courts and Parliament have developed procedures to try to ensure that such evidence is of a high quality. However, these procedures are a somewhat eclectic mix of common law and statute. Their development to some extent reflects the growing importance of scientific expertise in society as a whole.

Students should be aware of recent developments in civil and criminal law. The former includes the **Civil Evidence Act 1995** and the **Civil Procedure Rules (CPR) 1998**. As far as criminal law is concerned this is mainly a case law subject, but you should be familiar with **s. 30 of the Criminal Justice Act (CJA) 1988** as far as expert evidence and hearsay is concerned and **s. 35 of the CJA 2003** requiring notice by the defence of the intention to call expert witnesses. The **CJA 2003** has made some changes in this area. **Section 118(8)** preserves the common law rule under which in criminal proceedings an expert witness may draw on the body of expertise relevant to his field. **Section 127** relates to the preparatory work of experts. The Explanatory Note provides that it addresses the problem which arises where information relied upon by an expert witness is outside the personal experience of the expert and cannot be proved by other admissible evidence. The new statutory provision is based on the intention that rules about advance notice of expert evidence will be amended so as to require advance notice of the name of any person who has prepared information on which the expert has relied. In effect, an expert's opinion may be based on statements not prepared by him if:

- the statement was prepared for the purposes of criminal proceedings;
- the person who prepared the statement had, or may reasonably be supposed to have had, personal knowledge of the matters stated.

In answering a question in this area, you must be familiar with the differences between expert and non-expert opinion evidence. Be clear on when and in what circumstances both types of evidence are admissible and the questions that can be asked of the expert whilst giving evidence. The specific approach that should be taken after that depends on whether the question relates to civil or criminal trials.

You may also be expected to be familiar with the elements of probability theory. Of course, ideally evidence students should be mathematically literate, although it is revealing, if very worrying, that judges or counsel are not always necessarily equipped with those skills—any more than expert witnesses are always well-versed in criminal or civil justice principles.

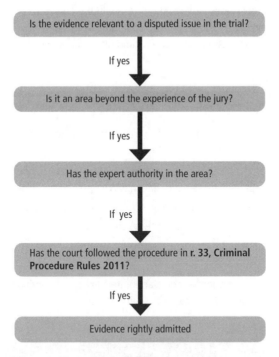

Diagram 6 Admissibility of expert evidence in criminal trials

Question 1

'An expert's opinion is admissible to furnish the court with scientific information which is likely to be outside the experience and knowledge of a judge or jury. If on the proven facts a judge or jury can form their own conclusions, without help, then the opinion of an expert is unnecessary.'

(*R v Turner* [1975] QB 834, per Lawton LJ, at 841.)

Critically examine the application of the approach outlined here in relation to the role of expert opinion evidence in criminal trials.

Commentary

This appears to be a relatively straightforward question. However, you should avoid the temptation to give a narrative account of the law and instead display your analytical knowledge of some of the controversies in this area, such as whether criminal trials should move towards court-appointed experts as in civil cases and whether the law in the area needs codifying. Recent cases about flawed expert evidence have shone the spotlight on this area of law, particularly on the question of whether the distinction between fact and opinion is a meaningful one.

Answer plan

- *Turner* illustrating traditional approach of courts, separating expert witness evidence and ordinary witnesses.
- In practice distinction is difficult to draw; and courts influenced by public opinion on what areas are acceptable for expert evidence—e.g. difficulty over psychiatric evidence.
- Arguably many witnesses give opinion evidence to some extent—the issue is to what extent scientific as opposed to eyewitness evidence is verifiable.
- Liberal approach of English courts to scientific expertise—contrast more jurisprudential approach in US.
- Assessment of reform arguments—court-appointed experts; scientific education for courts; stress that even scientific evidence cannot attain certainty.

Examiner's tip

Expert evidence is one area where it will improve your answers if you have some awareness of the law in the United States, in particular *Frye v US* **(1923) 293F, 1010** and *Daubert v Merrell Dow* **(1993) 509 US 579**. There the jurisprudence has been rather more developed and is influencing the law here as the following answer suggests.

Suggested answer

Expert opinion evidence is of growing importance in criminal trials. The Runciman Royal Commission's Crown Court Study (1993) found that in about one-third of all disputed trials scientific evidence played a part. Twenty years later the numbers have doubtless increased, particularly in the wake of the development of DNA profiling. As Roberts and Zuckerman put it: 'It is no exaggeration to regard DNA technology as the most revolutionary contribution to criminal investigation and forensic proof since the introduction of fingerprinting a century earlier' (2010, p. 470). The overall picture in relation to the use of expert evidence has changed since the landmark case of *Turner* quoted in the question, but the judicial approach to the admissibility of such evidence is still as expressed there. This expression, although accurate, indicates also the limitations of the current approach—some of which will be examined here. Lawton CJ points out here that expert evidence is only to be admitted on matters where a judge or jury cannot form their own conclusions. The essay will suggest that the distinction is not so easy to draw, particularly in certain scientific areas such as psychology. Further it will be argued that admissibility is only one aspect of the problematic nature of expert evidence, another being the way the courts, including the jury, handle such evidence. Finally the contribution of expert evidence to miscarriages of justice will be examined.

General rule of exclusion of opinion evidence and exceptions

The general rule is that a witness can only testify with respect to those matters which he or she actually observed or perceived. The witness is not entitled to give his or her own opinion on the matter. It is for the jury in a criminal trial to draw inferences from the evidence as the trier of fact, not the witness. There are a number of exceptions to this general rule. Munday (2011, p. 379) identifies four in addition to expert opinion. In the following areas a non-expert witness may give opinion evidence: identity, a witness's feelings, handwriting proved by a non-expert (see **Criminal Procedure Act 1865, s. 8**) and matters of impression and narrative.

The major exception to this general rule is in the case of expert witnesses. With regards to those matters for which the judge or jury may require assistance, the opinion of experts on those matters may be admissible. Examples of where the judge and jury may require assistance include scientific, medical and forensic evidence. The weight to be given to such evidence is a matter for the jury. It is apparent that this type of evidence is admissible because the jury would not be able to draw the appropriate inferences and form proper opinions from the facts requiring expert opinion: *Buckley v Rice Thomas* (1554) Plowd 118.

Who is an expert?

Before an expert witness can give opinion evidence relating to any particular issue, it is for the judge to decide whether that particular witness is an expert. This would be dependent on whether the witness had undergone a course of study giving the requisite expertise in that area or whether his experience is such as to make him an expert. It is not essential that in all cases the expert possess formal qualifications. In *R v Silverlock* [1894] 2 QB 766, opinion evidence from a solicitor was admitted, by the Court for Crown Cases Reserved, with respect to handwriting even though he did not possess any formal qualification in it but merely studied it as a hobby. The courts' liberal approach to expertise is illustrated more recently in *R v Hodges* [2003] 2 Cr App R 247, where the Court of Appeal allowed a police officer experienced in drug crime to give evidence as to the price and general supply procedure for heroin in the specific area. It is arguable that what is at issue here is not the rather simplistic distinction between expert and lay opinion suggested in *Turner*, but the more fundamental test of whether the evidence of the proposed witness is relevant. The Court of Appeal has set out the principles involving the admissibility of expert opinion evidence:

> For expert evidence to be admissible two conditions must be satisfied: first, that study the more experience will give a witness's opinion an authority which the opinion of one not so qualified will lack; and secondly the witness must be so qualified to express the opinion . . . If these two conditions are met the evidence of the witness is admissible, although the weight to be attached to his opinion must of course be assessed by the tribunal of fact. (*R v Lutrell* [2004] EWCA Crim 1344.)

Choo (2012, p. 313) summarises the two conditions as 'necessity and reliability' and adds 'the extent to which the twin issues of necessity and reliability are adequately accounted for in the law on the admissibility of expert opinion evidence is a question which ought to underlie any consideration of the law in this area' (p. 253).

Inadmissible expert evidence

Expert opinion evidence is not admissible per se in all criminal trials. Where the issue is one for which the jury is able to decide and does not require the assistance of experts, no opinion evidence from experts is admissible. The reason is because such evidence is usually unnecessary and irrelevant. In *R v Chard* (1971) 56 Cr App R 268, evidence from an expert with regards to the alleged inability of the accused to form the necessary *mens rea* of the offence was disallowed by the Court of Appeal. The court emphasised that where there was no issue of mental instability or illness, it is inappropriate to allow evidence from a medical witness as to the state of the accused's mind. Likewise in *R v Turner* [1975] QB 834 itself, where the accused's defence was one of provocation, the Court of Appeal excluded evidence from a psychiatrist because there was no issue as regarded his mental state. The issue of provocation was one for which the jury could decide. Lawton LJ stated in that case that the fact that an expert witness possessed impressive scientific qualifications did not necessarily make his opinion on matters of human nature any more helpful. These were matters which the jury was competent to decide.

The problem of credibility

The restriction on the admissibility of expert evidence on matters for which the jury requires no assistance includes a restriction on expert evidence on the credibility of a witness or the accused save in exceptional circumstances: *Lowery v R* [1974] AC 85. Although, in *Lowery*, such evidence was admitted, Murphy (2011, p. 399) regards this decision as applying only to the specific facts of the case rather than a general exception to the usual rule. This approach appears to be correct in the light of *R v Rimmer* [1983] Crim LR 250, where the trial judge refused to allow the evidence of an expert on the basis that this related only to the credibility of the accused. Murphy points to the case of *R v Weir, R v Somanathan* [2006] 1 WLR 1885, to illustrate the difficulty of applying the principle advocated here by Lawton CJ that expert evidence should not be allowed on issues within the jury's everyday knowledge, in particular that relating to the credibility of a witness. The case also illustrates that 'science' may be widely defined and that experts may be called to give evidence on social science, here, arguably, anthropology or religious studies. The case concerned the rape of a female member of his congregation by a Tamil Hindu priest. A professor of Hinduism was called as an expert witness by the prosecution to give evidence on how difficult it was for such a victim to make an allegation against a priest. The Court of Appeal held that the evidence was rightly admitted. Kennedy LJ stated (at para. 49) that counsel '. . . did not ask the witness to express a view about the truth or falsehood of the allegation, and he did not purport to do so, but the jury was entitled to know from an expert whether or not within the Hindu community an allegation of this kind was unusual.'

Murphy comments (2011, p. 401), 'With respect, whether or not the allegation was unusual (and whether or not it required courage, etc) was irrelevant to the case except in so far as it tended to confirm the credibility of the complainant. Thus, the only basis on which the court might have sought to defend the admissibility of the evidence was that the jury would be unable to assess the complainant's credibility without expert assistance. This would involve the proposition that the reluctance of a Hindu woman to accuse a priest of rape is a concept beyond the ordinary experience of most jurors, and so justifies a departure from the general rule expounded in *Turner*.'

What is meant by 'outside the expertise of the jury'?

Lawton LJ's observation in *Turner* correctly indicates how the courts call on experts for evidence on 'scientific information which is likely to be outside the experience and knowledge of a judge or jury.' However, it does not indicate how such areas can be identified. In practice the courts have had to consider the difficult question of at what point modish discoveries become a new science. In the United States for a long period the test set by *Frye v US* (1923) was that of 'general acceptance in the particular field to which it belongs'. English law did not have the same preoccupation with mainstream branches of science. Bingham LJ stated in *R v Robb* (1991) 93 Cr App R 161 that opinion evidence may be given in a wide range of areas, some 'far removed from anything which could be called a formal scientific discipline'. In *Robb* evidence of a voice identification technique was held to be properly admitted.

Another criticism made of *Turner* is that jurors might indeed welcome evidence within their broad general knowledge, such as human behaviour. In fact in practice this does happen. In *R v Stockwell* (1993) 97 Cr App R 260 the Court of Appeal allowed evidence from an expert about identifying a suspect by looking at video footage, which might be taken to be an everyday activity.

New areas of knowledge

In effect admissibility often turns on whether in society as a whole there is an acknowledgement of the importance of experts in a particular area. Some 'experts' such as psychiatrists are treated with more scepticism than others. One area of controversy that has generated recent case law is that of facial-mapping, illustrating that new areas of recognised expertise are continually developing. In *R v Mitchell* [2005] EWCA Crim 731 the court accepted that a facial-mapping expert can give an opinion, although this had been doubted in *R v Gray* [2003] EWCA Crim 1001. Ear print evidence is another contested area. It is important to realise that no evidence is infallible and that even fingerprint evidence may have a rate of error. As the *New Scientist* (2005) noted, 'fingerprint matching is undoubtedly a valuable tool for catching criminals but it suffers from one major flaw: nobody knows how often fingerprint examiners make a wrong call.' In *R v Gilfoyle (No. 2)* [2001] 2 Cr App R 57 the court held that evidence of a 'psychological autopsy' for the purpose of determining whether an alleged murder victim had in fact committed suicide was not admissible. Such autopsies did not have real scientific basis. (At the time of writing this case has been referred to the Criminal Cases Review Commission.)

The ultimate issue

At one time expert opinion evidence was inadmissible on the ultimate issue in the case. This was because the expert would be usurping the function of the jury: *M'Naghten's Case* (1843) 10 Cl & F 200. However, it is clear that whilst the rule is still referred to, in practice expert evidence on the ultimate issue is allowed. In *DPP v A & BC Chewing Gum Ltd* [1968] 1 QB 159, 164, Lord Parker CJ in the Divisional Court stated that:

> Those who practise in the criminal courts see every day cases of experts being called on the question of diminished responsibility, and although technically the final question 'Do you think he was suffering from diminished responsibility?' is strictly inadmissible, it is allowed time and time again without objection.

Section 3 of the Civil Evidence Act 1972 abolished the ultimate issue rule in civil proceedings. The position in criminal proceedings is that an expert can give his opinion on an ultimate issue within his area of expertise. In *R v Stockwell* (1993) 97 Cr App R 260 the Court of Appeal stated that evidence on the ultimate issue is admissible. This case also raises, however, a matter which is not covered in Lawton LJ's statement. What is the status of expert opinion evidence? In *Stockwell* the court said that the judge must make it clear that the jury must decide the issue and may reject the expert's evidence. This is the general rule. However, in *R v Tilly* **[1981] 1 WLR 1309** the Court of Appeal overturned a guilty verdict where the expert evidence was unchallenged and clearly suggested the verdict was unsustainable. In other words on occasion the expert evidence may determine the case.

It seems, however, that juries are on the whole more inclined to accept prosecution expert opinion evidence. Edmond (2002, p. 58) points out that 'Scientific evidence is an important component of most high profile miscarriage of justice cases.' He also points out (p. 59) that a 'common concern is that excessive reliance is placed on scientific evidence: that its potential fallibility is not recognised.' This is all the more significant in view of the 'meagre resources' available to the defence to challenge such prosecution evidence.

Difficulty of reform

It should be acknowledged that the current status of expert opinion evidence is by no means settled. A number of practical and theoretical issues demand attention. Some arguments have been put that a system of court-appointed experts (perhaps as well as party-appointed experts) should be established in criminal cases. Court-appointed experts were introduced in civil cases by the Woolf reforms in 1997/1998. But there are a number of difficulties. The criminal trial paradigm is still an adversarial one, with the search for a conclusion based on the conflict between two sides, and society is arguably not ready for trial by experts. In addition, it is a fallacy to think that there is necessarily only one version of scientific evidence. The question is most often that of probabilities, not certainties. As Howard (1991, p. 101) points out, 'It is slightly mysterious that it should be thought that experts are venal mountebanks when engaged by the parties but transformed into paragons of objectivity when employed by the court.'

What is undeniable is that there is increasing public attention and some unease about the treatment of expert evidence in criminal cases. In March 2005 the House of Commons Science and Technology Committee published a report entitled *Forensic Science on Trial*. The conclusions noted:

> 189. While we recognise that the number of miscarriages of justice associated with expert evidence may be relatively low, we are extremely concerned by the lack of safeguards to prevent such miscarriages of justice from happening, and the complacency of the legal profession in regard to these matters.

However, the committee was anxious that any failures should be recognised as systems failures and that 'focusing criticism on the expert has a detrimental effect on the willingness of other experts to serve as witnesses and detracts attention from the flaws in the court process and legal system which, if addressed, could help prevent future miscarriages of justice.'

The debate over reform has led to the publication in 2009 of a consultation paper by the Law Commission (*The Admissibility of Expert Evidence in Criminal Trials*) and proposals that the trial judge would exercise more of a gatekeeper role applying a test similar to that of the US case *Daubert v Merrell Dow* (1993). This might avoid what has been suggested is too ready an acceptance of expert evidence in cases such as *R v Atkins* [2010] Crim LR 141 where the Court of Appeal held that evidence from an expert on facial-mapping was rightly admitted.

Scientific literacy

The law on opinion evidence nearly 40 years after *Turner* is thus still evolving. Education in science for juries and legal personnel is one way forward but as the court in *Adams* [1996] 2 Cr App R 467 stressed, trials are about common sense, not mathematical or scientific reasoning. Thus Bayes' theorem was not appropriate for use in jury trials. (Bayes' theorem provides a way of calculating the conditional probability of an event. If there are two events A and B, the probability of A given B (written as P(A/B) in statistical shorthand, and always expressed as a positive number between 0 and 1) can be derived from the formula:

$$P(A|B) = \frac{P(B|A)\,P(A)}{P(B)}$$

Some look longingly at the more theoretically coherent approach in the United States, as seen in *Daubert v Merrell Dow* and **Federal Rule of Evidence 702** (see *R v Dallagher* [2002] EWCA Crim 1903). Perhaps the impetus for change will come from miscarriages of justice based in part on misconceptions about scientific opinion evidence. The Court of Appeal in *R v Clark* (2003) laid down clearer guidelines about procedure where there is dispute about scientific evidence and the case rests largely or entirely on this. In *R v Cannings* [2004] 1 WLR 2607 the Court of Appeal Criminal Division addressed the problem of disagreement between experts on the cause of infant deaths. It stated that, in such a situation, where death by natural causes could not be ruled out 'the prosecution of a parent or parents for murder should not be started or continued unless there is additional cogent evidence, extraneous to the expert evidence . . . which tends to support the conclusion that the infant, or where there is more than one death, one of the infants, was deliberately harmed.' However, in *R v Kai-Whitewind* [2005] 2 Cr App R 31 Judge LJ stated (at pp. 84–85), 'the logical conclusion of what we shall describe as the overblown *Cannings* argument is that where there is a conflict of opinion between reputable experts, the expert evidence called by the Crown is automatically neutralised. That is a startling proposition, and is not sustained by *Cannings*. In *Cannings* there was no evidence beyond the inferences based on coincidence which the experts for the Crown were prepared to draw.'

Roberts (2008, p. 443) points out that 'the principal weakness in the English law concerning the reception of expert evidence is that its development has been based on pragmatism rather than principle.' He deplores the way the courts draw 'vague analogies with approaches taken in other jurisdictions' and suggests the 'development of a judicial gate-keeping function in English civil procedure.' He argues that 'a central concern of any proposal for reform ought to be how best to address a lack of technical or scientific expertise on the part of those responsible for determining the admissibility of expert testimony.' Roberts recommends 'the adoption of pre-trial procedures which provide for direct involvement of experts in the gate-keeping process.' In short, there is a growing pressure for reform of the law in this area. Mistakes indeed seem to continue. Morrison (2012, p. 1), to give one example, cites *R v T* **[2010] EWCA Crim 2439** as a case where the Court of Appeal exhibited 'misunderstandings of statistics'. Naughton and Tan (2011) make the troubling observation that DNA evidence may be responsible for miscarriages of justice since 'it is not the panacea of criminal investigation that is popularly believed'. They write, 'The presumption of innocence that is claimed to lie at the heart of all criminal investigations and prosecutions dictates that this is more adequately recognized and acted upon by the criminal justice system to avoid causing wrongful convictions and to overturn those that have already occurred.'

The often controversial outcomes of attempts to introduce reforms over recent years, however, suggest that simply moving away from the restrictive proposition set out in *Turner* is not the solution. In conclusion it is arguable that the limitations of the approach suggested in the quotation from *Turner* is that admissibility is regarded as the central issue. As Roberts (2009, p. 558) points out in relation to the Law Commission proposals, 'the failure to identify and explore options that would bring about a fundamental change in the procedural arrangements for evaluating and receiving expert evidence is disappointing.' Similarly Edmond (2012) sees the problem of one of the need for a deep going cultural change in the legal profession and the criminal justice system, citing the need to address the reluctance to engage with 'exogenous (i.e. non legal knowledge)'. Reform has to be 'sustained' he argues. He calls for 'preventive interventions like those flowing from a more multi disciplinary advisory panel might be more useful than the case based contributions provided by occasional court based experts.' At the heart of this complex question of expertise is therefore not simply fairness to the parties but what Edmond calls 'the social legitimacy' of legal institutions.

  Question 2

Sarah (a minor) is suing Henfield Health Authority for damages for pain and suffering and loss of earnings as a result of negligent treatment she received as a patient in Henfield Hospital. It is alleged that the surgeon who operated on her was negligent in that what was supposed to be a simple surgical procedure resulted in partial paralysis of her left side. Her solicitors have sought the opinion of Dr Williams, who produced a written report concluding that in his opinion, the surgeon had not followed proper practice. The defence wishes to call evidence of Joan Soap, a psychiatrist, to the effect that Sarah is not to be trusted to speak the truth.

Advise the parties.

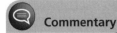

Commentary

This question requires a consideration of the application of the **Civil Evidence Act 1995**. This replaced and repealed **Part I of the Civil Evidence Act 1968** and **ss. 2(1), (2) and (3)(b) of the Civil Evidence Act 1972** and provides for the making of new rules governing the admissibility of expert opinion evidence. A working knowledge of the procedural rules governing the admissibility of expert reports under the **CPR 1998** will need to be shown.

Answer plan

- Admissibility of expert evidence in civil cases.
- Application of **s. 3(1) Civil Evidence Act 1972** which allows evidence on ultimate issue, applied in *Re M and R (Minors) (1996)*.
- Judge must establish expertise of Dr Williams and Joan Soap.
- Experts may rely on work of others, see *R v Abadom (1983)*.
- Application of **CPR, r. 35.1**.

Suggested answer

The general rule is that a witness cannot give his or her opinion on a fact in issue. To allow a witness to do so would be to usurp the function of the court, which is to draw an inference from the facts put before it. A witness should therefore only be allowed to give evidence of facts and that which he or she has observed. However, there are exceptions to this and the important exception that applies here is the admissibility of expert opinion evidence where it would assist the court in reaching its decision.

First, it should be noted that the expert evidence is admissible even though it may give an opinion on the ultimate issue. On the facts of the present case, it is arguable that Dr Williams, by concluding that the surgeon was negligent, is offering an opinion as to the ultimate issue. The difficulty faced in criminal trials is not present here. This is because **s. 3(1) of the Civil Evidence Act 1972** provides that where any person is called as a witness, his opinion on any relevant matter (which by **subs. (3)** includes an issue in the proceedings in question), on which he is qualified to give expert evidence, is to be admissible in evidence.

Jane Soap's evidence raises more difficult issues. In *Re M and R (Minors) (Sexual Abuse: Video Evidence)* [1996] 4 All ER 239, Butler-Sloss LJ held that a suitably qualified expert could give evidence as to the credibility of a child witness who had given evidence by way of a videotaped interview. The expert evidence fell within the ambit of **s. 3 of the Civil Evidence Act 1972**. Murphy (2011, p. 397) argues that this analysis is inaccurate but can be defended on the basis that this was expert psychiatrist and psychologist's evidence. He points out that the 'ultimate issue in such a case is not whether the child's evidence is credible but whether the alleged abuse occurred (though obviously the question of the child's credibility is of great importance in resolving the ultimate issue).' He goes on, however, to point out that the decision in the case can be defended on the basis that although expert opinion is not admissible on the issue of credibility since that is a lay matter, it is 'within the province of psychiatrists and psychologists to form an opinion about credibility because their diagnoses and recommendations for treatment or therapy are often based on the factual accounts given to them by their patients and clients.' Murphy suggests that 'the fact that such an expert witness believed what he was told is a fact which is essential to explain the formation of his opinion and can be admitted on that basis without considering the ultimate issue rule.' Murphy's approach suggests that expert psychiatric and psychological witnesses may be in a different position to that of other experts. The issue for the defence is relevance. If Sarah's testimony is disputed then arguably her credibility is a collateral issue and evidence may be taken on it.

It will be necessary to establish that Dr Williams and Joan Soap have the requisite expertise in the area in order to give their opinions on these matters: *R v Silverlock* [1894] 2 QB 766. This will be a question for the judge to decide prior to allowing the evidence to be admitted.

Another point to note is that an expert is entitled to rely on the work of others in reaching his conclusion. This was made clear in *R v Abadom* [1983] 1 WLR 126 (although a criminal case, the principle is likewise applicable here), where the Court of Appeal held that the expert opinion evidence was admissible although the expert had relied on statistics supplied by the Home Office Research Establishment. The court decided that the expert was entitled to rely on this research in forming his opinion and that this did not violate the rule against hearsay. In fact in civil proceedings hearsay statements are admissible under the **Civil Evidence Act 1995** since, with certain provisos, such statements are admissible as 'any representation of fact or opinion however made'.

The **Civil Procedure Rules (CPR) 1998** have made fundamental changes as to the admissibility of expert evidence in civil cases. **Rule 35.1 of the 1998 Rules** restricts expert evidence to that which is reasonably required to resolve the proceedings. One of these fundamental changes that the Rules have made is that in accordance with **r. 35.3** the duty imposed on the expert is to assist the court on those matters in which he has expertise. The fact that the expert is employed by one of the parties is dealt with by the rule that makes it clear that the duty to the court overrides any obligation to the person who instructed him. This is reinforced by the fact that the written expert reports must be addressed to the court. This requirement of objectivity, and the duty owed to the court, had been previously stressed by the court in *Vernon v Bosley (No. 1)* [1997] 1 All ER 577.

The **1998 Rules** have also made changes as to how the expert evidence is presented to the court. **Rule 35.5** provides that expert evidence shall be given by way of a written report in all cases unless the court orders otherwise. For cases that are on the fast-track the court will not permit oral expert evidence unless the interests of justice requires such oral testimony. **Rule 35.10** states that the report should contain a statement that the expert understands his duty to the court and has complied with it. It must also verify that the facts and opinions stated in the report are true and correct. The court will have to be satisfied that the experts are independent—in other words that although they are retained by the parties they give opinions in an objective and fair way and place their duty to the court beyond that to the parties. **Rule 35.3 of the CPR 1998** provides: '(1) it is the duty of an expert to help the court on the matters within his expertise. (2) This function overrides any obligation to the person from whom he had received instructions or by whom he is paid.' In *Liverpool Roman Catholic Diocese Trustees Inc v Goldberg (No. 2)* [2001] 4 All ER 950 the court held that a QC should not act as an expert witness on behalf of a member of his chambers. The latter was a defendant in an action for professional negligence and the proposed expert witness had expressed his sympathy for his colleague.

As regards whether the expert can be called to give evidence (for cases not on the fast track), this is governed by **r. 35.4**. This provides that no party shall call an expert without the court's permission. When permission is sought from the court, the party must identify the field in which he wishes to rely on the expert evidence and, where practicable, the expert in that field on whose evidence he wishes to rely.

In the present case, before the evidence of Dr Williams and Joan Soap can be adduced, permission will have to be obtained from the court and the way the evidence will be presented will be by way of a written report. If the parties wished to call experts to give oral testimony, then permission of the court has to be obtained and would depend on the circumstances of the case as to whether the court will allow such testimony to be given. Each can also appoint their own expert but the two experts will then have to meet to agree the reports to the court.

In civil cases there are strict rules about advance notice of expert evidence (see **Civil Evidence Act 1972, s. 2(3)**). Under the **CPR** a party who fails to disclose an expert's report may not use the report at trial or call the expert as a witness without the court's permission (**r. 35.11**).

Both Sarah and the Henfield Health Authority should be warned that they should be certain they want to use the experts' reports before disclosing them to the other side. Under the **CPR** any party to whom such a report is disclosed can put it in evidence, legal professional privilege being lost at that point (see **Chapter 11**). CPR, **r. 35.7(1)** states that 'where two or more parties wish to submit expert evidence on a particular issue, the court may direct that the evidence on that issue is to be given by one expert only.' It may well be the case that the parties wish to call evidence on these issues and if they cannot agree on the expert the court may select an expert from a list submitted by the parties or give directions on how the expert should be selected. Once selected each party can instruct the expert, although they must send copies of the instructions to the other side. Finally, both parties can expect the judgment to reflect the reasons why the views of the expert have been accepted. Lord Phillips of Worth Matravers MR stated the positions where two or more experts have been called as witnesses. The judge should:

provide an explanation as to why he has accepted the evidence of one expert and rejected that of the other. It may be that the evidence of one or the other accorded more satisfactorily with facts found by the judge. It may be that the explanation of one was more inherently credible than that of the other. It may simply be that one was better qualified, or manifestly more objective, than the other. Whatever the explanation may be, it should be apparent from the judgment. (*English v Emery Reimbold and Strick Ltd* [2002] 3 All ER 385.)

There may be grounds of appeal if the judge prefers lay opinion to uncontradicted expert opinion on a matter on which expert opinion is appropriate (*Re B (A Minor)* [2000] 1 WLR 790).

Further reading

Edmond, G., 'Judicial Representations of Scientific Evidence' (2000) 63 MLR 216.

Edmond, G., 'Constructing Miscarriages of Justice: Misunderstanding Scientific Evidence in High Profile Criminal Appeals' (2002) 22 OJLS 53.

Edmond, G., 'Is Reliability Sufficient? The Law Commission and Expert Evidence in International and Interdisciplinary Perspective'. Part 1 (2012) E & P 30.

House of Commons Science and Technology Committee 7th Report, *Forensic Science on Trial* (HL96–1) (London: TSO, 2005), www.publications.parliament.uk/pa/cm200001/cmselect/cmsctech/291/29102.htm.

Howard, N.M., 'The Neutral Expert: a Plausible Threat to Justice' [1991] Crim LR 98–105.

Law Commission Consultation Paper No. 190, *The Admissibility of Expert Evidence in Criminal Proceedings in England and Wales* (London: TSO, 2009).

Morrison, G., 'The Likelihood–Ratio Framework and Forensic Evidence in Court: A Response to *R v T*' (2012) 16 E & P 1.

Naughton, M. and Tan, G., 'The Need for Caution in the Use of DNA Evidence to Avoid Convicting the Innocent' (2011) 15 E & P 245.

New Scientist, 'The Myth of Fingerprints', 17 September 2005, 3.

O'Brian, E. Jr, 'Court Scrutiny of Expert Evidence: Recent Decisions Highlight the Tensions' (2003) 7 E & P 172.

Ormerod, D., 'Sounds Familiar—Voice Identification Evidence' [2001] Crim LR 595.

Pattenden, R., 'Conflicting Approaches to Psychiatric Evidence' [1986] Crim LR 92.

Redmayne, M., *Expert Evidence and Criminal Justice* (Oxford: OUP, 2001).

Roberts, A., 'Drawing on Expertise: Legal Decision-making and the Reception of Expert Evidence' [2008] Crim LR 443.

Roberts, A., 'Rejecting General Acceptance, Confounding the Gate-keeper: The Law Commission and Expert Evidence' [2009] Crim LR 551.

Ward, T., 'Usurping the Role of the Jury? Expert Evidence and Witness Credibility in English Criminal Trials' (2009) 13 E & P 83.

10

Issues in the course of trial

Introduction

This topic generally deals with the type of questions that can or cannot be asked in examination-in-chief or cross-examination in criminal trials.

Evidence courses vary in how they group the various aspects of the law of Evidence. In some courses competence and compellability (see **Chapter 3**) is covered along with other issues concerned with witness examination. That area overlaps considerably with criminal procedure and Evidence courses vary in the topics they cover. The areas covered in this chapter are:

Examination-in-chief

- refreshing memory;
- rule on previous consistent statements and exceptions;
- hostile witnesses.

Cross-examination

- rule on previous inconsistent statements;
- rule of finality to answers to collateral questions and exceptions;
- special rule for cross-examination of complainants in sexual offence cases;
- non-defendant's bad character.

Diagrams 7 and 8 should help you understand the input of statute and the common law to the law on previous consistent and previous inconsistent statements.

A particularly important aspect of this topic deals with the questions that can be asked about the complainant's sexual history in the case of a trial involving a sexual offence. For example, can the complainant be asked whether she is or was a prostitute? This will be considered in the light of **s. 41 of the Youth Justice and Criminal Evidence Act 1999 (YJCEA)**.

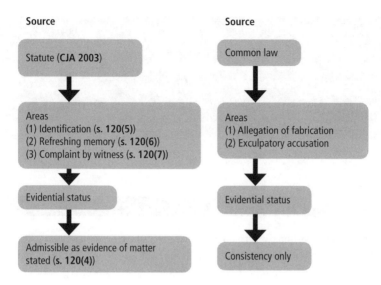

Diagram 7 Previous consistent statements

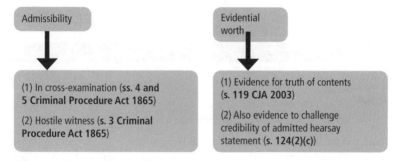

Diagram 8 Previous inconsistent statements

Question 1

Daniel, a police constable, in response to a call on his radio, went to investigate an alleged burglary at Henfield Road. As he drove up to the scene of the crime, he saw Henry dressed in a T-shirt and running shorts and carrying a holdall on his back, running in the opposite direction. Daniel chased after him but soon lost him. Daniel made a note of what he had seen in his notebook, but did not do so until nearly six months later, just before the trial. Just after the incident, following an appeal for witnesses, Henry went voluntarily to the police station and was interviewed. He said that the reason that he was in the area at the material time was because he had been out jogging, as he was training for the London Marathon and that the holdall contained bricks to weigh him down. Henry is subsequently arrested and charged with the burglary.

Advise on the following evidential matters:

(a) Can Daniel refresh his memory from his notebook outside court before giving evidence? If Daniel then gives evidence for the prosecution without referring to the notebook can the defence cross-examine him as to the contents of the notebook?

(b) Can Daniel refresh his memory from his notebook in court? And if so, can it be put in evidence?

(c) What use can the defence make of Henry's voluntary statement at the police station?

Commentary

This is a straightforward question concerning the witness refreshing his or her memory both inside and outside the courtroom and the use that the opposing counsel may make of the statements or documents used by the witness to refresh his or her memory. It also concerns previous consistent statements which are covered by both the common law and the hearsay provisions of the **Criminal Justice Act (CJA) 2003**.

Answer plan

(a) • Refreshing memory—relevant case law (1996); **CJA 2003** provisions—*R v McAfee* **(2006)**.

• Cross-examination and inspection permissible—see *Owen v Edwards* **(1983)**.

(b) • Conditions for refreshing memory—**CJA 2003**.

(c) • Inadmissibility of previous consistent statement unless falls within exceptions—**CJA 2003**.

• Arguable that exception applies as statement made at scene of crime.

Examiner's tip

This is an area which often lends itself to complex problem questions. Do not make the mistake of suggesting that the answer is always to be found in the massive **CJA 2003**. To give one example, previous consistent statements, the subject of part (c) of this question, are covered by both statute and common law. Exculpatory statements made at the scene of the crime are admissible under the common law as statements suggesting consistency. Unlike statements rebutting allegations of recent fabrication, they are not evidence of the truth of their contents. However **s. 114**, inclusionary hearsay discretion, may apply.

(a) Refreshing memory outside court

On the facts of the case, it would appear that Daniel will be called as a witness for the prosecution. The question that arises is whether he can refresh his memory from his notebook outside the court before giving evidence. It should be noted that it is common for witnesses to look at written statements which they have made, in order to refresh their memory, before testifying on the witness stand. This practice was recognised by the Court of Appeal in *R v Richardson* [1971] 2 QB 484. In any event, even if there was a rule prohibiting such action, the rule would be unenforceable.

In *Richardson*, four prosecution witnesses were given their statements prior to their testimony. The statements were not sufficiently contemporaneous for them to be used to refresh their memory in court. The accused argued on appeal, that as the statements were not contemporaneous for the purpose of the rule on refreshing memory in court, their evidence should not have been admitted. The Court of Appeal rejected this argument and approved the dicta in *Lau Pak Ngam v R* [1966] Crim LR 443. In that case, the Supreme Court of Hong Kong stated that if witnesses were deprived of the opportunity of checking their recollection beforehand by reference to statements or notes made near to the time of the events in question, testimony in the witness box would be no more than a test of memory, rather than of truthfulness. Further, refusal of access to the statements would create difficulties for honest witnesses, but would not hamper dishonest ones. The approach of the court in *Richardson* was later applied in the case of *Worley v Bentley* [1976] 2 All ER 449.

Subsequently, the court made it clear in *R v Da Silva* [1990] 1 All ER 29, that the judge has a discretion to allow a witness to withdraw from the witness stand in order to refresh his memory from a statement made near or at the time of the events in question. The judge has this discretion even where the statement is not contemporaneous with the events. Before he exercises his discretion, the judge must be satisfied that the witness cannot recall the events in question because of lapse of time, that the witness had made a statement near the time of the event representing his recollection of them, that he had not read the statement before testifying and that he wishes to read the statement before he continues to give evidence. In *R v South Ribble Magistrates' Court, ex parte Cochrane* [1996] 2 Cr App R 544, the Divisional Court made it clear that *R v Da Silva* did not lay down a rule of law that all four conditions must be satisfied. The court had a discretion whether to permit a witness to refresh his memory from a statement which was made non-contemporaneously.

Thus, it would appear proper for Daniel to refresh his memory from his notebook outside the court before testifying on oath. Even if it is unclear that Daniel made the note of the events contemporaneously with the events in question, this would not necessarily be fatal.

The next issue is whether the defence can cross-examine Daniel as to the contents of the notebook if he consults it before trial. The Court of Appeal in *R v Westwell* [1976]

2 All ER 812 decided that if the prosecution counsel is aware that his witness has refreshed his or her memory outside the court, it was 'desirable but not essential' that the defence should be informed of this fact. Failure to do so would not be a ground for acquittal. Once the defence is aware that Daniel has refreshed his memory from his notebook outside the court, they are entitled to inspect the notebook, and cross-examine Daniel on the relevant matters contained in it. This was so held by the Divisional Court in **Owen v Edwards** (1983) **77 Cr App R 191**.

However, the court in **Owen v Edwards** made it clear that if the defence counsel cross-examines a witness on material in the notebook or statement, which has not been used by the witness to refresh his memory, they run the risk of the notebook or statement being put in evidence. The court applied by analogy the rule applicable where the witness refreshes his or her memory in court. **Section 120(3) of the Criminal Justice Act (CJA) 2003** provides that if a witness's memory-refreshing statement becomes admissible as a result of cross-examination then it is admissible evidence of any matter stated of which oral evidence by the witness would be admissible.

Thus, provided the defence cross-examines Daniel on the part of the notebook which he has used to refresh his memory, the notebook will not be put in evidence. If the defence was to go beyond that, the notebook may be put in evidence.

(b) Refreshing memory in court

Daniel may be entitled to refresh his memory by referring to his notebook in court provided the pre-conditions are satisfied. This is now covered by the **CJA 2003, s. 139**. The common law test specified that a memory refreshing document requested by a witness giving oral evidence had to be contemporaneous. The new test allows a witness to consult a document if it was made when his recollection is likely to have been 'significantly better' when he made or verified it. In other words, the court will look at the quality of the evidence in the notebook rather than the time it was made. However, as Choo points out (2012, p. 74) the previous rule was 'liberally interpreted'. In *R v McAfee (John James)* [2006] EWCA Crim 2914 the Court of Appeal examined the question of what is meant by the witness's recollection being 'significantly better' when they make their note. The defence may argue that a note made shortly before the trial and many months after the incident would not satisfy this provision. The court noted that contemporaneity was not required and that the trial judge was best placed to pronounce on whether a witness's memory when he made the statement was likely to have been significantly better than when testifying. In this case the court approved the trial judge's decision to allow the memory-refreshing police document made four-and-a-half months after the incident. The court stated that it would not lightly interfere with the first instance judge's decision. They also stated that, 'A judge must have a residual discretion to refuse a **section 139** application even if the statutory conditions are met. But there were no good reasons for doing so in this case. The prosecution were entitled to present their best case to the jury. That is the object of many of the provisions in the **2003 Act**.' It is likely therefore that Daniel will be able to refresh his memory from his note.

The notebook should be handed to the defence counsel or the court so that it may be inspected and the witness cross-examined on its contents. The defence counsel can request that the jury be shown the notebook if it is necessary for the determination of an issue: *R v Bass* [1953] 1 QB 680.

Under the common law rule, which survives the **CJA 2003**, the notebook could not be evidence in the case. But it should be available for inspection by the defence. *R v Sekhon* (1987) 85 Cr App R 19 sets out guidelines whereby memory-refreshing documents may be shown to the jury to help them follow the cross-examination. If the cross-examiner only refers to parts of the document which the witness used in refreshing his memory then the party calling the witness cannot require that the document becomes evidence. If, however, the cross-examination uses other parts the witness has not relied upon then the party calling the witness may insist that the document becomes evidence (*Senat v Senat* [1965] P 172). Daniel should be advised that **s. 120(3) of the CJA 2003** would then apply and the document would be evidence not only of consistency, as under the common law, but of the truth of its contents. However, under **s. 122 CJA 2003** the document must not accompany the jury when they retire to consider their verdict unless all parties to the proceedings agree or the judge gives his permission. The risk is the jury will attach disproportionate weight to what is a hearsay statement. In *R v Hulme* [2007] 1 Cr App R 26 the Court of Appeal held that the judge had been wrong to allow a witness statement to be taken into the jury room.

(c) Previous consistent statements

The general rule is that a witness may not give evidence, during examination in-chief, of a previous consistent statement. The out-of-court statement may be excluded for two reasons: first, the rule against hearsay and second, the rule against narrative. The reason for the rule is that it can be easily manufactured; it adds nothing to the witness's testimony and is usually self-serving: *Corke v Corke and Cook* [1958] P 93 and *R v Roberts* [1942] 1 All ER 187. Although there are a number of exceptions to the general rule, the only one which may apply here is where the accused has made a statement on being accused of the crime. Where the accused makes an admission on being accused of the crime, this is admissible in evidence of the facts stated therein. Where the accused denies the charge, the statement, whilst it may be admissible in some circumstances, for instance to show the accused's reaction when taxed with incriminating facts, is admissible only to show consistency of the accused's testimony and goes only to credit. It is not evidence of the facts stated therein: *R v Storey* (1968) 52 Cr App R 334 and *R v Pearce* (1979) 69 Cr App R 365. The CJA 2003 has not affected this exception to the rule against narrative.

Is the statement exculpatory?

One issue is whether Henry's statement is taken to be exculpatory, inculpatory or mixed (see **Chapter 6**). It is assumed here that the defence is arguing that the statement is an exculpatory one. Henry should be warned that not all previous consistent exculpatory statements will be admitted. In *R v Tooke* **(1989) 90 Cr App R 417** a written statement was not admitted since it did not add to a previous oral statement. It is important that Henry appears to have made the statement promptly. In *R v Lowe* **[2003] EWCA Crim 3182** the Court of Appeal held that a statement which was made over four months after arrest was not admissible since it could not have been evidence of reaction to the accusation. On the facts, however, it is likely that the court may allow Henry to give evidence of his prior statement which he made in the police station, as evidence of his reaction when confronted at the police station and to support his not guilty plea. The statement is not evidence of the facts stated in it. However, Henry's statement may alternatively be admissible as evidence of the truth of its contents under **s. 114(1)(d) of the CJA 2003** if the 'interests of justice' test is satisfied.

Question 2

Frank is prosecuted for dangerous driving after he knocked down a pedestrian, Jennice. Jennice alleges that as she was crossing Middlefield Road, Frank hit her with his car, causing a fracture of her left leg. She states that Frank was driving his car at an excessive speed and without due care and attention. Frank's defence is that Jennice lurched out onto the road suddenly and appeared to be drunk. He was unable to avoid hitting her. He admits that the accident took place and the injuries suffered by Jennice.

Advise Frank on the following evidential matters:

(a) Dr Lee gives evidence for the prosecution that when he examined Jennice in the casualty department where she was brought after the accident, there were no signs of recent intoxication. Can he be cross-examined on the fact that he had told Lisa, a nurse at the hospital the next day, that Jennice appeared to be drunk when she was brought into the hospital? Can evidence in rebuttal be called if Dr Lee denies the conversation?

(b) Herbert, an eyewitness to the accident, has given evidence that he saw Frank driving erratically immediately prior to the accident. Can he be cross-examined that he was convicted of perjury seven years ago and that he had attempted suicide a few months ago?

(c) Before the trial, Paul, the manager of Toasters, a wine bar, has given a written statement to Frank's solicitor. In the statement, Paul said that he served Jennice three to four Singapore Slings, a cocktail, an hour before the accident. When testifying for the defence, he states that Jennice came into the wine bar to use the ladies room and did not have anything to drink. What use can be made of his written statement?

Commentary

The first issue here is whether a witness can be cross-examined as to a previous inconsistent statement and the evidential value to be put on such a statement. The second question involves the issue as to the admissibility of the previous convictions of a witness and the effect that it has on his testimony. The final issue relates to the question as to what the defence can do where the witness called by him does not come up to proof and the value of the testimony or the previous statement made by the witness.

Answer plan

(a) • Admissibility of previous inconsistent statement and its evidential value—**ss. 4 and 5 Criminal Procedure Act 1865** and **s. 119 CJA 2003**.

   • Admissibility of previous convictions of a witness—**s. 6 Criminal Procedure Act 1865** and **s. 100 CJA 2003**.

(b) • Application of **Rehabilitation of Offenders Act 1974** to criminal trials.

   • Application of **ss. 98 and 100** on bad character of non-defendant witness.

(c) • Witness does not come up to proof.

   • Position of 'hostile witnesses'—**s. 3 Criminal Procedure Act 1865**; **s. 119 CJA 2003**; *Joyce v Joyce* **(2005)**, *R v Gibbons* **[2008]**.

Suggested answer

(a) The issue here is whether Dr Lee's conversation with Lisa, which is inconsistent with his present testimony, can be admitted into evidence. This is governed by **s. 4 of the Criminal Procedure Act 1865** setting out the procedure to be followed. This states that if a witness is asked during cross-examination about a prior statement (whether oral or written) made by him which is inconsistent with his present testimony, and does not admit that he had made such a previous inconsistent statement, the cross-examining party may adduce evidence of that inconsistent statement. Before the inconsistent statement can be adduced into evidence, the procedure laid out in **s. 4** has to be complied with, namely, the circumstances in which the previous inconsistent statement was made must be put to the witness and he must then be asked whether he had made such a statement.

Thus, in this case, if Dr Lee denies making such a statement, evidence of the prior inconsistent statement can be adduced. This may take the form of calling Lisa as a rebuttal witness. If, on the other hand, Dr Lee admits making the statement, then the normal practice would be to ask him whether he still wishes to stand by his previous testimony. In most instances, when faced with such a situation, it is unlikely that the witness will stand by his previous testimony.

The next question is the value to be placed on the previous inconsistent statement. On the facts of this case, the previous inconsistent statement will help the defence's case that Jennice lurched suddenly onto the road, possibly because she was intoxicated. This would be the case if the previous statement is admissible as evidence of the facts stated in it. The **Criminal Justice Act (CJA) 2003, s. 119(1)** provides that a prior inconsistent statement which is admissible into evidence, is admissible as evidence of the facts stated therein and is not merely evidence of the consistency or inconsistency of the witness. Thus the statement by Dr Lee to Lisa would then be admissible as evidence of the fact that Jennice was intoxicated when she received treatment in the hospital.

(b) Presumably Hector will be a witness for the prosecution. Frank should be advised that under **s. 6 of the Criminal Procedure Act 1865**, a witness may be questioned as to whether he or she has been convicted of any felony or misdemeanour, and if he or she denies it or does not admit that fact, or refuses to answer the question, evidence can be adduced to prove such a conviction. Although the **Rehabilitation of Offenders Act 1974** does not apply to criminal proceedings, the court will take into account the length of time since the conviction. The court does retain a discretion not to allow the cross-examination of a witness regarding his or her previous spent conviction. The judge in considering whether to exercise his or her discretion should weigh the degree of relevance of the spent conviction against the prejudice it may cause against the witness. An unfair degree of prejudice may lead to an unfair trial.

Thus, whether Herbert can be questioned about his conviction for perjury would depend in part on whether it is a spent conviction under the **1974 Act** and whether, if it was a spent conviction, the court would be prepared to allow the cross-examination about it on the basis that justice could not otherwise be done. That is a question for the court to decide. However, bearing in mind that the conviction is for perjury, even if it is spent, it is likely that the court may allow the cross-examination of Herbert regarding it.

It should also be noted that it is a matter of judicial discretion how far the cross-examination of a witness may go about his or her previous conviction under **s. 6 of the Criminal Procedure Act 1865**. If Herbert does deny the previous conviction, this can be proved by a certificate from the court of the conviction under **s. 73 of the Police and Criminal Evidence Act 1984 (PACE)**.

However, Frank should be aware that cross-examination of witnesses in criminal proceedings is also now limited by **ss. 98 and 101 of the CJA 2003. Section 101(1)** provides that in criminal proceedings the bad character (as defined in **s. 98**) of a person other than the defendant is admissible if and only if it is important explanatory evidence, or it has substantial probative value in relation to a matter which is a matter in issue in the proceedings and is of substantial importance in the context of the case as a whole, or all parties to the proceedings agree to the evidence being admitted. A perjury conviction clearly falls within the **s. 98** definition as 'the commission of an offence or other reprehensible behaviour'. It is arguably relevant evidence in questioning Hector's credibility. However, attempting suicide probably does not fall within s. 98 as 'other reprehensible behaviour' and is prima facie admissible under the common law although its relevance would first have to be established (see *R v Hall-Chung* [2007] EWCA Crim 3429).

It is arguable that the perjury conviction would only be admissible if Frank denied that he was driving erratically and then it has substantial probative value in relation to an important issue.

In *R v Weir* [2006] 1 WLR 1885 the Court of Appeal held that the trial judge had erred in admitting evidence of a previous caution administered to a witness since it did not have substantial probative value in relation to the witness's credibility. However, in the light of a very strong summing-up on the defendant's convictions the conviction was not unsafe.

Thus, an application to have Herbert's convictions admitted would have to be made to the court. Here it is arguable that the perjury conviction has 'substantial probative value' and is admissible under s. 100(1)(b) in that it is of 'substantial importance in the context of the case as a whole'.

(c) In this situation, Frank should be advised that his witness, Paul, is not coming up to proof. The general rule is that a party may not impeach his own witness. This means that Frank cannot call evidence from another source to show that Paul is lying, forgetful or mistaken. He can, of course, call other witnesses who may be able to testify as to what Jennice drank at the wine bar, if there were any. The court must be satisfied that Paul is a hostile witness and not one who does not give evidence through fear (*R v Honeyghon and Sayles* (1999) Crim LR 221).

There are, however, exceptions to this general rule. In order for the exceptions to apply, it is necessary to determine whether Paul is merely an unfavourable witness or a hostile one. In the former case, the witness is one who is not coming up to proof whether because they are mistaken, foolish or forgetful. In such a case, the witness cannot be attacked as to his credit or challenged as to his previous inconsistent statement. However, if the witness is regarded as a hostile witness, at common law the previous inconsistent statement can be put to him and leading questions to test his memory and perception may be asked. A witness is regarded as hostile when he is not desirous of telling the truth at the instance of the party calling him.

In view of the fact that his previous statement to the solicitor is clear and unambiguous, it is possible that Paul may be treated as a hostile witness. However, this is a matter for the judge to decide. The procedure in such a situation is for counsel to make an application to the judge, to treat the witness as hostile. The judge can decide whether the witness is hostile by looking at the prior statement, the witness's demeanour and attitude.

If the judge decides that Paul is a hostile witness, then he may be asked leading questions and may be cross-examined by the defence as to his previous inconsistent statement (see *R v Thompson* (1976) 64 Cr App R 96) under s. 3 of the Criminal Procedure Act 1865 (which applies only in cases of hostile witnesses; see *Greenough v Eccles* (1859) 5 CB (NS) 786, a case on the identically worded s. 22 of the Common Law

Procedure Act 1854), before the defence can prove that Paul made a previous inconsistent statement, he must be reminded of the circumstances of the previous statement sufficient to designate the particular occasion and must be asked whether or not he has made such a statement.

If Paul refuses to admit making such a statement, **s. 3 of the 1865 Act** allows the party calling the witness, the defence in this case, to prove that such a statement was made by the witness. The Act sets out the procedure for cross-examining a hostile (described here as 'adverse') witness on 'a statement inconsistent with his present testimony'. This will apply whether Paul gives testimony that differs from the earlier statement or says nothing at all (*R v Thompson* (1976) **64 Cr App R 96**). Paul may then be cross-examined on the earlier statement. **Section 4** deals with proof of 'contradictory statements of adverse witnesses' and **s. 5** with cross-examination on a previous statement in writing.

The prosecution should be reminded that cross-examination is only allowed on previous inconsistent statements on matters relevant to facts in issue—not to those on credibility (*R v C & B* [2003] **EWCA Crim 29**).

In *Joyce v Joyce* [2005] **EWCA Crim 1785** the Court of Appeal considered the impact of **s. 119 of the CJA 2003**, which allows previous inconsistent statements to be admissible as evidence of the truth of any matter stated even if the maker of the statement does not accept that it was true. This is a change from the previous law, which only allowed such statements to be evidence of lack of credibility. The case involved eyewitnesses who had given pre-trial statements identifying the accused. However, they retracted their statements at trial and became hostile witnesses. The judge sanctioned the admission of their pre-trial identification under **s. 119** as evidence of their truth, on which the jury could decide. The Court of Appeal upheld the decision that the jury could 'evaluate, separately and together the quality of the three witnesses' oral evidence and to be able to rely, if they thought fit on the terms of the original statement.' The defence may also rely on *R v Gibbons* [2008] **EWCA Crim 1574**. The Court of Appeal held that under **s. 11 CJA 2003** the jury could decide whether the contents of a prior statement of a hostile witness were true even where the witness did not accept making it. Finally, as *Gibbons* makes clear, even if Paul is not declared a hostile witness **s. 119** would allow the statement to be adduced as evidence of its truth if he admits making it. The court must, however, consider fairness to the proceedings in terms of admissibility, **ss. 125 and 126 CJA 2003, s. 78 PACE**. It is important that the correct directions should be given to the jury about relying on previous inconsistent statements for the truth of their contents (see also *R v Billingham* [2009] **EWCA Crim 19**).

? Question 3

John is charged with the attempted rape of Patricia. He denies the offence and claims that he was chatting innocently to her about her dog. He claims that she invented the attempted rape.

(a) Advise on the likely admissibility of evidence from Patricia's flatmate that Patricia came home sobbing and when asked what was the matter said she had been 'assaulted a week ago'.

(b) When first arrested John makes the claim that he stopped Patricia simply to chat about her dog when she was out walking. He says he had an identical breed of dog. The prosecution accuse him of having made this up. Advise the defence.

(c) The defence wish also to call evidence that Patricia had made previous allegations of sexual assault which turned out to be fabricated. Are they likely to succeed?

Commentary

This question involves the types of questions that the prosecution and the defence can ask either in examination-in-chief or in cross-examination in a rape trial. In part (a), it will be necessary to discuss the general rule with respect to the admissibility of prior consistent statements and the exception to that rule in cases involving sexual offences. In the next part of the question, the discussion is centred around the question as to whether evidence can be given of John's immediate reaction and his subsequent admission. Students, especially for part (c), would have to be familiar with **s. 41 of the YJCEA 1999**.

Answer plan

(a) • Admissibility of previous consistent statement.

     • Exception for recent complaints by certain witnesses and conditions of admissibility— **ss. 120 and 114 CJA 2003**.

(b) • Admissibility of John's statement to rebut allegation of fabrication—**s. 120(2) CJA 2003**.

(c) • Permissible cross-examination of rape victims on previous sexual history and previous false allegations.

     • **YJCEA, s. 41**.

Suggested answer

(a) The general common law rule was that a witness may not be asked in examination-in-chief whether he or she had made a prior statement, either oral or written, consistent with his or her testimony. The reason for the rule is that it can be easily manufactured, it adds nothing to the witness's testimony and is usually self serving: *Corke v Corke and*

Cook [1958] P 93 and *R v Roberts* [1942] 1 All ER 187. There are a number of exceptions to this general rule. It may therefore be possible for evidence to be given of Patricia's statement to her flatmate under one of these exceptions in statute which replaced the common law in this area.

In cases involving sexual offences, evidence of a recent complaint by the victim could be given even though this was a self-serving statement: *R v Osborne* [1905] 1 KB 551. It was suggested by Holmes J in *Commonwealth v Cleary* (1898) 172 Mass 175, the reason this exception was permitted is because of the 'survival of the ancient requirement that a woman should make hue and cry as a preliminary to an appeal of rape.' The recent complaint could be oral or written and included a note given by mistake to a friend: *R v B* [1997] Crim LR 220.

In order for the complaint to be admissible, it had to have been made voluntarily (i.e. it should not have been elicited by questions of a leading and intimidating nature) and at the first reasonable opportunity that offers itself. Whether these conditions were satisfied was a question of fact depending on the circumstances of the case. This would include the character of the complainant and the relationship between the complainant and the person to whom she might have complained. In *R v Valentine* [1996] 2 Cr App R 213, the Court of Appeal recognised that some complainants might find it impossible to complain to the first person they encounter after the alleged attack. (In *R v Birks* [2002] EWCA Crim 3091 a complaint made from six months to a year after the final attack in a series of sexual assaults was too long.) The requirement that the complaint had to be made voluntarily did not rule out the complaint being procured by questioning, but only where the questions were of a leading and intimidating manner. Thus questions such as 'Why are you crying?' would be permitted but not 'Did A sexually assault you?' In *R v Osborne*, a complaint by a girl of 13 of an indecent assault to a friend was permitted where she was asked 'Why are you going home?' This area is now covered by s. 120 of the Criminal Justice Act (CJA) 2003. Section 120(4)(b) admits a statement which consists of a complaint about conduct made by a witness (whether to a person in authority or not) who claims to be a person against whom an offence has been committed. The statement must consist of a complaint made by the witness about conduct which would, if proved, constitute the offence or part of the offence. It should not be made as a result of a threat or a promise and before the statement is adduced the witness must give oral evidence in connection with its subject matter. Whilst giving evidence the witness must indicate that to the best of his belief he made the statement, and that to the best of his belief it states the truth. There are two significant departures from the common law; s. 120(8) provides that it is irrelevant that the complaint was elicited by a leading question. The requirement that the complaint was made as soon as reasonably practicable was abolished in 2009.

On the facts of the present case, therefore, it would appear that Patricia's complaint to her flatmate would be admissible. The prosecution may rely on *R v Xhabri* [2005] EWCA Crim 3135. In this case the complainant alleged she had been raped and forced to work as a prostitute. She had made a number of telephone calls to her parents and others about her plight and the question was whether the evidence of the receivers of the calls could be received. At trial the judge allowed them in under **s. 120(5)** (previous identification), **s. 120(6)** (a fresh statement when the witness could not be expected to recall) and **s. 120(7)** (recent complaints).

The court held that **s. 120(7)** was rightly applied but not **s. 120(5) and (6)**. The court also noted that the evidence could have been admitted under **s. 114(1)(d)**. There was no conflict with **art. 6**. The hearsay provisions under the statute applied to both defence and prosecution and so the principle of the equality of arms was upheld. **Article 6(3)(d)** did not give a defendant an absolute right to examine every witness whose testimony was adduced against him. The touchstone was whether fairness of the trial required that in the present case almost all the hearsay evidence derived directly or indirectly from the complainant. She was available for cross-examination and so this satisfied the requirements of **art. 6(3)(d)**.

In *R v O* **[2006] 2 Cr App R 27**, the Court of Appeal held that **s. 120(7)** allows more than one complaint to be admitted. It also stated that 'this is no longer a question of considering whether a complaint is made as soon as could be reasonably expected after the alleged complaint, which is a different test.' The complaint if admitted will be evidence of the truth of its contents, as an exception to the rule against hearsay.

(b) The first question to address is whether the prosecution is simply arguing that John should not be believed or whether it is alleging he has made up this explanation. If it is the latter then the rule against the admissibility of previous consistent statements applies. In *R v Oyesiku* **(1971) 56 Cr App R 240** it was held that a previous statement may be admissible to disprove the accusation of 'recent fabrication'. The statement was not evidence of the truth of its contents but of the credibility of the witness (*R v Y* **[1995] Crim LR 155**). This area of law, however, has been changed by **s. 120(2) CJA 2003**. Admissibility is not affected. That is a matter for the judge. However, this status of the evidence is changed. In *R v Athwal* **[2009] EWCA Crim 789** the Court of Appeal considered the relationship between common law principles and the **CJA 2003**. In that case defence counsel made an allegation against a prosecution witness and the trial judge applied *Oyesiku* but did not consider **s. 114(1)(d) and s. 120(1)(2) CJA 2003**. Under the latter provision 'if a previous statement by the witness is admitted as evidence to rebut a suggestion that his oral evidence has been fabricated, that statement is admissible as evidence of any matter stated of which oral evidence by the witness would be admissible'. Alternatively, the statement would have been admitted under the inclusionary discretion under **s. 114**. Thus John is advised to rely on **s. 120(2)** which would admit his previous statement as evidence of the truth of its contents.

The Court of Appeal in *Athwal* emphasised that it was not necessary to consider how 'recently' the account had been fabricated, as was the issue under the common law. Maurice Kay LJ stated (at para. 58), 'There is no margin in the length of time. The touchstone is whether the evidence may fairly assist the jury in ascertaining where the truth lies. It is for the trial judge to preserve the balance of fairness and to ensure that unjustified excursions into self-corroboration are not permitted, whether the witness was called by the prosecution or the defence.'

(c) The defence is also claiming that the complainant is making a false allegation and that she has made it before. Here s. 41 may not apply since making a false allegation is not 'sexual behaviour'. This was established in *R v MH* [2002] Crim LR 73. The Court of Appeal set out guidelines for questioning on false allegations in *R v C & B* [2003] EWCA Crim 29. The defence should establish that the previous allegations were made and were false and that there is an evidentiary basis for the claim.

But there is the question of whether the proof of falsity of the previous allegation is supported by evidence other than previous sexual behaviour. If proof of falsity requires questions on sexual behaviour, then s. 41 would apply. In *R v H* [2003] EWCA Crim 2367 the court observed: 'However, it has been established that the fact that a complainant has fabricated allegations of sexual conduct in the past would not be prohibited by **section 41(4)** as the questions would not be about "sexual behaviour" but about lies.'

John must be warned that there should be a proper evidential basis for the assertion that Patricia has made previous false allegations. As the court in *R v T* [2001] EWCA Crim 1877 accepted even this would not 'provide a watertight guarantee' that evidence about prior sexual behaviour as opposed to that about allegedly false allegations would be excluded.

The courts took a restrictive approach in *R v E* [2004] EWCA Crim 1313 in holding there was no evidential basis for cross-examination on previously false allegations.

However, in *R v Garaxo (Shino)* [2005] EWCA Crim 1170 the Court of Appeal held that the trial judge should have allowed cross-examination on two previous allegations of sexual assault made by the complainant. Although the judge held there was insufficient evidence that these were untrue the Court of Appeal noted that, depending on the answers given by the complainant, a jury could have concluded the allegations had been false. If the defence wish to cross-examine on previous false allegations they may have to satisfy the conditions of s. 100 CJA 2003. The non-defendant witness can only be questioned on bad character on the grounds set out in the statute which set a high test for admissibility and which also requires leave of the court. However, Patricia should note that s. 112(3)(b) CJA 2003 provides that s. 100 does not affect the exclusion of evidence under s. 41 on grounds other than the fact that it is evidence of a person's bad character.

Thus, whether s. 41 applies or not depends on the circumstances of the previous complaints which the defence claim have been made by Patricia. **Section 41 of the Youth Justice and Criminal Evidence Act 1999 (YJCEA)** provides that if at trial a person is charged with a sexual offence no evidence can be adduced nor questions asked in cross-examination about any sexual behaviour of the victim without leave of the court. **Section 41(2)** makes it clear that the court will not grant leave unless it is satisfied that the evidence is of the kind specified in s. 41(3) which applies where the issue is other than consent, as is the case here. In short, in order to have the false allegations admitted John will have to satisfy the court that he is not trying to bring in questions about sexual behaviour. More information is required to establish whether the perfidious allegations would also reveal sexual behaviour which satisfies the high tests in s. 41(3) YJCEA 1999.

Question 4

'Rather than tightening up the admissibility criterion for sexual history evidence—as was Parliament's intention—it seems as though [s. 41 YJCEA 1999] has actually loosened it.'

(Redmayne, 'Myths, Relationships and Conferences. The New Problems of Sexual History' (2003) 7 E & P 75 at 95.)

How far do the current evidential rules in relation to rape victims ensure fairness?

Commentary

Essay questions are not usually set on issues in the course of trial. One possible question, however, on this subject relates to the effect of the new **s. 41 of the YJCEA 1999**, which replaced **s. 2 of the Sexual Offences (Amendment) Act 1976**. It is important that students are able to demonstrate to the examiner a clear understanding of the Act and the courts' approach to this statutory provision. You should assess whether the **Human Rights Act 1998** has had an impact in this area, particularly in the light of *R v A* **[2001] UKHL 25**. It is important that you adopt an analytical approach and have a clear structure for your answer.

Answer plan

- Background to reform of law in 1999 and weakness of **s. 2 Sexual Offences (Amendment) Act 1976**. Question requires an analysis of fairness to defendant, complainant and public.
- Particular difficulties of rape trials where there is usually no third party witness and where what are called 'myths' of female behaviour are prevalent (see *R v Seaboyer* **(1991) 83 DLR 193**).
- Analysis of relevant provisions, **s. 41 YJCEA**, Special Measures, removal of corroboration rules, **s. 100 CJA 2003**.
- Arguments to suggest that is unfairness to defendant—high test **s. 41**.
- Arguments to suggest there is unfairness to complainant, e.g. low conviction rate, loosening of admissibility of prior sexual behaviour after *R v A* **(2001)**.
- Conclusion: additional provisions needed, see academic argument: Temkin, Redmayne, Dennis.

Suggested answer

The history of the law of evidence and rape cases illustrates the difficulties of achieving trials which are demonstrably fair. That history largely turns on two areas. These are: first, the exercise of judicial discretion to admit evidence of prior sexual behaviour of the complainant and Parliament's attempts to control that discretion; secondly, the law has attempted to give particular protection to complainants in these cases in relation to the way they give evidence, and here the protection of anonymity and the availability of protection such as screens and video links have been provided. Despite a plethora of measures in recent decades there remains ongoing controversy in this area, not least because the conviction rate for rape is considered by many to be unacceptably small (the recent Stern Review cited this as 6 per cent). The question of fairness is also complex since many would argue that while defendants have the right to a fair trial victims are only entitled to courtesy and humane treatment.

Against this there is a powerful lobby for the installation of rights of victims even where these might appear to take away those of the defendant.

There was undoubtedly general agreement that **s. 27 of the Sexual Offences (Amendment) Act 1976** was ripe for reform. It had been introduced as a result of the Heilbron Committee report (Report of the Advisory Group on the Law and Rape, Cm 6352, 1975) and recommended changes to the common law which allowed the victim to be cross-examined on her previous sexual relationships and evidence to be called to contradict her. This was especially so where it was alleged that the victim was a prostitute or was a person who was 'notorious for want of sexual chastity'. The committee recommended changes which resulted in **s. 2 of the 1976 Act**. This drew a distinction between questions or evidence concerning the victim's sexual relationship with the accused and with other men. In the case of the latter, leave of the court had to be obtained before the victim could be asked such questions.

The shortcomings in **s. 2 of the 1976 Act**, were illustrated in *R v Viola* [1982] 3 All ER 73. Temkin ([1993] Crim LR 3) criticised *Viola* in that it allowed evidence of sexual history, which she argued was scarcely relevant. She was of the view that the Court of Appeal in *Viola* attributed too much relevance and undue significance to such evidence. Further, the court's approach to **s. 2** and the issue of leave was not necessarily consistent: *R v Barton* (1987) 85 Crim App R 5, compared with *Viola*. In *Barton*, the court suggested that the judge's decision whether to grant leave was an exercise of the judge's discretion but in *Viola*, the court suggested that it was an exercise of the court's judgment. A significant body of comment (e.g. Sue Lee's *Carnal Knowledge: Rape on Trial* (London: Penguin, 1996)) criticised the operation of **s. 2 of the Sexual Offences (Amendment) Act 1976**. Research showed that the cases which were the most difficult to prove were those where there had been some prior relationship between the complainant and the accused. **Section 2 of the 1976 Act** was replaced by **s. 41 of the Youth Justice and Criminal Evidence Act (YJCEA) 1999**. This introduced broader provisions to this area of law and, unlike the earlier law, applies to any sexual offence as defined in **s. 62 of the 1999 Act**. It provides that if at trial a person is charged with a sexual offence, no evidence can be adduced nor question asked in cross-examination about any sexual behaviour of the victim except with the leave of the court. **Section 41(2)** makes it clear that the court will not grant leave, unless it is satisfied that the evidence is of a kind specified in **s. 41(3) or (5)**, and a refusal of leave might render unsafe a conclusion of the jury on any relevant issues in the case. This is a very high test. **Section 41(3)** deals with evidence relevant to an issue in the case and a distinction is drawn between issues that are issues of consent and those that are not. Criticism of the Act in terms of fairness fell into the following areas. First, the Act arguably is not fair to the defendant in that it does not draw a distinction between questions relating to the victim's sexual relationship with the accused and other men. The emphasis of **s. 41** is on the relevance of the evidence in order for leave to be granted.

Section 41(3) provides that where the issue is consent and **s. 41(2)** is satisfied, leave to adduce or cross-examine on previous sexual behaviour may be allowed in situations where it occurred at or about the same time as the event (**s. 41(3)(b)**) or is so similar to the event which forms the basis of the charge against the accused (**s. 41(3)(c)**) that it cannot be explained on the basis of a coincidence. The purpose of this is clearly to restrict evidence, which is relevant to the issue of whether there was consent. It has been argued that the prohibition contained in **s. 41** as well as the specific prohibition on cross-examination by the accused in person (**ss. 34–39**) contravenes the accused's right to a fair trial. The Government claimed that it had taken account of the Canadian case of *R v Seaboyer* [1991] 2 SCR 577, where a provision which allowed sexual history evidence only in limited and predetermined circumstances was held to be a violation of the right of the accused to a fair trial.

Arguably, the statute is an instance where the desire to balance the rights of defendants and victims has tipped the scales too heavily and jeopardises the integrity of the criminal trial.

The issue was referred to the House of Lords (see *R v A (No. 2)* [2001] 2 WLR 1546). Lord Steyn pointed out that, 'The genesis of the problem before the House was that **s. 41** imposed identical exclusionary provisions in respect of a complainant's sexual experiences with the accused as with other men.' This posed 'an acute problem of proportionality'. The House concluded that it was a matter for the trial judge in each case to actually determine whether or not the evidence was sufficiently probative to merit admission. In a judgment which showed the impact of the **Human Rights Act**, it declared that since ordinary canons of statutory interpretation of **s. 41** did not allow admission of such evidence, the section should be interpreted in the light of **s. 3 of the Human Rights Act 1998** to allow compliance with the provisions of **art. 6**.

In a unanimous judgment a number of the speeches indicated that excluding such evidence might jeopardise the fairness of the trial. Lord Steyn declared that evidence may be 'so relevant to the issue of consent that to exclude it would endanger the fairness of the trial'. It is indeed the case that relevance depends on context and that legislating too narrowly on it may be unwise. The House of Lords addressed the problem by stretching the interpretation of **s. 41(3)(c)**, the similar facts section, to allow questioning on the previous sexual encounter. They applied **s. 3 of the Human Rights Act 1998**, which as Lord Steyn put it 'requires the court to subordinate the niceties of the language of **s. 41(3)(c)** and in particular, the touchstone of coincidence, to broader considerations of relevance judged by logical and common sense criteria of time and circumstances'.

The House's approach has been criticised as unprincipled by a number of commentators who suggest that the reasoning is tortuous and that a declaration of incompatibility would have been preferable. Criticism of the current 'rape-shield' provisions centres on this landmark judgment and its interpretation in later cases. Redmayne is one of the critics who deplores in particular the use of similar fact concepts and the 'coincidence' test as it was applied in *R v A*. He noted (2003, p. 100) that 'once the requirement that the coincidence be relativised to the complainant's non-consent is loosened the section lurches back to unrestricted admissibility.' In a contentious argument Redmayne suggests that the reason for the use of similar fact concepts in relation to prior sexual behaviour is the desire to avoid concentration on probative value. He writes (p. 90), 'If you are convinced that unchaste women are no more likely than other women to consent to intercourse, then you will be loath to sign up to an admissibility test which refers to probative value, because it might suggest that sexual history generally does have probative value on the issue of consent.'

In *R v Mukadi* [2003] EWCA Crim 3765 the weakness of the 'coincidence' test was displayed. The Court of Appeal held that evidence that the complainant had some hours before the alleged rape climbed into the car of an older male driver and exchanged telephone numbers with him should have been admitted. As Redmayne points out, it is difficult to see why the argument that she found men attractive could be used to suggest she had consented to sex with the defendant.

The current law can be criticised therefore in moving to greater admissibility of prior sexual behaviour with what Redmayne has called 'an unstable approach' (p. 100) in that it is logically weak.

Special Measures Directions are arguably a more generally acceptable way of protecting complainants, since they are automatically assumed to be in 'fear and distress' (s. 17(4) YJCEA 1999) and entitled to measures such as screens in court. However, this again may be unfair to the defendant since it might impinge on the jury's perception of the case and also hamper meaningful cross-examination. The measures contrast with those available to vulnerable defendants. The complainant in sexual cases is treated differently from other victims. In some ways she is more protected, as this account has shown; in others she is trusted, for example by the removal of corroboration warnings in 1994. Overall, however, it has been suggested that the problem of the low conviction rate is caused not so much by evidential provisions which are unfair to victims but by judicial and social attitudes. Even after three decades of statutory changes, the position is still contentious.

Kelly, Temkin and Griffiths, in the Home Office Report on the operation of this law, give some figures on applications under s. 41. Defence applications were made in one-quarter of the trials studied and two-thirds were granted. More applications were made where a pre-existing relationship between the complainant and the defendant is claimed and these applications were granted more often.

Dennis (2006, p. 869) comments, 'Defence lawyers do not generally come well out of this report; they are accused at various points of evading the legislation by not making necessary applications, or flouting the judges' rulings, or of using devious ploys to attack the complainant's credibility in contravention of s. 41(4). Such judgments will inevitably be contested.' Dennis acknowledges, however, that 'there is clearly still scope for improvement, even if one does not support the authors' recommendations for further tightening of the section.' In a lengthy reflection on the current state of the law in this area, Choo (2012, pp. 392–393) suggests the discussion needs broadening beyond just a review of **s. 41**. He points out that it is not simply a matter of 'tighter legislation'. 'What is required is a change in judicial attitudes, possibly through better judicial training, as well as a change in the attitudes of other lawyers involved in the system.' He calls into question also the very nature of the trial process, particularly the conduct and control of cross-examination. To meet the problem of defence lawyers using various stratagems to circumvent **s. 41**, Choo cites also the proposal from Kelly, Temkin and Griffith (2006, p. viii) that 'A new exception to the rule of exclusion should be inserted into **section 41** allowing for evidence of previous or subsequent sexual behaviour with the accused.' Redmayne's comment thus illustrates the sometimes contradictory and ongoing effects of poorly drafted legislation which has brought some uncertainty and therefore unfairness to the law in this area.

Further reading

Birch, D., 'Rethinking Sexual History Evidence: Proposals for Fairer Trials' [2002] Crim LR 531.

Cook, K., 'Sexual History Evidence: The Defendant Fights Back' (2001) 151 NLJ 1133.

Dennis, I., 'Sexual History Evidence: Evaluating Section 41' [2006] Crim LR 869.

Durston, G., 'Previous (In)Consistent Statements' [2005] Crim LR 206.

Hoyano, L.C.H., 'Striking a Balance between the Rights of Defendants and Vulnerable Witnesses: Will Special Measures Directions Contravene Guarantees of a Fair Trial?' [2001] Crim LR 948.

Kelly, L., Temkin, J. and Griffiths, S., 'Section 41: An Evaluation of New Legislation Limiting Sexual History Evidence in Rape Trials', Home Office Online Report 20/06 (London: Home Office, 2006).

Kibble, N., 'The Sexual History Provisions: Charting a Course Between Inflexible Legislative Rules and Wholly Untrammelled Judicial Discretion' [2000] Crim LR 274.

Kibble, N., 'Judicial Perspectives on the Operation of s. 41' [2005] Crim LR 190, 263.

Redmayne, M., 'Myths, Relationships and Conferences. The New Problems of Sexual History' (2003) 7 E & P 75.

Temkin, J., *Rape and the Legal Process* (Oxford: OUP, 2002).

11

Privilege and public policy

Introduction

This chapter deals with evidence which is excluded for policy or public interest considerations. A party or witness or even a non-participant in the proceedings may refuse to disclose information, papers or answer questions even though such material may have a high degree of relevance and reliability.

As far as privilege is concerned, the areas which are most likely to occur in Evidence courses are privilege against self-incrimination and legal professional privilege. The former includes the right to silence of the defendant (see **Chapter 6**) and the compellability of witnesses (see **Chapter 3**). The privilege against self-incrimination generally is upheld by common law and by implication by **art. 6 of the European Convention on Human Rights (ECHR)**. Note that the privilege does not extend to objects that exist independently of the will of the person from whom it was obtained, such as documents or blood samples. Legal professional privilege is a common law exclusionary rule principle which applies in both civil and criminal proceedings. Communications between a legal professional adviser and his client may not be disclosed. The purpose of the rule which is implicitly but not explicitly contained in **art. 6**, is to ensure that parties to a legal action are not constrained in preparing their case.

Murphy (2011, p. 482) points out that apart from the privilege against self-incrimination and legal professional privilege, 'English law has a distinctly illiberal attitude to the matter of protecting confidential communications from compelled disclosure at the instance of an opponent.' On the other hand, **art. 10 of the ECHR** has had some effect on this area, allowing a limited privilege for journalists with respect to their sources of information (**Contempt of Court Act 1981, s. 10**).

Exclusion of evidence on grounds of public interest immunity (PII) arises where the court, not the parties or witnesses, accepts a duty of non-disclosure for the public good. Primarily, the issue is one of non-disclosure of documents rather than oral testimony. The original objection to the disclosure may be made by the court itself or by any person or body including government departments, even though not taking part in the proceedings. The court will itself scrutinise the claim. There is some conflict of authority on whether the immunity can be waived, though the prevailing view seems to be that this depends on the nature of the document. Those whose disclosure would endanger national security, for example, probably fall outside the category of those that can be waived, whereas those protecting confidentiality in order to promote candour, could fall inside. In fact, PII claims are more often made in civil litigation. The Matrix Churchill trial highlighted the difficulties of applying the doctrine in criminal cases.

Although they are often taught together, you must bear in mind the differences between legal professional privilege and PII as illustrated in **Table 12**.

Your Evidence course may require you to have some knowledge of the complicated area of disclosure in criminal and civil trials. You should be aware, therefore, of the provisions in **s. 3 of the Criminal Procedure and Investigations Act 1996** as amended by the **Criminal Justice Act (CJA) 2003** which covers prosecution disclosure of unused material. Defence disclosure is also governed by this statute. **Rule 31.19(1) of the Civil Procedure Rules (CPR)** covers disclosure in civil proceedings.

Table 12 Public interest immunity and legal process privilege compared characteristics

	PII	LPP
1. Is non-disclosure a duty or a right?	Duty	Right
2. Can non-disclosure be claimed by a non-party?	Yes	No
3. Does the existence of the disputed document have to be disclosed to the other side?	No	Yes
4. Can secondary evidence of the relevant document be adduced?	No	Yes
5. Should disclosure be made in order to prevent a possible miscarriage of justice?	Yes	No

 Question 1

Emily is suing Heathcliff Translation Services for failure to deliver the translation of her novel. Rochester, a Heathcliff employee, is refusing to respond to interrogatories because he fears his involvement in submitting invoices for work that had not been done may expose him and his wife to fraud charges. Rosa, Rochester's wife, worked as a secretary for Heathcliff. At the same time Heathcliff is subject to investigation by the (imaginary) Translators Regulatory Body (TRB), an organisation set up under statute. The TRB argue that Heathcliff do not comply with their minimum standards. The TBA has statutory powers for their inspectors to examine documents and records. Carlyle, the owner of Heathcliff, at first refuses to allow an inspection, claiming his privilege against self-incrimination, but he then allows the search to go ahead. Inspectors examine Carlyle's computers and find evidence of both child pornography and fraudulent business practices. Carlyle asks his lawyer for advice on whether he can prevent the material being handed to the police. James, who works in the lawyers' offices, and who is Emily's brother, sends her a copy. Emily wants to use aspects of the document as part of her case against Heathcliff.

Advise the parties.

Commentary

You have a clue that this question involves privilege in the reference in the question to refusing to give evidence. A more complex question is the refusal to allow inspection of documents. This area has a close affinity with that covered in **Chapter 6** in relation to inferences drawn from silence, but here we are looking at the privilege in relation to civil proceedings. The issue has aroused some recent controversy, which makes it a likely examination question. The second part of the question deals with another head of privilege, namely legal professional privilege between lawyer and client: you need to trace carefully the stages whereby privilege may be threatened but then possibly reclaimed.

Answer plan

- Privilege against self-incrimination in civil proceedings—see *R v Director of the Serious Fraud Office, ex parte Smith* (1993); *C Plc v P (Attorney General intervening)* [2007] 3 WLR 437.
- Does application of privilege deprive the claimant of her remedy—see *AT&T Istel v Tully* (1993)?
- Impact of **Human Rights Act 1998**—*Saunders v UK* (1996).
- Legal professional privilege may apply to note of discussion between Carlyle and company lawyer but does not apply to copies.
- Possibility of *Ashburton v Pape* (1913) injunction.

Suggested answer

Privilege against self-incrimination

These are civil proceedings and Rochester and Carlyle are seeking to exercise the privilege against self-incrimination. The privilege is based on common law and is acknowledged in s. 14(1) Civil Evidence Act 1968. This states: '(1) The right of a person in any legal proceedings to refuse to answer any question or produce any document or thing if to do so would tend to expose that person to proceedings for an offence or for the recovery of a penalty— . . . (b) shall include a like right to refuse to answer any question or produce any document or thing if to do so would tend to expose the husband or wife of that person to proceedings for any such criminal offence or for the recovery of any such penalty.'

The privilege which they seek to exercise is the second of the six aspects identified by Lord Mustill giving the House of Lords judgment in *R v Director of Serious Fraud Office, ex parte Smith* [1993] AC 1, 30: 'A general immunity, possessed by all persons and bodies, from being compelled on pain of punishment to answer questions the answers to which may incriminate them.' The justification for the existence of the privilege, according to Lord Templeman in *AT&T Istel Ltd v Tully* [1993] AC 45, is first that it discourages the ill-treatment of a suspect and second that it discourages the production of dubious confessions.

The scope of the privilege was set out by the Court of Appeal in *Blunt v Park Lane Hotel* [1942] 2 KB 253, 257 per Goddard LJ:

> The rule is that no one is bound to answer any question if the answer thereto would, in the opinion of the judge, have a tendency to expose the deponent to any criminal charge, penalty or forfeiture which the judge regards as reasonably likely to be preferred or sued for.

Its scope was limited in civil proceedings by the **Civil Evidence Act 1968**, which provides by **s. 14(1)** that:

> The right of a person in any legal proceedings other than criminal proceedings to refuse to answer any question or produce any document or thing if to do so would tend to expose that person to proceedings for an offence or for the recovery of a penalty—(a) shall apply only as regards criminal offences under the law of any part of the United Kingdom and penalties provided for by such law.

Refusal to attend to interrogatories

Dealing first with the refusal to respond to interrogatories, it is for Rochester to persuade the judge that the privilege should apply because his answers might expose him and Rosa to criminal proceedings. Thus, in *Rank Film Distribution Ltd v Video Information Centre* [1982] AC 380, the House of Lords upheld the claim for privilege because there was a real danger of a criminal charge of conspiracy to defraud against the defendant.

A consideration which will be relevant to Rochester is how far the application of the privilege may restrict the recovery of money or property by Emily. The House of Lords in *AT&T Istel Ltd v Tully* [1993] AC 45 established that there is no reason to allow a defendant in civil proceedings to rely on it, thus depriving a claimant of his rights, where the defendant's own protection can be secured in other ways. As Lord Templeman said (at p. 53):

It is difficult to see any reason why in civil proceedings the privilege against self-incrimination should be exercisable so as to enable a litigant to refuse relevant and even vital documents which are in his possession or power and which speak for themselves.

Referring to the defendant, Lord Templeman said:

... Mr Tully would be entitled to rely on [the privilege against self-incrimination] if but only if and so far as compliance with the order of Buckley J would provide evidence against him in a criminal trial. There is no reason why the privilege should be blatantly exploited to deprive the plaintiffs of their civil right and remedies if the privilege is not necessary to protect Mr Tully.

In that case a plaintiff was making a claim for damages and repayment of money obtained by fraud. At the same time, a police investigation was set up. The plaintiffs were granted orders requiring the defendants to disclose all dealings concerning the money. The order contained a condition that it would not be used in the prosecution of a criminal offence. The order was later varied and the plaintiff appealed against the variation. The House of Lords varied the order after the Crown Prosecution Service gave an informal assurance that it would not seek to use the divulged material. Thus, if here the judge were assured that the answers would not be relied on in criminal proceedings, there might be no obstacle to the requirement that Rochester answer the questions.

If no such undertaking had been given by the Crown Prosecution Service, Rochester's failure to answer questions involves then a clash between two principles, namely the duty to testify and the privilege against self-incrimination. The question then arises as to whether Emily will succeed in getting an order to compel Rochester to answer, violation of which would be contempt of court. There is no indication that the statute in this case has abolished the privilege. The privilege, therefore, if it applied here, would also cover answers to questions which might tend to implicate Rosa.

In *Versailles Trade Finance Ltd v Clough* [2001] EWCA Civ 1509 the court stressed the need to bear in mind the interests of the claimant, as well as the potential unfairness to the reluctant witness should a criminal trial take place. Whether Rochester was ordered to respond or not would therefore depend on the likelihood of his facing a criminal trial and the extent of the potential prejudice should he do so.

Carlyle and Rochester should be aware, however, that the privilege has been subject to judicial criticism. In *Tully* Lord Templeman stated (at p. 53): 'I regard the privilege against self-incrimination exercisable in civil proceedings as an archaic and unjustifiable survival from the past when the court directs the production of relevant documents and requires the defendant to specify his dealings with the plaintiff's property or money.'

Disclosure of computer material

Recent case law suggests that Carlyle may be on particularly weak ground in resisting disclosure of the material found as a result of the search. In *C Plc v P (Attorney General intervening)* [2007] EWCA Civ 493 the Court of Appeal drew a distinction between response to questions and 'independent' evidence. In this case a search order issued to discover materials relating to copyright infringement unexpectedly revealed child pornography. The court stated (at p. 34): 'The privilege can be invoked to refuse to answer interrogatories or to refuse to disclose matters which are ordinarily discoverable; those matters may be documents or other "things", but independent matters coming to light in the course of executing a proper order of the court are in an altogether different category.'

The pornography could therefore be handed to the police. Carlyle is likely to be the subject of a police investigation.

Legal professional privilege

The final issue in the problem involves the note of the discussion between Carlyle and the company lawyer. Legal professional privilege attaches to certain communications between lawyer and client provided the purpose of the consultation is not the furtherance of crime. Though it is a common law privilege, its scope is authoritatively said to be summarised by **s. 10 of the Police and Criminal Evidence Act 1984**. The House of Lords so held in *R v Central Criminal Court, ex parte Francis & Francis* [1989] AC 346. Carlyle is seeking immunity for communications with the lawyer for the purpose of giving or receiving advice. The fact that the lawyer is employed by the company does not exclude his communications from the scope of the privilege. However, copies of the communications are not privileged: *Calcraft v Guest* [1898] 1 QB 759. But until they are actually before the court, Carlyle could be granted an injunction to restrain the use of the documents, which were clearly obtained in breach of confidence as the Court of Appeal held in *Lord Ashburton v Pape* [1913] 2 Ch 469. However, Carlyle may not need to apply for an injunction. **Rule 31.20 of the Civil Procedure Rules 1998** allows such documents to be used only with permission of the court. Hence, when Emily seeks to use the document, Carlyle may be able to object to its use on the ground of privilege.

? **Question 2**

(a) Brenda is charged with unlawful possession of pornographic photographs discovered after a legally conducted police raid on her flat. Her defence is that they were sent through the post to her unsolicited and she, although disgusted and puzzled, had put them on one side and had forgotten to destroy them. She noted that they purported to be from an organisation called the Partners Exchange. She recalls that a member of her sports club, Archie, who had made several unwelcome sexual advances to her, had mentioned that he belonged to the Partners Exchange, which he said arranged 'interesting introductions'. Having spurned his advances she thought no more of the matter but now she suspects that Archie, who was known to the police as a drug user, may have sent the mail and then informed on her.

Advise Brenda.

(b) Geraldine is facing prosecution for carrying out unauthorised cosmetic surgery at her home. Joan and Jack, police officers, will give evidence about keeping watch on her house and seeing young women emerge heavily bandaged. The prosecution do not wish to reveal that they used Sanjay's shop opposite Geraldine's house for observation. Joan dressed in a milkwoman's uniform and kept the house under surveillance from a fake milk float in the street. Geraldine denies the charge.

Advise Geraldine.

Commentary

English law has long protected the anonymity of informants in matters relating to public prosecutions, or civil proceedings arising from them. There is clearly a public interest in protecting such sources because the information might otherwise dry up. There is a presumption of non-disclosure and it is for the accused to show there is good reason, arising from the defence case, to breach it. In these instances the court must, as in all cases involving PII, balance the rights of the accused against any countervailing public interest in protection of sources. In this question, as in all practical questions, you should state the basic rule, citing if you can authority to back up your point. Then you look at possible exceptions to the principle of protection and consider the question of fact in this case, namely would disclosure help the defendant's case? The question requires you to have knowledge of the specific case law on disclosure of details of police observation. There are only a few cases on this but you should be familiar with them.

Answer plan

(a) • Rule on naming informers—**Marks v Beyfus (1890)**; **Conway v Rimmer (1968)**; **R (on the application of WV) v Crown Prosecution Service [2011] EWHC 2480**.

• Duty of disclosure—**R v Ward (1993)**.

• **Criminal Procedure and Investigations Act 1996**, as amended by the **CJA 2003** and the **CPR 2011**.

• Issue is will identity of informer contribute to issue before the jury? See **R v Slowcombe (1991)**.

• **Article 6** case law on right to a fair trial and the House of Lords guidance in **R v H, R v C [2003] UKHL 3**, on procedure to be followed when prosecution refuse to reveal material. On this last point, **Diagram 9** will help you.

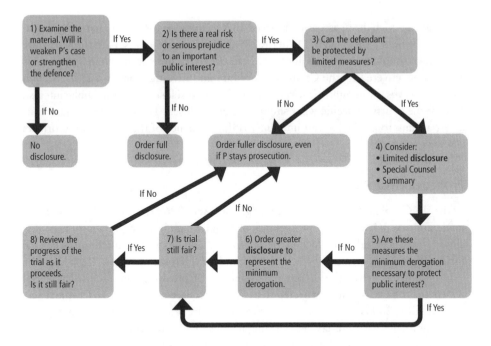

Diagram 9 Procedure to be followed when prosecution refuse to reveal material

Source: *Evidence Concentrate: Law Revision and Study Guide*, 2nd edition, Maureen and John Spencer, Oxford University Press, 2012, p.162.

(b) • How to apply the leading case of **R v Johnson** (1988) to the facts in relation to the observation from the neighbouring shop.

   • Is there any reason not to disclose details of Joan's movements as a fake milkwoman?

 **Suggested answer**

(a) A long-established rule prevents witnesses being asked, or answering, questions about the names of informers or the nature of the information given. The rule applies to criminal proceedings. It has been acknowledged that in criminal proceedings the identity of police informers may be excluded if the public interest requires it. This applies as long as the information is not necessary to establish guilt. Lord Esher MR stated in **Marks v Beyfus** (1890) 25 QBD 494, 498: 'If upon the trial of a prisoner the judge should be of the opinion that the disclosure . . . is not necessary or right in order to shew the prisoner's innocence, then one public policy is in conflict with another public policy and that which says that an innocent man is not to be condemned when his innocence can be proved is the policy that must prevail.' The rationale of the rule was explained by Lord Reid in **Conway v Rimmer** [1968] AC 910, 953: 'The police are carrying on an unending war with criminals many of whom are today highly intelligent. So it is essential there should be no disclosure of anything which might give any useful information to those who organise criminal activities.' However, **R v Ward** [1993] 1 WLR 619 placed the prosecution under an obligation to disclose to the defence all the material on which the prosecution is based. In *R v Horseferry Road Magistrates' Court, ex parte Bennett (No. 2)* [1994] 1 All ER 289 the Divisional Court set out the procedure the Crown should follow for voluntary disclosure of documents in criminal cases. This area is now covered by the **Criminal Procedure and Investigations Act 1996**. **Section 21(2)** preserves the common law rules as to whether disclosure is in the public interest. It is for the courts to decide what should not be disclosed. The prosecution must thus assert a claim to public interest immunity (PII) if evidence of the identity of informers is to be excluded.

Procedure for PII

Under the **Criminal Procedure and Investigations Act 1996** primary disclosure must be made under **s. 3(1)(a)** of any prosecution material which has not previously been disclosed to the accused and which in the prosecutor's opinion might undermine the case for the prosecution against the accused. Secondary disclosure under **s. 7(2)(a)** is to be made following delivery of a defence statement, of previously undisclosed material which might be reasonably expected to assist the accused's defence. The **Criminal Justice Act (CJA) 2003** amended **s. 3(1)(a)** so as to require primary disclosure of any previously undisclosed material 'which might reasonably be considered capable of undermining the case for the prosecution against the accused or of assisting the case for the accused'. The rules are now enshrined in the **Criminal Procedure Rules 2011**.

Brenda may find some support in the principle of the right to a fair trial enshrined in **art. 6(1) ECHR**. The Strasbourg Court had discussed the issue in a number of cases, including *Rowe and Davis v UK* (2000) 30 EHRR 1, *Jasper v UK* (2000) 30 EHRR 441 and *Fitt v UK* (2000) 30 EHRR 480. In *Fitt v UK* (para. 45) the following observation was made:

> The entitlement to disclosure of relevant evidence is not an absolute right. In any criminal proceedings there may be competing interests, such as national security or the need to protect witnesses at risk of reprisals or keep secret police methods of investigation of crime, which must be weighed against the rights of the accused. In some cases it may be necessary to withhold certain evidence from the defence so as to preserve the fundamental rights of another individual or to safeguard an important public interest. However, only such measures restricting the rights of the defence which are strictly necessary are permissible under **art. 6(1)**. Moreover, in order to ensure that the accused receives a fair trial, any difficulties caused to the defence by a limitation on its rights must be sufficiently counterbalanced by the procedures followed by the judicial authorities.

Brenda may be assisted by the House of Lords ruling in *R v H, R v C* [2003] UKHL 3, where the House set out the procedure to be followed when the prosecution refuses to disclose evidence on the grounds of public interest. It held that: 'In considering any disclosure issue the trial judge had to constantly bear in mind the overriding principle that derogation from the principle of full disclosure had always to be the minimum necessary to protect the public interest in question and must never imperil the overall fairness of the trial.' It considered also the possibility of partial disclosure and the option of discontinuing the prosecution in order to avoid making a disclosure. Lord Bingham stated (para. 18) that if information on informers and undercover agents 'cannot be disclosed without exposing individuals to the risk of personal injury or jeopardising the success of future operations . . . some derogation from the golden rule of full disclosure may be justified but such derogation must always be the minimum necessary to protect the public interest in question and must never imperil the overall fairness of the trial.'

The prosecution is placed under an obligation to reveal first any evidence that might undermine the prosecution case and, later, information which assists the defence case. The **CJA 2003** has changed the pre-trial disclosure regime, making new demands on defence and prosecution. The procedure differs according to the sensitivity of the material. The judge may hear an application for disclosure either *inter partes*, or in extremely sensitive cases *ex parte*. On the facts this would appear not to be a situation which required the defence counsel to be present. A procedure introduced under the **Special Immigration Appeals Commission Act 1997** allows for the appointment of an independent special counsel, who will be shown the disputed evidence but may not communicate it to the defendant or his legal advisers. This way of dealing with the awkward problems posed by disclosure is likely to become more widespread, though its unsatisfactory nature is obvious enough.

Where the revelation of the existence of an informer would otherwise require the abandonment of the prosecution, application can be made *ex parte* by the Crown without notice to the defence: *R v Davis* [1993] 1 WLR 613. The court will normally exclude evidence of an informer's identity, but where the judge is of the opinion that disclosure is necessary to establish the accused's innocence, it is a rule of law that the judge must allow the question to be asked and require an answer: *Marks v Beyfus* (1890) 25 QBD 494. It is for the accused to show that there is good reason to expect that disclosure is necessary to establish his innocence. This should normally be done before the trial in proceedings to set aside a witness summons or subpoena for the appropriate Crown witness: *R v Hennessy* (1978) 68 Cr App R 419. Brenda may rely on *R v Agar* (1989) 90 Cr App R 318, where it was held on appeal that disclosure of the name of an informer in a drugs case was necessary where the defendant claimed to have been set up by the informer and the police acting together. In reaching its decision whether to allow disclosure, the court can take into account the informer's willingness to be named, but this is not conclusive: *Savage v Chief Constable of Hampshire* [1997] 1 WLR 1061.

Here, Brenda is claiming that Archie framed her and not just that he informed. In *R v Slowcombe* [1991] Crim LR 198, where the identity of the informer would have contributed little or nothing to the issue before the jury, disclosure was refused. If Brenda is able to put up some evidence that Archie did set the police onto her, the jury may well conclude that her story may be true, so her counsel should be permitted to ask the police whether Archie was the informant. The association with the Partners Exchange may well be relevant evidence and lead to an inference of Archie's involvement. If Archie was not the informer, the police would not be required to name the informer, however, and the jury would be asked to believe Brenda's case without that knowledge.

Brenda should be assured that the final decision on disclosure is with the judge. In the recent case of *R (on the application of WV) v Crown Prosecution Service* [2011] **EWHC 2480** the importance that is attached to protecting the identity of informers was affirmed. The informant should have his identity protected and the Crown Prosecution Service had been wrong to seek to break this confidentiality. As Hungerford-Welch commented on this case (2012, p. 460), 'the reality is that where the judge is satisfied that the defence need to know the identity of the informant in order to put forward their case properly (and so have a fair trial), but revealing the identity of the informant would place him (or his family) at grave risk, the prosecution are left with little choice but to discontinue the proceedings altogether.'

(b) Geraldine's right to a fair trial is also arguably threatened by the operation of PII.

The shop as observation post

Geraldine should be advised that the courts have established that PII may apply to police observation posts since residents who might include business proprietors may wish to remain anonymous for their security or financial interest and the supply of posts might dry up if addresses were revealed. However, in *R v Rankine* [1986] 2 **WLR 1075** the Court of Appeal held that if the accused can convince the court of a relevant evidential reason why he should know the identity of the post then it should be revealed. If Geraldine is claiming mistaken identification of the condition of the women allegedly leaving her premises then the court might decide this should be tested in cross-examination by revealing the address of Sanjay's shop. In *R v Johnstone* [1988] 1 **WLR 1377** the Court of Appeal set out the information which should be given in a voir dire in order to assist the court in deciding whether to uphold the PII claim. The sergeant in charge of the surveillance should give evidence that he had spoken to the residents before the operation began and ascertained their views on disclosure of their identity. Also a senior officer should give evidence that, just before the trial, he had spoken to the occupants to confirm their wishes. If the judge rules that disclosure should not be made he must explain the reasons to the jury and the effect of his ruling.

The milk float as observation post

Geraldine might have more success in determining the identity of the milk float, relying on *R v Brown* (1987) 87 **Cr App R 52**. In that case the court held that if the occupants are police then they do not need protection. On the other hand, the prosecution may argue that there is a public interest in protecting police methods which here include disguise as a milkwoman.

Question 3

The social services department of the Henfield Borough Council have applied to the court for an order placing Gertrude's children into care. She wishes to bring into evidence a tape-recording of a meeting held at the Henfield Borough Council's Family Unit attended by Gertrude and a number of other parents. She argues that the tape-recording demonstrates that the children were happy when they were with her. Henfield Borough Council refuses to allow the tape to be admitted into evidence on the grounds of PII. The council want to call Gertrude's husband, Fred, to give evidence at the hearing.

Advise Gertrude.

How would your advice differ if Gertrude is facing criminal charges arising from the same facts?

Commentary

This is a straightforward question about PII. It is important that you show that you are aware that PII can also apply to bodies other than government bodies. As Lord Hailsham remarked in **D v NSPCC [1978] AC 171**, 'the categories of public interest are not closed and must alter from time to time whether by restriction or extension as social conditions and social legislation develop' (at p. 230).

You should explain the different approaches of the courts according to whether the proceedings are civil or criminal. The reference to the calling of Fred requires you to consider the privilege against self-incrimination in relation to spouses.

Answer plan

(a) • Difference between PII and privilege.

• Rules on disclosure.

• Confidentiality and tape-recording—see **Campbell v Tameside (1982)**.

(b) • PII in criminal cases.

• **Article 6** consideration—see **Rowe and Davis v UK (2000)**.

Suggested answer

Certain types of evidence, though relevant, are not admissible because their disclosure is held to infringe a public interest. The so-called public interest immunity (PII) differs from other types of privilege. The judge of his own motion can exclude the evidence if he thinks the public interest so demands: *Conway v Rimmer* [1968] AC 910. The court made it clear that in reaching this decision, it had to balance the interests of the parties in order to decide whether to withhold or to compel disclosure.

Public policy

PII can apply where the party concerned is not a central government department, as the House of Lords held in *D v NSPCC* [1978] AC 171.

Need to display a legitimate interest

A party seeking disclosure must show that he or she has a legitimate interest in seeking disclosure. Under **r. 31.6 of the Civil Procedure Rules 1998** a party must disclose all relevant documents. Under **r. 31.17(3)**, an order for disclosure can be made only where the documents or the evidence, in relation to which disclosure is sought, are likely to support the case of the applicant or adversely affect the case of one of the other parties. Further, the disclosure must be necessary to fairly dispose of the claim or to save costs.

There is no doubt that the tape-recording of the meeting is capable of being subject to PII. The argument for non-disclosure is likely to be that the workings of the social services department should be kept secret so that people will deal with them in confidence. There appears to be less force in the argument here, because the tape records a meeting in which Gertrude herself took part, but the council may be worried that future participants may not want to take part if the tape-recordings may be admitted as evidence. In *Campbell v Tameside MBC* [1982] QB 1065, the Court of Appeal was presented with an application for PII concerning records of a local education authority, but upheld their disclosure since they were necessary for the plaintiff's case. The records here concerned children and the courts have frequently held such records to be protected from disclosure because there is an important public interest in keeping confidential this sensitive work. It is possible that the interests of the children rather than those of Gertrude will be paramount. However, even if the courts acknowledge on inspection that PII applies, it is arguable that it is open to them to accept a waiver, although there is no clear authority on this. In *Campbell v Tameside MBC*, Lord Denning, obiter, said there was a difference between claims affecting documents which should be kept secret on grounds, for example, of national security and those of a lower level of confidence. Immunity should, in the latter, be capable of being waived. Thus, the local authority could agree to submit the tape-recording.

With regard to Fred's position as a witness to the civil hearing, the parties will need to take note of the **Children Act 1989, s. 98**. This provides that in proceedings concerning the care of children a person cannot refuse to answer questions on the grounds either that the person or his or her spouse would be incriminated. The welfare of the children is of paramount importance.

One final controversial issue is whether pre-trial statements are protected as well as evidence in the proceedings. The answer in *A Chief Constable v A County Council* [2002] EWHC 2198 (Fam) appears to be 'yes'.

In criminal cases, the court is generally the final arbiter of the question as to whether the evidence should be excluded on the basis of PII: *R v Davis* [1993] 1 WLR 613. The Court of Appeal in *Davis* stated that the prosecution should make disclosure of all relevant material and inform the defence that an application to withhold evidence which they regard as being subject to PII would be made. The defence would have a right to be heard when the application is being considered. In exceptional cases, an *ex parte* application can be made without the defence being informed. This decision can be reviewed by the judge during the trial. The guidance in *Davis*, as well as the decision in the case of *R v Ward* [1993] 1 WLR 619, are now incorporated in the **Criminal Procedure and Investigations Act 1996**. This introduced rules in respect to pre-trial disclosure of evidence in criminal cases and treatment of sensitive material, including evidence subject to PII. It should be stressed that the court, not the prosecution, must decide on the claim to withhold evidence, otherwise a failure to do so would be a violation of the accused's right to a fair trial: *Rowe and Davis v UK* (2000) 30 EHRR 1.

In assessing whether the evidence ought to be withheld on the grounds of PII in criminal cases, the balance of competing interests should be made. In the present case there is clearly a need to afford greater protection to Gertrude, as an accused, than as a party to civil proceedings. The courts must balance the public interest and the rights of the individual affected. In *R v Governor of Brixton Prison, ex parte Osman* [1991] 1 WLR 281, the weight to be attached to the interests of justice was very great where the documents were necessary to the defence in a criminal case. However, Lord Taylor in *R v Keane* [1994] 1 WLR 746 at p. 751 commented in the Court of Appeal, that the right answer must result from 'performing the balancing exercise not from dispensing with it'. He said 'if the disputed material may prove the defendant's innocence or avoid a miscarriage of justice then the balance comes down resoundingly in favour of disclosing it.'

The position thus seems to be that a PII claim may be made in criminal cases. Murphy comments (2011, p. 452): 'The withholding of evidence, especially evidence which might assist the defence, is a serious step and one which should be taken only where a strong public interest in withholding it clearly outweighs the general obligation of disclosure.' Significantly, the Court of Appeal allowed the appellants' appeal against conviction in the light of the judgment of the Strasbourg Court in *Rowe and Davis v UK* [2000] Crim LR 584. The failure to allow judicial scrutiny of material sought to be withheld under PII had violated the right to a fair trial. As was stated in *Ex parte Osman*, the public interest in the administration of justice will weigh very heavily in the balance if the liberty of the defendant is at stake, particularly here where there is no question of national security.

Leigh (1995) pointed out that British procedures in this area are a 'patchwork' and suggested it would be 'better to introduce a comprehensive code integrating the safeguards, such as the US **Classified Information Procedures Act, 18 USC app 1–18 (1982)**.'

The House of Lords has given attention to the problem of PII in criminal trials in *R v H* (2004) although for Choo (2012, pp. 210–11) it was 'disappointing' that the House 'did not take the opportunity to dispel uncertainty in this area'. He acknowledged, however, that the House strongly implied that the material in question in a criminal case must be inspected by the judge. The House also anticipated that special counsel may be appointed in rare cases. It set out detailed guidance for making PII claims in criminal cases.

Section 98(2) of the Children Act 1989 protects Gertrude if she faces criminal charges. Any evidence given by Fred in the civil care proceedings is not admissible in subsequent proceedings except perjury. Fred is, however, a compellable witness against Gertrude in any criminal proceedings if the alleged offences involve children under the age of 16 years.

? Question 4

(a) Mr X is suing the Rural Retreat nursing home for negligently causing the death of his wife. He alleges that Gloria, a nursing auxiliary, administered a drug overdose. He wishes to adduce in evidence a letter and a report for the home's insurers made after the death of Mrs X in preparation for a health and safety inquiry in which other staff gave evidence that there was lax management in the home and bottles were often mislabelled. The report and papers were also sent to the nursing home's lawyer. Jane, Mr X's neighbour, works as a clerk for the lawyer. She took a secret photocopy of the papers and sent them anonymously to Mr X.

Advise on the report's admissibility, along with correspondence between the lawyers and the nursing home.

(b) Olaf (O), Patrick (P) and Sarah (S) were charged with conspiracy to rob. They all con-sulted solicitors separately and all planned initially to plead not guilty. O claims that S told him that that she told her solicitor that he, O, had nothing to do with the con-spiracy. S now denies having said this to O. S had subsequently entered into an agree-ment with the prosecution to plead guilty and give evidence against O and P who both plead not guilty. At the start of the trial S gives evidence-in-chief for the prosecution. In preparing to cross-examine S, Mary (M), O's defence counsel, wants discovery of the interview files between S and her solicitor. M also plans to use as evidence an email which S had written to her solicitor after giving evidence in which she said that she could not be sure that she had given correctly the dates of meetings she had said had taken place between O and S as part of the alleged conspiracy. Dispute over the tim-ings of these alleged meetings is part of O's defence case. S had sent the email by mistake to O instead of to her solicitor. S is refusing to grant permission to see the interview transcript and is questioning the admissibility of the misdirected email.

Advise O's defence on how the judge is likely to rule.

Commentary

The specific questions here on legal professional privilege are: how far does it stretch to correspondence with third parties? What is the status of copies? If the privilege is lost can use of the document be restrained by an injunction on grounds of confidentiality? How does the **CPR 1998** affect this? This second part of the question requires you to have knowledge of the law governing legal professional privilege in criminal proceedings and in particular the principle that it still holds even in the face of a possible miscarriage of justice. Note that there are two contested documents here, the record of the initial interview between S and her solicitor and the misaddressed email. You must deal with each separately.

Answer plan

(a) • Legal professional privilege and third parties.

 • Status of copies.

 • 'Inadvertent' inspection.

 • Conduct of third party.

 • **CPR, r. 31.20**.

(b) • Are the disputed documents relevant?

 • If yes are they covered by legal professional privilege or has that been waived intentionally or inadvertently?

 • If either or both are covered by legal professional privilege does this still hold if they may contribute to establishing innocence?

Examiner's tip

(The point behind this tip applies to all your answers!)

The suggested answer to part (b) particularly illustrates the general point that to get a high grade it is important to read widely during your course. *R v Tomkins* **(1977)** is only dealt with in a footnote by Choo but the diligent student will have read the report of the case and thus appreciated how appropriate it is to the facts of this problem question. Remember that examiners may draw on the factual scenarios of recent cases which may not have been taught in the course when drafting questions. A conscientious reading of the *Criminal Law Review* as part of your examination preparation would have uncovered the case of *R v Daniels* **[2011] Crim LR 556**.

Suggested answer

(a) The report contains cogent evidence of the state of affairs in the home at the time of Mrs X's death and would clearly be useful to Mr X in the litigation.

Legal professional privilege and third parties

Third party or litigation privilege is directed at communications with potential witnesses and covers communication between the party and a third party, or communications between the party's lawyer and a third party.

However, it may be argued in answering this question that the home would have been entitled to claim legal professional privilege for the report by its insurers. The House of Lords in *Waugh v BRB* [1980] AC 521 held that this would be so, provided the report was compiled with a view to pending or contemplated litigation with the dominant purpose of obtaining legal advice. In that case the defendants were sued under the **Fatal Accidents Act 1976**. The plaintiff's husband had died in a railway collision. The widow asked for discovery of an internal report by the defendants submitted to the railway inspectorate and the ministry. However, the report was also intended to give details to the Railway Board's solicitor so he could give advice. There was no privilege because the intended or contemplated litigation was not on the facts 'at least the dominant purpose' of creating the document.

The fact that it was sent to the home's legal department would not confer on the report legal professional privilege which it did not already possess (otherwise every litigant could protect embarrassing documents merely by sending them to his legal representatives, as the Divisional Court held in *R v Peterborough JJ, ex parte Hicks* [1977] 1 WLR 1371). In *Ventouris v Mountain* [1991] 1 WLR 607 the Court of Appeal held that legal professional privilege could not attach to original documents which did not come into existence for the purposes of the litigation but already existed before the litigation was contemplated or commenced. Each case will turn on its facts but it appears here that the likelihood is that the insurers were anticipating legal proceedings and that is the dominant purpose for which the papers came into being.

Meaning of legal proceedings

Mr X should be advised that the courts have taken a strict view on what amounts to legal proceedings. In *Re L (A Minor) (Police Investigation: Privilege)* [1997] AC 16 the House of Lords decided that legal professional privilege applies only in adversarial proceedings and therefore would not apply to advice concerning investigations and inquiries. It may be argued here that the communication was in anticipation of a public inquiry. In *Re L* the majority of the House of Lords held that while legal professional privilege in the form of communication between lawyer and client was absolute it did not apply to confidential communications with third parties in relation to proceedings brought under the **Children Act 1989**. One issue was the use of the document in possible criminal proceedings against a mother who had communicated confidentially with an expert. However, the rule in *Re L* has been criticised by Murphy (2003, p. 494) as being 'a judicial creation' which undermines the basic rights of the parties.

The correspondence between the lawyers and nursing home management are also privileged if they are for the purposes of legal advice. The courts interpret this to mean 'dominant purpose' (see *Three Rivers District Council v Bank of England (No. 5)* [2003] QB 1556).

Copies and privilege

However, the privilege extends only to the original document. The contents of a privileged document can be proved by secondary evidence, including the production of copies, following the Court of Appeal decision in *Calcraft v Guest* [1898] 1 QB 759. This rule was explained in *Lord Ashburton v Pape* [1913] 2 Ch 469 by Cozens-Hardy MR, as arising from the fact that the court in an action where it is sought to prove the contents of a privileged document from secondary sources, is not trying the circumstances under which the document was produced. But that rule, as he pointed out, had no bearing on a case where the whole subject matter of the action is the right to retain the copy of a document which is privileged. *Ashburton* established the availability of equitable relief to restrain the use of copies of documents which were subject to a duty of confidence and possession of which it had been wrongfully obtained. Despite some attempt to reconcile these principles, uncertainty arises as to the result in such cases. This has now been simplified by the **Civil Procedure Rules (CPR) 1998**.

Rule 31.20 of the 1998 Rules provide that where a party inadvertently allows a privileged document to be inspected, the party who has inspected the document may use it or its contents only with the permission of the court. The consequence of this is that a party seeking to restrain the use of a privileged document, whether a primary or secondary copy, does not have to apply for an injunction to restrain its use. Under this rule the court can of its own motion, or on the application of a party to the case, order the return of the document which is privileged without separate proceedings being commenced. It should be noted that this rule does not affect the question as to how the court decides whether a document is privileged.

The difficulty is that the court must decide whether the document has been 'inadvertently' inspected. There remains the question as to whether this applies to cases where the document has been obtained by fraud or trick. At common law, the court took the view that how the document was obtained was not relevant and the issue was whether the party claiming its return was entitled to have it: *Goddard v Nationwide Building Society* [1987] QB 670.

The Court of Appeal in *Derby & Co Ltd v Weldon (No. 8)* [1990] 3 All ER 362 emphasised that no balancing exercise is required when a party seeks to vindicate privilege in documents mistakenly disclosed. As Dennis (2010, p. 432) comments, 'It is clear that the conduct of the third party is not a critical issue . . . some innocent recipients of privileged documents disclosed by mistake may be restrained from using them in the same way as a party who acquired them by fraud.' It should be noted that under **r. 31.20 of the CPR**, if a party inadvertently permits a privileged document to be inspected, it may only be used with the permission of the court by the party who has inspected it.

It is clearly the case here that Jane, the clerk, is subject to the duty of confidence as against her employer. She has broken her obligation of secrecy in passing the document to Mr X, even if the documents had been obtained without any reprehensible conduct. The home could ask for the return of any privileged documents when Mr X seeks leave of the court to use the document under **CPR r. 31.20**. Mr X should be warned that the courts have taken a rather strict approach since the **CPR** were introduced (see *USP Strategies v London General Holdings* [2004] EWHC 373 (Ch)). Mr X's counsel may be under ethical restraints under the Code of Conduct for the Bar, which may prevent him using communications that have come into Mr X's hands by such unorthodox means.

(b) The disputed evidence is arguably relevant and therefore disclosure is likely to be requested.

The transcript of the interview with the solicitor

This goes to an issue in the trial, namely how far S's evidence truthfully gives an account of O's involvement. O's defence barrister will want to cross-examine S on the alleged verbal statement to O which S now denies having made. The record of the interview could be used as a previous inconsistent statement (see **Chapter 10**). It appears that they are covered by legal professional privilege which is defined in **s. 10 of the Police and Criminal Evidence Act 1984 (PACE)** and which include under **s. 10 (1)(a)**, 'communications between a professional legal advisor and his client or any person representing his client made in connection with the giving of legal advice to the client.' There is no information that S has waived the privilege. The courts take an absolutist stance in relation to non-disclosure of material subject to legal professional privilege as illustrated by the case of *R v Grant* [2005] 3 WLR 437. In that case the Court of Appeal quashed a conviction because the police, in recording G's conversations with his solicitor had violated the privilege. It was not material that G's defence had not been prejudiced as a result of the disclosure. In the more recent case of *R v Daniels* [2011] 1 Cr App R 18 the Court of Appeal held that waiver could not be implied in a situation whereby the appellant had entered into an agreement to give evidence against alleged accomplices. The court acknowledged, however, that there was a question mark over the reliability of prosecution evidence obtained in such circumstances. It will not benefit O to claim that the record of the interview is required to prevent a possible miscarriage of justice. In *Derby Magistrates' Court, ex parte B* [1996] AC 487, 507, Lord Taylor of Gosforth CJ stated the rationale for legal professional privilege:

> The principle which runs though all these cases, and the many other cases which were cited, is that a man must be able to consult his lawyers in confidence, since otherwise he might hold back half the truth. A client must be sure that what he tells his lawyer

in confidence will never be revealed without his consent. Legal professional privilege is thus much more than an ordinary rule of evidence, limited in its application to the facts of a particular case. It is a fundamental condition on which the administration of justice as a whole rests.

In that case the stepfather in a murder trial was expected to give evidence against the defendant and the evidence covered by legal professional privilege could, if admitted, have been used as Murphy points out (2011, p. 515) either as a previous inconsistent statement or as admissible hearsay under **s. 114(1)(d) of the CJA 2003**. The advice to O is that the evidence is unlikely to be admitted.

The misdirected email

This evidence is clearly relevant in that it could raise reasonable doubt about the veracity of S's evidence for the prosecution. The email falls into the same category of evidence, namely protected by legal professional privilege, as identified earlier. There is one difference here, however, that the answer to the question, has the privilege been waived, is yes. Legal professional privilege will be lost when evidence falls into the hands of the other side innocently or by mistake on the part of the party claiming privilege. O can rely on the case of *R v Tomkins* **(1977) 67 Cr App R 181** where the privilege was lost. The prosecution was able to use in cross-examination the contents of a note which a legal assistant had found on the floor of the courtroom. The defendant had written a note to his barrister which arguably contradicted his testimony.

? **Question 5**

(a) Alice, the 4-year-old daughter of Mrs Y, is badly injured in a playground incident at Treasure Island Nursery. Mrs Y is suing the nursery. An internal report has been prepared by the Department for Education as part of its routine inspection of private nursery schools. In this report the department indicates concern about management procedures and lack of proper vetting of staff at Treasure Island Nursery. The department claims that the report is covered by public interest immunity because to disclose it would prejudice the conduct of future inspections in that it would deter witnesses from giving evidence. A 'mole' in the department sent a photocopy of key sections of the report to the pressure group Childwatch which is helping Mrs Y and they have offered to let her have a copy.

Advise on the admissibility of the report.

(b) Jane has been the victim of an unlawful drugs raid although no charges were preferred after it. She was badly hurt in the raid. She believes the raid occurred as a result of an article she wrote after an interview with a Mr Big detailing the extent to which drug dealers were plying their wares among schoolchildren. Jane is considering suing the police, having already made a complaint to the Independent Police Complaints Commission (successor to the Police Complaints Authority), which it has investigated.

> She wonders if she will be able to obtain copies of the investigation and is worried that at the trial she may be forced to disclose the name of Mr Big since she had promised him anonymity.
>
> Advise Jane of her legal position.

 Commentary

The first part is a straightforward question about PII. Note that PII attaches to copies of documents, unlike the position in relation to legal professional privilege, which only extends to an original document. The second part requires you to be reasonably familiar with the landmark decision in *R v Chief Constable of the West Midlands*, *ex parte Wiley* **[1995] AC 274**. Otherwise, there is a real danger you will be citing overruled authorities. This is an instance when it is vital to check that your textbook and lecture notes are up to date. In this case, judicial review had been sought of the refusal of chief constables to give undertakings that material relating to complaints against the police would not be used to prepare defences to civil claims on police misconduct. The House of Lords decided that no class immunity applied to police complaints procedure documents and cases which held otherwise were overruled. It was acknowledged that in some cases a 'contents' claim might be appropriate and that there may be a 'class' claim for sub-groups of documents. Subsequently, this latter view was accepted for reports of officers investigating a complaint in *Taylor v Anderton (Police Complaints Authority intervening)* **[1995] 1 WLR 447**. The other part of the question deals with journalists' sources, and whether or not you are allowed to take a statute book into the examination; you must be reasonably familiar with the text of the **Contempt of Court Act 1981, s. 10**.

 Answer plan

(a) • General rule on PII.

 • **CPR 1998, r. 31.6**.

 • Report may be subject to PII on grounds of confidentiality in the public service. Is it material Mrs Y has a copy?

(b) • General rule on PII.

 • Difference between class and content claims.

 • PII and police complaints—see *Ex parte Wiley* **(1995)**.

 • Modification made in *Taylor v Anderton* **(1995)**.

 • **Contempt of Court Act 1981, s. 10**.

Suggested answer

(a) Public interest immunity (PII) protects the nation or the public service against the harm which can arise by disclosure of certain documents. It is not material to the claim that the party making it is not a party to the proceedings as here. It is also irrelevant here that the report is in the form of a copy. The argument of the Department for Education is that staff and owners of nurseries would in future be less candid with their inspectors if they knew their statements were likely to be used in litigation.

Procedure for disclosure

The Crown is not a party to the proceedings here, so should give notice that it intends to contest the production of the report. Under **r. 31.19 of the Civil Procedure Rules (CPR) 1998** any person, including the Crown, may apply for an order that he is entitled to withhold a document on the ground of PII.

The application to exclude should be supported by evidence. Under **r. 31.19(6) of the 1998 Rules,** the court may require that the documents or evidence be produced for its inspection so it can decide where the public interest lies. The claim can be either on a 'class' or a 'contents' basis, saying either that the document belongs to a class of documents whose production is not in the public interest or that its production is objectionable because of its specific contents. Although in the wake of the Scott Report the Lord Chancellor announced in 1996 that the Government would not attempt to justify withholding documents on a class basis, this does not apply to non-governmental organisations although, as Murphy (2009, p. 459) pointed out, 'it is to be hoped [they] will follow suit'.

The claim here appears to be of the 'class' type but Lord Reid in *Conway v Rimmer* **[1968] AC 910**, indicated that courts are likely to be more sympathetic if the claim is of the 'contents' type. The court has power to inspect the documents and in a class claim is likely to do so. The courts are not obliged, since *Conway v Rimmer* abrogated the rule in *Duncan v Cammell Laird* **[1942] AC 624**, to accept without question the minister's certificate.

Evidence and relevance

Mrs Y in this case would have to show that the report was 'necessary either for disposing fairly of the cause or matter or for saving costs', which is not a difficult hurdle on the present facts: see *Air Canada v Secretary of State for Trade (No. 2)* [1983] 2 AC 394. In addition, the application for disclosure should not be a 'fishing expedition', though plainly that does not apply in the present case. The argument that if it became known that confidential reports might be disclosed for the purposes of private litigation, the elements of frankness and candour in their preparation might be lost, carries less weight after *Conway v Rimmer*. In *Science Research Council v Nassé* [1980] AC 1028 that reasoning was rejected by Lord Salmon. Lord Fraser saw the need to prevent disclosure as only a private interest of the individuals who prepared the documents. But the need for candour was strongly defended by Lord Wilberforce (dissenting) in *Burmah Oil Co. Ltd v Bank of England* [1980] AC 1090, so might still have some foundation.

Mrs Y can clearly argue that the report is relevant. She may be able to rely on waiver by the witnesses. In *Alfred Crompton Amusement Machines Ltd v Customs and Excise Commissioners* [1974] AC 405 the documents in question were business documents submitted by third parties to the Commissioners as part of a valuation of the plaintiff's machines. In this case, the balance of interests fell evenly and the House was inclined to hold in favour of the claim for public interest. However, Lord Cross thought that a person for whose benefit the objection was made could waive the immunity, although this was doubted by Lord Simon in *Rogers v Home Secretary* [1973] AC 388. The authorities thus conflict on this point of the availability of waiver. The fact that the report which is in the hands of Mrs Y is a copy is not material to the question of disclosure since immunity attaches to copies also, unlike the position on legal professional privilege.

Finally, it might be difficult to argue here that there is a public interest in non-disclosure since revealing the weakness in the nursery's procedures may well assist the well-being of children more than anonymity for whistleblowers.

(b) The application of PII to police complaints records has been the subject of recent case law.

Class and contents claims

The House of Lords in *R v Chief Constable of the West Midlands, ex parte Wiley* [1995] AC 274 overruled previous authorities and decided that it was no longer necessary to impose a general class PII on documents generated in the course of an investigation by the Police Complaints Authority of a complaint against the police. What has to be decided is whether the particular documents in this case are covered by PII. This is a matter for the court hearing Jane's civil action for assault. Jane's case will not be helped by *Taylor v Anderton* [1995] 1 WLR 447, where the Court of Appeal held that a 'class' immunity applied to a sub-group of documents, namely reports of officers investigating a complaint. Any immunity which does attach to any of the documents is limited to the disclosure of the documents or their contents rather than the use of knowledge obtained from them. Jane may be refused sight of the documents on grounds of PII, namely that preserving the confidentiality of the reports outweighed the public interest in disclosure in that they were not necessary for fairly disposing of the case or saving costs. The important point is that it is for the court to inspect the documents and decide accordingly whether or not to admit them, following the current **Civil Procedure Rules**.

Confidentiality of sources

Jane is also worried that she will be forced to disclose the identity of Mr Big. The courts have been very reluctant to acknowledge privileged confidential relationships apart from that between a lawyer and client. One area of concern has been confidentiality between journalists and their sources. The attempt to assert a general journalistic immunity based on public policy, protecting, for example, dissemination of information by granting sources anonymity, failed in *British Steel Corporation v Granada Television Ltd* [1981] AC 1096. The House of Lords, recognising the importance of protecting certain confidences while also recognising that it had a discretion to order disclosure, ordered Granada to disclose the identity of an informant. In this case, the majority felt Granada's conduct was irresponsible in using the 'leaked' confidential reports on the national steel strike. The House agreed, with Lord Salmon dissenting, that although the courts had a wish to respect journalistic sources, no public policy immunity existed which would override the public policy of making relevant evidence available to the court. British Steel Corporation had a worthy case. Disclosure of the source of information contained in a publication is now governed by statute.

Section 10 of the Contempt of Court Act 1981 provides that:

> No court may require a person to disclose, nor is any person guilty of contempt for refusing to disclose, the source of information contained in a publication for which he is responsible, unless it be established to the satisfaction of the court that disclosure is necessary in the interests of justice or national security or for the prevention of disorder or crime.

Parliament, according to Murphy (2011, p. 520), 'took the most remarkable step of introducing a new statutory privilege'.

The section will thus give Jane as a journalist a presumption against disclosure of the identity of Mr Big. The police if they wish disclosure will have to convince the court that one of the four reasons in the section applies, the two most likely being necessary either in the interests of justice or the prevention of crime. As regards the former, the majority of the House of Lords in *Secretary of State for Defence v Guardian Newspapers* [1985] AC 339 held it to mean technically the administration of justice in the course of legal proceedings in a court of law, tribunal or other such body. However, Lord Bridge in *X v Morgan-Grampian (Publishers) Ltd* [1991] 1 AC 1 did not think resort to actual legal proceedings was required. In any case, it will be difficult for the police to establish that they need Mr Big's identity either for their defence against Jane or to exercise another legal right. The court may, however, consider that the police require the identity for the prevention of crime. It will then have to balance the interests of a free press in non-disclosure of sources against the police contention. This approach was followed by the Court of Appeal in *Camelot Group plc v Centaur Communications Ltd* [1998] 1 All ER 251. However, the European Court of Human Rights came to a different conclusion in *Goodwin v UK* (1996) 22 EHRR 123 at p. 436. This aspect of s. 10 was considered in *Re an Inquiry under the Company Securities (Insider Dealing) Act 1985* [1988] AC 660. Inspectors carrying out a criminal investigation contended that disclosure of the sources of a journalist's article about insider dealing was 'necessary in the interests of the prevention of . . . crime'.

This area of law has been influenced by the **Human Rights Act 1998**. In *Ashworth Hospital Authority v MGN Ltd* [2001] **1 WLR 515** the Court of Appeal held that the interpretation of **s. 10** should accord with **art. 10 of the European Convention on Human Rights** and set out an overall test. The House of Lords affirmed the decision of the Court of Appeal (see [2002] **1WLR 2033**). Murphy (2011, p.524) commented 'The Court of Appeal attempted to lay down an overall test for the application of s10, having regard, not only to art.10 of the Convention, but also to the incorporation of the Convention rights into the law of the UK by the **Human Rights Act**, a factor in the decision which makes it particulary important.'

Three aspects of the House of Lords ruling are relevant to Jane's concern: first, **s. 10** applied to all types of proceedings; secondly, the 'prevention of crime' could refer to crime in general and, thirdly, 'necessary' meant somewhere between 'indispensable' and 'expedient'. (On the last point it is arguable that the definition reduces the standard enacted by Parliament.) If the police decide that Mr Big's identity is necessary for their general investigations into drug dealing, then Jane may be ordered to disclose it.

Further reading

Allen, T.R.S., 'Abuse of Power and Public Interest Immunity: Justice Rights and Truth' (1985) 101 LQR 200.

Brown, Sir Simon, 'Public Interest Immunity' [1994] PL 579.

Forsyth, C., 'Public Interest Immunity: Recent and Future Developments' (1997) 56 CLJ 51.

Hungerford-Welch, P., 'Case Comment, *R (on the application of WV) v CPS*' [2011] Crim LR 456.

Leigh, I., 'Reforming Public Interest Immunity' [1995] 2 Web JCLI; http://webjcli.ncl. ac.uk/articles2/leigh2.html.

Murphy, P., *Murphy on Evidence* (OUP, 11th edition 2009).

Redmayne, M., 'Rethinking the Privilege against Self-incrimination' (2007) 2 OJLS 209.

Scott, Sir Richard, *Report of the Inquiry into the Export of Defence Equipment and Dual-Use Goods to Iraq and Related Prosecutions* (HC 115) (London: TSO, 1996).

Spencer, M., 'Bureaucracy, National Security and Access to Justice: New Light on *Duncan v Cammell Laird*' (2004) 55(3) NILQ 277.

Sprack, J., 'The Criminal Procedure and Investigations Act 1996. (1) The Duty of Disclosure' (1997) Crim LR 308.

Tapper, C., 'Prosecution and Privilege' (1996) 1 E & P 5.

Taylor, C., 'In the Public Interest. PII and Fair Trials' (1999) 63 JCL 67.

Tomkins, A., 'Public Interest Immunity after Matrix-Churchill' [1993] PL 650.

Zuckerman, A., 'Legal Professional Privilege: the cost of Absolutism' (1996) 112 LQR 535.

Mixed questions

Introduction

Examination questions in evidence papers frequently cover several issues. There is no way you could anticipate any particular combination of topics so the questions will be a test of your skill in identifying what specific areas of knowledge will be needed. Obviously, you will not be able to cover each area in the same depth as the single issue questions. It is most important, therefore, that you spend some time in listing the various matters which raise a point of law, then specify the appropriate statute or case law and finally apply the law to the facts in the question.

The skill lies in identifying all the relevant areas—you will lose marks if you ignore one. A well-crafted question will not contain any redundant information, so you should be prepared to comment on all parts of the question. You are not generally being asked in these questions to evaluate or criticise the law as it is, but to identify the legal issues in the narrative as you are given it and apply the law to each of them. However, it may be appropriate to refer to academic commentary, particularly in new areas of law.

Table 13 reminds you of the areas you need to have in mind.

Table 13 Identifying legal issues in mixed questions

Area of evidence	Comment
1. Relevance	The pre-condition of all admissibility. It may be appropriate to show your powers of logical analysis and fact management by explaining why a particular piece of evidence is relevant to the trial

Area of evidence	Comment
2. Burden and standard of proof	Always a key area and you are generally expected to say something about them. You might be given an extract from a statute, including an imaginary one, which refers to the need to 'prove' and be expected then to construe the wording in the light of the changes brought about by the **Human Rights Act 1998** to the allocation of legal and evidential burdens
3. Confessions/silence of defendant	Bear in mind that confessions can be made to non-state agents, may be ambiguous and could even, under the common law, involve silence if the parties are on 'even terms'. Only apply **CJPOA** if the silence is in the face of questioning by officials charged with this task
4. References to spouses, co-defendants who are reluctant to testify	This indicates that competence and compellability may be in issue
5. Character evidence	Usually only questioned in criminal cases but be aware also of similar fact in civil cases. Note the rules on admissibility of character evidence by a non-defendant witness in criminal trials
6. Improperly obtained evidence	Usually only raised in criminal evidence questions with suggestion of impropriety or illegality by the police and **s. 78 PACE** may apply to prosecution evidence
7. Supporting evidence	The formal rules here have now been either abolished or simplified but you should still be prepared to comment on the desirability of supporting evidence, particularly in relation to identification evidence, lies told by the defendant, admissible hearsay and inferences from silence
8. Examination and cross-examination	There are many procedural rules here. The special rules relating to vulnerable witnesses, such as alleged victims in sex cases, are perhaps the most significant. Make sure you know the details of Special Measures Directions
9. Out-of-court statements	When there is a reference to an out-of-court oral or written statement, including one made by a witness who is testifying, think hearsay. But bear in mind that the important question is not the *form* the statement is in but the *purpose* for which it is being tendered in evidence. Note that civil and criminal rules are different
10. Communications with lawyer	This raises legal professional privilege. In civil cases, communications with a third party may also be privileged if there is pending litigation. In criminal cases, bear this in mind in considering **ss. 34–38 CJPOA 1994**

Area of evidence	Comment
11. Public interest immunity	This may come up in questions on civil or criminal evidence, more usually the former. In the latter there are often questions in relation to police informers
12. Opinion evidence	This usually refers to expert evidence and is easily recognised. The grey areas include the admissibility of expert evidence in relation to human behaviour and psychology

Question 1

Jones and Watkins are both accused of the murder of Simpson. Both blame the other for the offence. Jones has three previous convictions for disorderly behaviour, while Watkins has five previous convictions for robbery, in two of which he had been part of a gang which had used knives and pick-axes and had threatened their victims. Freda, aged 19 years, was a witness to the killing of Simpson and she gave a statement to the police but also claimed that Jones afterwards threatened to harm her if she told what she had seen. Jones denies this. Watkins's counsel wishes to adduce evidence that Jones had pleaded not guilty to all the previous charges of disorderly behaviour of which he had been convicted. Watkins had previously worked as a security guard in a college. The prosecution wish to call evidence of an internal college disciplinary hearing over an allegation of assault on a student. As a result, Watkins had been dismissed. At the investigation stage Jones had refused to answer police questions but his solicitor read out a prepared statement. Freda has a conviction for shoplifting. She states she is too afraid to give evidence at trial. Jones had pleaded not guilty to the previous charges on which he was convicted.

Advise on evidence.

Commentary

The question covers three areas. You need to consider the application of the new character provisions of the **Criminal Justice Act (CJA) 2003**, the provisions on silence in the **Criminal Justice and Public Order Act 1994 (CJPOA)** and the special provisions relating to witnesses who claim they are afraid to give evidence.

Answer plan

- Jones and Watkins (co-defendants) and Freda as witness—various instances of criminal convictions and behaviour not leading to a criminal charge are given (the assault on the student and the alleged threats to Freda). Do these fall within the definition of bad character in **CJA 2003, s. 98**?

- Freda is a non-defendant—what are the provisions relating to the admissibility of her bad character? See **s. 100 CJA 2003**. If Jones or Watkins adduce this consider **s. 101(1)(g)**.

- Watkins and Jones operate a 'cut throat' defence. Consider the operation of **s. 101(1)(e)**, *R v Randall* **[2003] UKHL 69**, *R v Robinson* **[2005] EWCA Crim 3233** and *R v Lawson* **(2006) LTL 25/8/2006**.

- Watkins's previous offences are arguably of the same nature as the current charge—are they admissible under **s. 101(1)(d)**? Does his disciplinary charge count as 'bad character'? Consider also whether Jones's previous offences are admissible.

- Freda is afraid to give evidence—operation of **s. 116 CJA 2003**; current law on anonymous witnesses.

- Jones refuses to answer police questions—consider **s. 34 CJPOA 1994** and *R v Knight* **[2004] 1 WLR 340**.

- Finally, it will be necessary to consider how the judge should direct the jury in relation to any evidence which is admissible.

 Suggested answer

Prior record

The two co-defendants, Jones and Watkins, and the witness, Freda, have previous convictions and/or instances of reprehensible behaviour. Before examining whether these are likely to be admissible at trial it is necessary to examine whether they fall within the sort of behaviour which is covered by **s. 98 of the Criminal Justice Act (CJA) 2003**. The definition covers evidence of, or a disposition towards, misconduct. The term 'misconduct' is further defined in **s. 112** as the commission of an offence or other reprehensible behaviour. The Explanatory Note to the Act specifies that, 'This is intended to be a broad definition and to cover evidence that shows that a person has committed an offence, or has acted in a reprehensible way (or is disposed to do so) as well as evidence from which this might be inferred.' Thus the definition is likely to cover all the behaviours cited, namely the previous convictions and Watkins's disciplinary charge. However, with regard to the alleged threat made by Jones, para. 357 of the Explanatory Note makes it clear that this evidence is likely to be regarded as evidence relating to the facts of the offence and so does not come within **s. 98**. It reads, 'Evidence that the defendant had tried to intimidate prosecution witnesses would also be admissible outside this scheme [**s. 98**] as evidence of misconduct in connection with, as appropriate, the investigation or the prosecution of the offence, as would allegations by the defendant that evidence had been planted.'

Jones and Watkins should be aware that the **CJA 2003** applies in relation to the admissibility of their bad character whether they give evidence or not.

Character of non-defendant

To take first the position of Freda, the non-defendant, the first question is whether evidence of her shoplifting offence is admissible. **Section 100 CJA 2003** specifies that evidence of the bad character of a person other than a defendant is not to be given without the permission of the court (**s. 100(4)**) and this can only be given if it meets one of three conditions: They are:

- it is important explanatory evidence;
- it is of substantial probative value to a matter in issue and that issue is one of substantial importance in the case; or
- the prosecution and defence agree that the evidence should be admitted.

Here we are told that there is a dispute between Jones and Freda as to what happened. It is arguable therefore that if Jones's counsel applies to have the evidence admitted under the second head above, the court may give permission. Jones should then be aware, however, that it may be arguable that he has now 'attacked the character of another person' and that the prosecution may seek to have his previous convictions admitted under **s. 101(1)(g)**. This is dealt with later.

Special Measures

Freda is frightened to give evidence. This may bring into play **s. 19 of the Youth Justice and Criminal Evidence 1999**, which covers Special Measures for the giving of evidence by fearful witnesses. The question then arises as to whether Freda falls into one of the categories of witnesses, not including the defendant, who are eligible for 'special measures'. Her age does not qualify her for **s. 16(1)(a)** since she must be under 18. We are not told she has mental, or physical, impairment, so **s. 16(2)** will not apply. She is not a complainant in a sexual offence so **s. 17(4)** does not apply. She is, however, a witness to a violent offence so will be covered by the amendment, not yet in force, to the **Coroners and Justice Act 2009**. This extends the category of automatically eligible witnesses to those who were witnesses to killing/GBH/ABH or other assaults using a firearm or knife. Freda may thus fall within **s. 17** and the court will consider the relevant criteria applying to witnesses where the quality of their evidence is likely to be diminished by reason of fear or distress.

The judge may consider the use of such measures as live links or video screens. An alternative approach is for Freda's pre-trial statement to be admitted under the hearsay provisions of the **CJA 2003**. **Section 116(2)** sets out a procedure which may apply where 'through fear the relevant person does not give (or does not continue to give) oral evidence in the proceedings, either at all or in connection with the subject matter of the statement, and the court gives leave for the statement to be given in evidence.' Fear is to be 'widely construed'. The admissibility of Freda's evidence in this way will depend upon the exercise of the court's discretion, which will include a consideration of fairness in view of the impossibility of cross-examining Freda. The court may exercise its discretion not to allow this hearsay evidence since Freda will not be cross-examined, thus arguably undermining the defence. Evidence of Freda's lack of credibility may be given even if she does not appear.

Jones and/or the prosecution may try to have Watkins's previous convictions admitted as evidence. The prosecution may argue that they are admissible under **s. 101(1)(d)** as relevant to an important matter in issue between the defendant and prosecution. The test for admissibility has been set out in *Hanson* [2005] 1 WLR 3169.

1. Does the history of conviction(s) establish a propensity to commit offences of the kind charged?

2. Does that propensity make it more likely that the defendant committed the offence charged?

3. Is it unjust to rely on the conviction(s) of the same description or category; and, in any event, will the proceedings be unfair if they are admitted?

In this case the previous convictions arguably show a propensity to violence if not to murder, but the Court of Appeal in *Hanson* stressed that 'In referring to offences of the same description or category, **section 103(2)** is not exhaustive of the types of conviction which might be relied upon to show evidence of propensity to commit offences of the kind charged. Nor, however, is it necessarily sufficient, in order to show such propensity that a conviction should be of the same description or category as that charged.' Even if the judge decides the offences are eligible to be considered under this head she must apply her discretion under **s. 101(3)**: 'The court must not admit evidence under **subsection (1)(d)** if on an application by the defendant to exclude it, it appears to the court that the admission of the evidence would have such an adverse effect on the fairness of the proceedings that the court ought not to admit it.' She must also consider **s. 103(3)**, which refers to 'the length of time since the conviction or for any other reason, that it would be unjust for it to apply in this case'. If the evidence is admissible under this head then Jones may make use of it also to try and establish his innocence.

However, even if the court ruled the convictions and the disciplinary charge inadmissible for the prosecution under this section it would still be open to the co-defendant Jones to put in an application to have the character of Watkins put in evidence. The relevant section is **s. 101(1)(e)**. Under this, evidence must have substantial probative value in relation to an important matter in issue between the defendant and the co-defendant. Since each blames the other for the offence it is likely that Jones will argue that Watkins's previous convictions and the reason for his dismissal demonstrate a propensity to violence which he, Jones, does not have.

Co-defendants and criminal record

With regard to the evidential value of the bad character evidence, in *R v Randall* [2003] **UKHL 69** the House of Lords made it clear that where two defendants were jointly charged with a crime and each blamed the other for its commission, one accused could rely on the more significant criminal propensity of the other in order to prove his innocence. In that case, the co-defendants were charged with murder and each claimed the other had killed the victim. The evidence of the antecedents of the co-defendant was relevant not only to lack of credibility but also to the issue of which of them was more likely to have committed the offence. That case was decided upon under the **Criminal Evidence Act 1898**, but it was relied upon in *R v Dennis Robinson* [2005] **EWCA Crim 3233** under the **CJA 2003**. There the Court of Appeal held that the judge had been entitled to direct the jury to consider all the evidence, including evidence adduced by one of the co-defendants as to the bad character of her co-accused. The exclusionary discretion in relation to **s. 101(3)** does not apply to **s. 101(1)(e)**.

Jones's convictions arguably do not show a propensity to extreme violence and so may not be admissible under the above heads. Jones may decide to put his conviction in evidence on the basis that they do not demonstrate a propensity to such violence. This would be covered by **s. 101(1)(b)**. Alternatively, the evidence may be admissible by the prosecution under **s. 101(1)(g)** since Jones has adduced Freda's convictions. In this case the court has discretion not to admit the evidence under **s. 101(3)**. The explanatory note on **s. 101(1)(g)** states that such evidence 'will primarily go to the credit of the defendant'. However, it adds 'Currently a jury would be directed that evidence admitted in similar circumstances, under the **1898 Act**, goes only to credibility and is not relevant to the issue of guilt. Such directions have been criticised and the new statutory scheme does not specify that this evidence is to be treated in such a way. However, it is expected that judges will explain the purpose for which the evidence is being put forward and direct the jury about the sort of weight that can be placed on it.' Depending on how the evidence is treated in the trial it is possible that even if it is not admitted under **s. 101(1)(e)** that Watkins's counsel may be able to cross-examine Jones on it. In a controversial decision the Court of Appeal held in *R v Highton* [2005] **EWCA 1985**, 'Once evidence of bad character became admissible through one of the "gateways" in the **Criminal Justice Act 2003** the use to which it could be put depended upon the matters to which it was relevant rather than upon the gateway through which it was admitted. Accordingly, evidence of an offender's bad character admitted under **s 101(1)(g)** could be used, if relevant, to show the offender's propensity to commit offences of the kind with which he was charged.'

However, it may be that Watkins can argue that the fact that Jones pleaded not guilty in the previous trials is of substantive probative value to the matter in issue between the two defendants. The issue is who is telling the truth. **Section 104** further explains 'matter in issue between the defendant and a co-defendant'. It states that 'Evidence which is relevant to the question whether the defendant has a propensity to be untruthful is admissible on that basis under **section 101(1)(e)** only if the nature or conduct of his defence is to undermine the co-defendant's defence.' That seems to be the case here. In *R v Hanson* the Court of Appeal considered the meaning of 'propensity to untruthfulness', which was 'not the same as propensity to dishonesty'. It stated (para. 13),

> It is to be assumed, bearing in mind the frequency with which the words honest and dishonest appear in the criminal law, that Parliament, deliberately chose the word untruthful to convey a different meaning, reflecting a defendant's account of his behaviour, or lies told when committing an offence. Previous convictions, whether for offences of dishonesty or otherwise, are therefore only likely to be capable of showing a propensity to be untruthful where, in the present case, truthfulness is an issue and, in the earlier case, either there was a plea of not guilty and the defendant gave an account on arrest, in interview, or in evidence, which the jury must have disbelieved, or the way in which the offence was committed shows a propensity for untruthfulness, for example by the making of false representations.

Thus, further information is needed to assess whether the earlier not guilty pleas indicate that degree of untruthfulness on the part of Jones. In *R v Lawson* [2007] **1 WLR 1191** the Court of Appeal held that a judge was correct to allow the prosecution to adduce bad character evidence in order to establish a defendant's propensity as to truthfulness where there were inconsistencies between the defences of the two co-accused and the evidence was of substantive probative value. Here the bad character evidence was a previous conviction for unlawful wounding. It was noted in *R v Campbell* [2007] **EWCA Crim 1472** that as a result of the **CJA 2003** it has been much more common for evidence of the accused's bad character to be admitted at trial. However, in that case a restrictive stance was taken to **s. 103(1)(b)**. It held that to suggest that a propensity for untruthfulness makes it more likely that a defendant has lied to the jury is not likely to help them. If they apply common sense they will conclude that a defendant who has committed a criminal offence may well be prepared to lie about it even if he has not shown a propensity for lying, whereas a defendant who has not committed the offence charged will be likely to tell the truth, even if he has shown a propensity for telling 'lies'. It followed that a propensity for untruthfulness will not normally be of assistance in assessing guilt.

Finally, with regard to Jones's refusal to talk to the police at interview and his submission of a statement, Jones may rely on *R v Knight*, where the Court of Appeal discussed what was meant by the defendant's failure to mention at interview facts later relied on for his defence under **s. 34 of the Criminal Justice and Public Order Act 1994**. It held that the failure was not meant to be that of refusing to answer questions. Accordingly a statement given to the police at the time of the refusal to answer questions and put later in evidence read out by the judge in the summing-up meant that inferences could not be made under **s. 34**.

Question 2

Alerted by a burglar alarm, police from a nearby station arrive at a house in Meadow Way at 9.00 p.m. on Thursday night. They find a smashed window and while two officers search the house a third searches the street for suspects. Meanwhile the owner of the house, Jack, is pursuing someone running down the street. He sees Wayne running several yards away, catches up with him and grabs him. 'You rat,' Jack shouts, 'you've tried to burgle my house.' Wayne says nothing but tries to shake Jack off. Wayne is arrested and cautioned. At the police station he is questioned in a series of interviews beginning at 4.00 a.m. on Friday 2 April. He is cautioned before all the interviews. Before the first interview Wayne requests access to a solicitor, but this is denied by Inspector Brown on the grounds that they suspect Wayne had an accomplice who could be alerted by calling a solicitor. At the first interview, Wayne refuses to cooperate with the questioning. At the second interview Wayne is again denied a solicitor, but offers to 'tell what he knows', if the police promise to put in a good word for him to the judge. The Inspector nods his assent. Wayne then says that he was out playing football with his friends on the night in question and when making his way home he kicked the ball through the window of Jack's house. He ran off because he was scared. The second interview ends at 12 noon on Saturday. He is given no food. Wayne is later charged with attempted burglary. At trial the prosecution put it to him that Jack had had an affair with his wife.

Advise on evidence.

Commentary

Among the issues you must consider here are whether fleeing can constitute adverse evidence and what is the evidential value of silence in the face of questioning both by persons in authority and an ordinary citizen. You must recall both the common law rules and also the provisions under **ss. 34 and 37 of the CJPOA 1994**. In addition, you will have to deal with the possibility of breach of **s. 58 of the Police and Criminal Evidence Act 1984 (PACE)** and the Codes of Practice. The Codes are very comprehensive and you will obviously not be able to remember all the details, but you must touch on the main points, considering possible breaches in the period of detention and the related question of whether the offence here is an indictable offence. The circumstances of the obtaining of Wayne's statement, and whether it is inadmissible under **s. 76 or 78 PACE** should be considered. You must identify the various legal issues first and then in turn consider the relevant law in relation to the narrative of events. In these questions it is useful to prepare a plan for your answer to ensure your coverage is comprehensive.

Answer plan

- Implied assertion by conduct—is 'fleeing' a statement or the circumstances of the alleged offence?
- Evidential value of silence in face of questioning by persons in authority and ordinary citizens—**CJPOA 1994** and common law.
- Possible breaches of **s. 58 PACE** and Codes of Practice (revised periodically).
- Investigate whether an earlier silence at interview when replaced by an explanation is admissible; no solicitors present—Code C Annex C.
- Wayne's statement 'mixed'—**R v Sharp (1988)**; possible exclusion under **s. 76 or 78 PACE**.
- Wayne presented by prosecution of the fact of wife's affair—does **s. 34** apply?

 Suggested answer

The case concerns the question of whether various items of evidence are likely to be admissible for the prosecution. This essay takes each issue in turn.

Assertive behaviour

Wayne is seen fleeing from the scene of the crime. Does this have evidential significance? A confession is defined in **s. 82(1) of the Police and Criminal Evidence Act 1984 (PACE)**. It 'includes any statement wholly or partly adverse to the person who made it whether made to a person in authority or not and whether made in words or otherwise.' It is arguable that this definition is wide enough to include an admission by conduct. The Criminal Law Revision Committee in its 11th Report (Cm 4991, 1972) gave as an example, a possible admission by conduct, a nod of the head. But that is clearly an express statement by conduct. It is unlikely that an implied statement by conduct such as running away will be accepted as a confession. In *Preece v Parry* **[1983] Crim LR 170** the Divisional Court held that violent behaviour on arrest was capable of being a confession. This is generally regarded as an unusual case.

Clearly, however, the fact that Wayne is running away along the street is part of the circumstances of the alleged offence and is therefore relevant as an integral part of the events forming part of the basis of the charge. It would arguably be admissible under **s. 98(a) of the Criminal Justice Act (CJA) 2003** as evidence which 'has to do with the alleged facts of the offence with which the defendant is charged'. See also **s. 101(1)(c)**.

Silence at common law

Wayne's silence in the face of accusations from Jack is more likely than his fleeing to amount to an admission. The common law rule is that a statement made in the presence of the accused cannot amount to evidence against him, except in so far as he accepts what has been said, as the House of Lords held in *R v Christie* [1914] AC 545. However, if in certain circumstances a reply or rebuttal would reasonably be expected, silence can be taken to be a confession. The test of admissibility of this type of silence is whether the parties are speaking on even terms: see *R v Mitchell* (1892) 17 Cox CC 503 and the Privy Council decision in *Parkes v R* (1977) 64 Cr App R 25. The court will thus have to decide first whether Jack and Wayne were speaking on even terms, which does seem likely. Thus, any direction by the judge that the silence could amount to a confession is arguably proper. The judge, however, must be careful to direct the jury to consider, first, whether the silence does indicate acceptance of what Jack said and, if so, whether guilt could reasonably be inferred from what he had accepted. It was the failure of the judge to leave these two issues to the jury and his suggestion that the defendant's silence could indicate guilt which led the Court of Appeal to quash the conviction in *R v Chandler* [1976] 1 WLR 585.

Silence and statute

This common law principle is not affected by **s. 34 of the Criminal Justice and Public Order Act 1994**, which covers questioning under caution by a police constable. **Section 34(5) of the 1994 Act** provides that the section does not:

> prejudice the admissibility in evidence of the silence or other reaction of the accused in the face of anything said in his presence relating to the conduct in respect of which he is charged ... or preclude the drawing of any inference from any such silence or other reaction of the accused which could properly be drawn apart from this section.

Under the **PACE** Code of Practice C para. 11.1, following a decision to arrest, the suspect must not be interviewed except at a police station unless the 'emergency' exceptions apply. It appears Wayne's treatment accords with this. Furthermore, Wayne should take account of paras 11.4 and 11.4A, which provide that at the beginning of an interview carried out in a police station the interviewing officer, after cautioning him, is to put to the suspect any 'significant statement or silence' which occurred before the start of the interview. Wayne should be given an opportunity to confirm or deny any preinterview silence or statement.

In addition, European human rights law must be considered under the **Human Rights Act 1998**. The right to a fair trial under **art. 6** extends to pre-trial as well as trial proceedings. Evidence obtained at interview may be excluded if it affects the fairness of the proceedings. The Strasbourg Court has placed much emphasis on the right of access to legal advice specifically in relation to the admissibility of silence as evidence, leading to changes in UK legislation (*Murray v UK*).

Interview and Code

Some possible procedural flaws arise in relation to Wayne's interviews at the police station. Wayne maintains silence at first and then makes a statement. It is necessary to consider the application of **ss. 34 and 37 of the 1994 Act**, Wayne's failure to account for his presence in the street at the initial interview may be admissible under **s. 37**, since the court is permitted to draw inferences, whether or not the accused gives another version of events at trial. The investigating officer must give the additional special warning set out in para. 10.10 of Code C. **Section 34**, on the other hand, does not allow inferences to be drawn from silence, per se, but only when the accused for his defence in later proceedings relies on evidence, which evidence could have been provided in answer form during earlier questioning. The statute in fact does not make it clear whether an earlier silence in an early interview albeit replaced by an explanation at a later one is admissible, although it would seem rather harsh to interpret the statute against the defendant in this way. The evidential value of silence which is shortly replaced by an explanation, as is the case here, must be low. For **s. 34** to apply there must be, inter alia, a 'fact' relied on by Wayne at trial which he could reasonably have been expected to have raised earlier. The purpose of the legislation is to prevent 'ambush defences' or concocted evidence in situations where the prosecution will not have been able to properly mount a challenge. It does not apply to situations where the new fact is true. Presumably the prosecution wishes to imply a motive of revenge on the part of Wayne and make a possible defence of accidentally breaking the window less likely. If Wayne simply accepts the prosecution evidence at trial that Jack was having an affair with his wife he is probably not running the risk of having an inference of guilt drawn from his failure to mention it at interview. It is the case that under **s. 34** a fact may be relied upon by the defendant which is not put in evidence on his behalf (see *Chenia* [2002]). However, in *Betts and Hall* [2001] 2 Cr App R 257 the Court of Appeal held that if the defendant simply admits at trial a fact asserted by the prosecution, even if he failed to mention it at interview, that in itself should not lead to **s. 34** applying. Note also that no inference should be drawn if the fact relied on is true (*Webber* [2004] UKHL 01). However, the most significant consideration is that **s. 34** should not apply here in any case since there has apparently been a serious breach of criminal procedure in the failure to allow access to requested legal advice. Silence at interview is admissible only if, inter alia, the suspect has been given the opportunity to consult a solicitor (**s. 34(2A)**). It appears that this has been wrongly denied to Wayne so the silence may be inadmissible.

Mixed statements

Wayne's subsequent statement takes a form which is partly exculpatory and partly inculpatory in that he accepts he was at the scene but not that he was attempting to burgle. Following the House of Lords decision in *R v Sharp* [1988] 1 WLR 7, such mixed statements are admissible as evidence of the facts related. It is possible that the whole statement itself should be excluded. Confessions may be excluded under several provisions of **PACE**. The grounds are oppression under **s. 76(2)(a)**; unreliability under **s. 76(2)(b)**, both of which operate as a rule of law; and unfairness under **s. 78**, which operates as the exercise of discretion. There appear to be no grounds of oppression here, but **s. 76(2)(b) PACE** may be appropriate. Arguably, Wayne has been induced to confess by a promise of a favour. In *R v Barry* (1991) 95 Cr App R 384, the promise of bail led to a confession being held potentially unreliable by the Court of Appeal. It must be shown that there is a connection between what was said or done and the confession. It is arguable that Wayne was induced to confess by the indication of favourable treatment by the Inspector. Thus the 'something said or done evidence' is the possible inducement. The 'circumstances' are arguably the absence of a solicitor with whom Wayne could discuss the offer (*R v Mathias* [1989] **Crim LR 64**). If the judge accepts this as an arguable proposition, then the burden of proof is on the prosecution to prove in a voir dire beyond reasonable doubt that the confession was not so obtained. The test is an objective one of whether any confession obtained in such circumstances would be likely to be unreliable.

Even if **s. 76(2)(b) PACE** is not applicable there may be sufficient breaches of other sections of the statute and the Code to warrant exclusion under **s. 78 PACE** by the exercise of the court's discretion. The circumstances in which the statement was obtained reveal a number of possible breaches of the statute and Codes of Practice.

First, Wayne has his access to a solicitor denied. Delay in obtaining legal representation is only permissible under **s. 58 PACE** if the offence is an indictable offence. Following the introduction of the **CJA 2003** detention without charge is permitted for up to 36 hours for indictable offences without reference to a magistrate. The reason for delaying legal advice given by the police, namely fear of alerting another suspect, does appear to comply with **s. 58(8)(b) PACE** but the police must put up cogent evidence to justify such a fear (see *R v Samuel* [1988] QB 615). (Prior to the **2003 Act** the court had to determine whether the attempted burglary amounted to a serious arrestable offence. Further information would have been needed on the relative status of the victim and perpetrator, to determine whether the offence would cause serious financial gain or loss.) As the offence does constitute an indictable offence, the reason for delay in access to a solicitor appears appropriate, as long as the delay has been authorised by a senior officer. Further, Wayne should have been allowed eight hours' rest in any 24 hours free of questioning, with breaks for refreshment and periodic checks during the questioning.

The courts appear to take the attitude that to justify exclusion under **s. 78 PACE**, the breach or breaches must be 'significant and substantial', as the Court of Appeal held in *R v Keenan* [1990] 2 QB 54. A key issue is whether the police acted in bad faith: *R v Alladice* (1988) 87 Cr App R 380. In *R v Canale* [1990] 2 All ER 187 the Court of Appeal held that the officers had shown a cynical disregard of the Code, which they had breached flagrantly. The court held that the confession should have been excluded under **s. 78 PACE**. **Section 76(2)(b) PACE** was not appropriate since the accused had been in the Parachute Regiment and was not therefore in the position of a vulnerable defendant in the face of police questioning.

Here, there also appear to be breaches of the conditions of detention. In the absence of bad faith, the court will be concerned to look at whether the breaches were operative in leading to potential unreliability under **s. 76(2)(b) PACE** or unfairness to the proceedings under **s. 78**.

Thus Wayne's silence in the face of the accusation from Jack is probably admissible. The cumulative effect of the possibly wrongful denial of legal advice, the apparent inducement and breach of the statute and Code C are together likely to lead to Wayne's initial silence at interview and his partly inculpatory statement being held inadmissible.

 Question 3

John is an inmate of a hostel for young stablehands employed by Harry, who trains horses. Harry has set up and owns the hostel, to provide accommodation for his staff. Ann, the residential care worker at the hostel has, unknown to Harry, been allowing the residents to watch 'pirate' videos she has bought in a car boot sale. A quarrel breaks out in the hostel recreation room one evening while students are watching a violent video which Ann has brought in. John, sickened by the violence, wants the video to be turned off so he can play snooker but Ann refuses. A scuffle breaks out and John is poked in the eye by Fred, another employee who is holding a snooker cue. It later becomes apparent that John has been blinded in one eye. After the incident, the snooker table is removed from the residents' lounge. At the same time Harry offered John £5,000 compensation 'without prejudice', but John rejected this as too low. Harry writes to Sally, his solicitor, after the accident and sends Fred's job application, which reveals that he had been sacked from a previous post at a residential hostel after allegations of violence against the inmates. Harry also sends the snooker cue to the solicitor for 'safe keeping'. John is suing Fred and Harry as being vicariously liable for the incident and for assault. The case is set down for trial. Ann is refusing to answer questions on the issue or to appear as a witness.

Discuss the evidential issues involved, not the matters of substantive law.

 Commentary

You are not told what the evidential issues are so you must be careful to identify the relevant ones. You are clearly warned not to discuss the matters of liability in negligence, even if you feel you could shine in that area! This is a civil case in which you would be quite justified in referring to the burden and standard of proof as a basic question of evidence. The refusal of Ann to appear prompts you to dwell on the compellability of witnesses and since there is a suggestion of criminal activity on her part, you need to bear in mind the privilege against self-incrimination on which there has been some recent case law under the **Human Rights Act**. You also need to consider whether the removal of the snooker table after the incident is a relevant piece of evidence. Explicit questions uniquely on relevance are rare but you should not ignore a possible part-question. The exchange with the lawyer raises the issue of legal professional privilege, both in relation to the correspondence and the sending of the snooker cue. As for Harry's without prejudice offer of compensation, you need to consider whether this can be disclosed in court. The approach you should adopt is to list the issues in the order in which they appear in the question and work systematically through them.

Answer plan

- Ann's refusal to appear—compellability as witnesses—possible privilege against self-incrimination.
- Relevance of removal of snooker table after incident.
- Exchange with lawyer—legal professional privilege—correspondence and sending of snooker cue.
- Can without prejudice offer of compensation be disclosed?
- Burden of proof in civil cases.
- Fred's earlier sacking—consider similar fact in civil cases.

Suggested answer

Relevance

All admissible evidence must be relevant, although not all relevant evidence is admissible. The removal of the snooker table is arguably not relevant to the facts in issue. To qualify for admission it should increase or diminish the probability of the existence of a fact in issue. Deciding on relevance is a matter of drawing generalisations from experience. Does the removal of the table make it more or less probable that Harry was vicariously liable in negligence or that Fred had assaulted John? Relevance is a matter of logic not law, but it may be appropriate to cite *Hart v Lancashire and Yorkshire Railway Co.* (1869) 21 LT 261. There, a runaway engine ran into a stationary train on a branch line, injuring the plaintiff. He sued the railway company and used as evidence the fact that the company had subsequently changed the points system. On appeal, the evidence was held to be wrongly admitted since, as Bramwell B said (at p. 263):

> People do not furnish evidence against themselves simply by adopting a new plan in order to prevent the recurrence of an accident.

It is therefore likely that the removal is not legally relevant.

Burden of proof

In this civil case John has the legal burden of proof on both suits (*Miller v Minister of Pensions* [1947] 2 All ER 372). There is an issue as to whether the standard of proof in these two suits of negligence and assault is the same. In *Hornal v Neuberger Products* [1957] 1 QB 247, CA, a case of fraudulent misrepresentation, Denning LJ said, 'The more serious the allegation the higher the degree of probability that is required.' The case law does seem to suggest that the more serious the allegation, the more cogent is the evidence required to overcome the unlikelihood of what is alleged and thus to prove it. However, the standard of proof is still the balance of probabilities. In *Re Del-low's Will Trusts* the issue in the civil case was whether the husband had been killed unlawfully by the wife. Ungoed Thomas J stated, 'there can hardly be a graver issue than that'. The standard of the balance of probability was applied. In *Re H and Others* [1996] AC 563 a majority of the House of Lords held that there was no third standard in some civil cases. With regard to the assault charge therefore, the gravity of the issues is part of the circumstances which the court has to take into consideration in assessing the balance of probabilities.

Privilege against self-incrimination

Ann is reluctant to appear as a witness possibly because she is afraid that evidence of her wrongdoing, namely showing pirate videos, may be revealed. These in themselves are relevant to the suits in that they were the cause of the quarrel. Their criminal origin is not relevant. In *Blunt v Park Lane Hotel* [1942] 2 KB 253 Goddard LJ expressed the scope of the common law rule, that no one is bound to answer any question if the answer thereto would, in the opinion of the judge, have a tendency to expose the deponent to any criminal charge, penalty or forfeiture which the judge regards as reasonably likely to be preferred or sued for. In practice, of course it is only the exposure to possible criminal charges which is of concern. The right is referred to in the **Civil Evidence Act 1968, s. 14(1)(a)**, which provides that if the claim is made in civil proceedings the offence must be provided for by law of any part of the UK. If the pirate videos are held to be relevant to the proceedings and counsel wish to pursue a line of questioning on this, Ann may be permitted to refuse to answer (*Rank Film Distributors Ltd v Video Information Centre* [1982] AC 380). If a witness is wrongly compelled to answer a question in breach of the privilege against self-incrimination, the answer will be inadmissible in subsequent proceedings against him (*R v Garbett* (1847) 1 Den CC 236). In *AT&T Istel v Tully* [1993] AC 45 Lord Templeman (at p. 53) condemned the privilege against self-incrimination in civil proceedings as archaic and unjustifiable. That case involved the disclosure of documents rather than the appearance of witnesses, but it does suggest that the judiciary will not apply the privilege too readily. As Lord Griffiths said (at p. 57) the law was in need of 'radical reappraisal'. However, the House of Lords conceded that any abrogation of the privilege in such cases could only be made by statute.

There is clearly a public interest in speedy settlement of civil litigation and the law does offer some protection to communications which are aimed at achieving this. Obviously, there is a danger that an offer of settlement may be later interpreted as an admission of liability. Because of this, communications between parties, namely Harry's offer of settlement, may not be ordered to be disclosed on discovery and will not form part of the documents placed before the court, as the House of Lords held in *Rush & Tompkins Ltd v Greater London Council* [1989] AC 1280. The privilege is that of the parties, so it only applies if Harry requests it. However, although without prejudice correspondence may not be admissible on the issue of liability, it may be admissible on other grounds such as costs, where delay or unreasonable refusal to settle may be material (see **RSC Order 22 r. 14**). This rule applies the proposal made by Cairns LJ in *Calderbank v Calderbank* **[1976] Fam 93**.

Legal professional privilege

It is a common law rule that communications passing between lawyer and client about materials prepared for the purpose of litigation are privileged. In this question, the first aspect of legal professional privilege applies, namely, that communications between lawyer and client made in the course of seeking and giving advice within the normal scope of legal business are privileged if the client seeks the privilege. Thus, any advice that Sally gave to Harry could not be disclosed (*Minter v Priest* **[1930] AC 558**). **Section 10 of the Police and Criminal Evidence Act 1984** gives statutory recognition to legal professional privilege. However, Harry cannot claim the privilege for material objects so the snooker cue is not covered, nor can there be a claim of privilege for Fred's job application, since these did not arise in the course of his relationship with the lawyer (*R v King* **[1983] 1 WLR 411**). In that case, the court expressed doubts about the earlier decision, *Frank Truman Export Ltd v Commissioner of Police for the Metropolis* **[1977] QB 952**, where Swanwick J held that pre-existing documents which might be relevant in evidence against the plaintiff, were privileged in the hands of the plaintiff's solicitor to whom they had been delivered for his consideration in relation to likely criminal charges.

Similar fact

The job application is likely to be highly probative and admissible as 'similar fact' evidence (*Mood Music Publishing Co. Ltd v de Wolfe* **[1976] Ch 119**). In that case, Lord Denning MR, after referring to what was then similar fact evidence in criminal cases, stated:

> In civil cases the courts have followed a similar line but have not been so chary of admitting it. In civil cases the courts will admit evidence of similar facts if it is logically probative, that is if it is logically relevant in determining the matter which is in issue: provided that it is not oppressive or unfair to the other side: and also that the other side has fair notice of it and is able to deal with it.

The House of Lords reconsidered this area of law in *O'Brien v Chief Constable of South Wales Police* **[2005] 3 All ER 931**. The House stressed the difference between the civil and criminal tests for the admissibility of previous misconduct to show propensity. The latter has now been changed in the **Criminal Justice Act 2003**. Lord Phillips stated at para. 53:

> I would simply apply the test of relevance as the test of admissibility of similar fact evidence in a civil suit. Such evidence is admissible if it is potentially probative of an issue in the action.

He went on, however, to acknowledge that the 'policy considerations that have given rise to the complex rules . . . in **sections 100 to 106 of the 2003 Act**' may have a part to play and referred to the objective of dealing with cases justly in **CPR r 1.2**. The court will consider, therefore, whether the prejudicial effect of admitting the earlier allegations of violence against Fred will generate unfairness. In *O'Brien* earlier evidence of impropriety on the part of a chief constable was admitted in a suit for misfeasance in public office and malicious prosecution.

 Question 4

Tanya witnessed an attempted break-in of an off-licence and claims she saw a car speed away from the scene. She phoned the police and dictated the car registration number to PC Ford, who wrote it down in his notebook. Tanya also wrote down the number in her diary. PC Ford found a cigarette lighter with the initials RS at the scene of the crime. The car is traced to a Richard Smith, who claims it was taken without his permission by his neighbour Harold and that he had nothing to do with the crime. The prosecution had obtained evidence from another customer, Joan, who claims to have seen the attempted break-in at the off-licence. Joan described the driver of the car which sped away as 'an old man with white hair'. Richard is 30 years old and has red hair. The prosecution have decided not to call Joan as a witness since they believe she is unreliable. Richard claims Harold told him that he, Harold, had used Richard's car on the night of the burglary. Harold now denies he said this.

Richard is charged with burglary. Advise on evidence.

 Commentary

This question requires the student to consider a number of different evidential issues. The first part requires a discussion on whether a witness can refresh his or her memory from a number of possible sources. There is also a need to consider whether this infringes the rule against hearsay. The cigarette lighter as evidence should be considered and the status of Harold's statement as possible hearsay.

 Answer plan

- Can witness refresh memory when in witness box—**CJA 2003**?
- Application of hearsay rule to PC Ford's statement to Richard—**CJA 2003**.
- Admissibility of lighter and initials—real evidence.
- Does the prosecutor have to disclose Joan's evidence to the defence?

Suggested answer

Memory refreshing

The first issue relates to the admissibility of Tanya's statement to the police. It is clear that whilst testifying in court, Tanya is unable to remember the registration number and it is therefore necessary for Tanya to be able to refresh her memory by using PC Ford's notebook or her own diary. One issue is whether Tanya verified Ford's entry. In *Jones v Metcalfe* [1967] 1 WLR 1286, the Divisional Court refused to allow a police officer's testimony regarding the registration number of a lorry which had been told to him by an eyewitness. This was because the statement was hearsay and since the police officer had failed to read the number back to, and have it verified by, the witness, it could not also be used to refresh the eyewitness's memory. **Section 139 of the Criminal Justice Act (CJA) 2003** now replaces the common law provisions on memory-refreshing documents. In effect Tanya may refresh her memory from a document while giving oral evidence providing she confirms that the document represents her recollection at the time she made it and her recollection was likely to have been significantly better at that time than it is while she is giving oral evidence. It is likely that she can rely on either the extract from the notebook entry if she had verified it, or her diary. If the defence inspect these documents and cross-examine her on parts not relied on to refresh her memory, then the party who called the witness may have the document admitted (*Senat v Senat* [1965] 1 WLR 981). Under **s. 120(3) CJA 2003** the document then is evidence of any matter stated of which oral evidence would be admissible.

The entry in the diary should ideally have been made at the first practicable opportunity at a time when the events were still fresh in Tanya's mind. The earlier common law provision applied the principle of contemporaneity but the wording of the **CJA** does not indicate such a strict approach.

The diary or notebook should be handed to the defence counsel or the court so that it may be inspected and the witness cross-examined on its contents. The defence counsel can request that the jury be shown the notebook if it is necessary for the determination of an issue: *R v Bass* [1953] 1 QB 680. Finally, the document should be the original. However, if the original has been lost, it seems that a verified or accurate copy can be used (see *R v Cheng* (1976) 63 Cr App R 20).

Real evidence

With respect to the finding of the cigarette lighter, it is submitted that this is a piece of real evidence, which should be admitted into evidence for the jury to draw their own inferences. The difficulty is whether this may be inadmissible because of hearsay. It is unclear whether the identifying marks, names or initials on the item make any statement as to identity. In *R v Rice* [1963] 1 QB 857, the Court of Criminal Appeal allowed into evidence an airline ticket bearing the accused's name. The court rejected an argument that the airline ticket should not be admitted because it was hearsay. It was of the view that the ticket was admissible as relevant albeit circumstantial evidence to show that a person with the name of the accused had flown at the time and date stipulated on the air ticket. If *Rice* is correct then the cigarette lighter would be admissible provided that the court can be convinced that it was relevant to the facts in issue. Presumably, if the lighter had the appearance of just being lost, then there is a strong argument for its admission into evidence. However, if it appears that the lighter had been lost some time ago, then it is unlikely to be admitted because it may be irrelevant. The prosecution argument presumably is that it could have been lost at the same place as the scene of the burglary sometime prior to the commission of the offence.

Hearsay

Can Richard give evidence of what Harold allegedly told him? The purpose of adducing the statement would be to suggest it was true; that is, that it was Harold who committed the offence. It would thus arguably fall within the definition of hearsay in **s. 114 CJA 2003**. It may, however, be admitted under one of the statutory exceptions, one possibility being **s. 114(1)(b)**, the common law exception of *res gestae*. The prosecution may argue that the statement is a third-party confession and that the courts have shown reluctance to admit such statements on the grounds of inadmissible hearsay or irrelevance. Alternatively, the statement may be admitted under the inclusionary discretion **s. 114(2)(a)–(d)**. It was established *R v Xhabic* [2005] EWCA Crim 3135, that this may be relied upon even if the statement is inadmissible by another section. On the facts it does not appear that **s. 116** would apply since there is no reason not to call Harold as a witness. There is a difficulty, however, in that the courts are reluctant to admit third-party confessions. In *R v Blastland* the House of Lords took a restrictive view of relevance in ruling that what an absent third party said to a number of individuals, which if true would have tended to exonerate the accused, was inadmissible because it was evidence of a state of mind and emotion which was irrelevant to the facts in issue. Here it seems the defence is arguing that Harold was the perpetrator. If he is called as a witness he could be cross-examined and if he denies taking the car his alleged previous inconsistent statement to Richard could be put to him under the procedure set out in **s. 4 Criminal Procedure Act 1865**. The statement may be evidence of the truth of its contents following **s. 119 CJA 2003**.

Disclosure

The prosecution proposal not to call Joan as a witness raises the question of disclosure of evidence to the defence. Non-disclosure of evidence by the prosecution to the defence has been a major cause of miscarriages of justice. In *R v Maguire* [1992] QB 936 failure to disclose material which weakened the prosecution case was held to be a material irregularity. The **Criminal Procedure and Investigations Act 1996, s. 3(1)(a)** imposes a duty to disclose prosecution material which might reasonably be considered capable of undermining the case for the prosecution against the accused or of assisting the case for the accused. The section was amended by the **CJA 2003** to introduce a one-stage objective test, replacing the previous two-stage test which relied on 'the prosecutor's opinion' on the usefulness of the material to the defence. It is likely that the prosecution will be required to disclose the eyewitness evidence from Joan which supports the defence denial of involvement.

Question 5

Fred is charged with sexually assaulting Amanda, a colleague at work. He claims she had engaged in sexual banter with men at work and had invited him to her flat and consented to sexual intercourse. He claims she was showing her gratitude to him for help he had given her at work. He also claims she has a suggestible personality and had been persuaded to invent the assault by work colleagues who knew his past. Fred has a previous conviction for sexual assault on a female co-worker, five years ago. The prosecution are considering calling Amanda's mother to testify that Amanda was very reclusive and she never had a boyfriend. She is also a volunteer youth worker. The prosecution want to call evidence from a psychiatrist that Amanda does not have a 'suggestible' personality. Fred is considering whether to testify.

Advise on evidence.

Commentary

The issues include the evidence that can be brought to support a non-defendant witness, such as good character evidence. Expert evidence is also at issue, and the previous convictions of a defendant. Bearing in mind this is a sexual assault case you should consider the cross-examination of the complainant under **s. 41 Youth Justice and Criminal Evidence Act 1999 (YJCEA)**. Fred's decision on whether to testify at trial involves **s. 35 CJPOA 1994**.

Answer plan

- Can Amanda's good character be admitted, consider **s. 41 YJCEA 1999**?
- Fred's previous conviction—effect of **CJA 2003**.
- Expert evidence on questions of 'personality'.
- Defendant's failure to testify, **s. 35 CJPOA 1994**.

Suggested answer

Good character

The prosecution wish to claim that Amanda is of good character. The common law governs the admissibility of good character of a non-defendant witness (see *R v Hamilton* (1998) **The Times, 25 June**). In general, although a defendant can call evidence of his good character, that is not the case in relation to a witness. However, the prosecution may rely on a developing line of authority in cases involving sexual assault which has to some extent undermined the strict common law position. Thus, in *R v Tobin* [2003] **EWCA Crim 190** where a defendant alleged the complainant had initiated sexual activity the Crown was allowed to call evidence of her good character. **Section 41 Youth Justice and Criminal Evidence Act 1999 (YJCEA)** is relevant here. **Section 41(5)(a)** refers to the prosecution adducing evidence about the sexual behaviour of the complainant. In *Tobin* the defendant, a married man of 36 years, alleged that the complainant, a young girl, had initiated sexual activity in thanks for a lift. The Court of Appeal held that the trial judge had been right to allow the complainant's mother to give evidence about her good character. It is possible therefore that the prosecution may be allowed to call Amanda's mother.

Sexual activity

Any reference to Amanda's lack of boyfriends may be judged to be a 'reference' to sexual activity under **s. 41(5)(a) YJCEA 1999**. If the prosecution lead on Amanda's good character then by **s. 41(2) and (5) YJCEA 1999** the defence may apply to the court for leave to adduce evidence concerning the complainant's sexual behaviour. Thus Fred may raise the allegation of her flirting at work and cross-examine her on that. If the prosecution do not lead on that issue it is likely the court would refuse such cross-examination. The evidence from the psychiatrist raises the problem of the admissibility of expert testimony. The law does not admit expert evidence of witness credibility unless there are special circumstances. In *R v Robinson* (1994) **98 Cr App R 370** the Court of Appeal held that evidence from an educational psychologist that the complainant in a rape trial was 'not suggestible' should not have been admitted. The court stated 'the Crown cannot call a witness of fact, and then, without more, call a psychologist or psychiatrist to give reasons why the jury should regard that witness as reliable.' It does not appear here that Amanda is suffering from a mental illness which would permit expert evidence to be admitted.

Previous convictions

Fred's previous conviction for sexual assault may be admissible under the provisions on bad character in the **Criminal Justice Act (CJA) 2003**. As a conviction it satisfies the test of bad character under **s. 98** and Fred may have triggered its admissibility under two heads and these considerations will apply whether he testifies or not. First, the prosecution may argue that the conviction is admissible under **s. 101(1)(d)** as being relevant to an important matter in issue between prosecution and defence. This section equates to the earlier common law provisions on similar fact, although it is clearly the intention of the new Act that more of such evidence will be admitted (see *R v Hanson* [2005] 2 Cr App R 21). The current test for admissibility is set out in *Hanson*. The court should consider three matters:

- Did the history of the convictions establish a propensity to commit offences of the kind charged?
- Did that propensity make it more likely that the defendant had committed the offence charged?
- Was it just to rely on the conviction(s) of the same description or category; and in any event would the proceedings be unfair if they were admitted? **Sections 101(3) and 103(3)** allow the court an exclusionary discretion. One factor would be how long ago the offence was.

Fred's conviction of a sex offence appears to fall into the same category of offence as the current charge, although the current **Categories of Offences Order 2004 (SI 2004/3346)** issued under the **CJA** lists only offences of dishonesty and sexual offences against children. In *Hanson* the Court of Appeal stated that 'In referring to offences of the same description or category, **section 103(2)** is not exhaustive of the type of conviction which might be relied upon to show evidence of propensity to commit offences of the kind charged' (see also *R v Weir*). The prosecution will rely on recent case law which does indicate a low threshold for admissibility. In particular, where the offence is a sexual one previous sexual behaviour seems almost routinely to be admitted. In *R v Weir* the Court of Appeal held that evidence of an earlier caution for taking an indecent photograph of a child was rightly admitted in a trial where the defendant was charged with sexually assaulting a 13-year-old girl. It is not fatal to the prosecution's application that Fred has only one previous conviction, especially since this is a charge of a sexual offence. In *Hanson* the Court of Appeal stated, 'There is no minimum number of events necessary to demonstrate such a propensity. The fewer the number of convictions the weaker is likely to be the evidence of propensity. A single previous conviction for an offence of the same description or category will often not show propensity. But it may do so where, for example, it shows a tendency to unusual behaviour or where its circumstances demonstrate probative force in relation to the offence charged' (compare *DPP v P* [1991] 2 AC 447, 460E–461A).

The question also arises whether Fred's conviction could be admitted under **s. 101(1)(g)**. The defendant has made an attack on another person. If Fred is allowed to cross-examine Amanda on her alleged behaviour at work because the prosecution had introduced the matter of her sexual activity then it may be that **s. 101(1)(g)** is triggered, which would allow another route of admissibility of the previous conviction. Under **s. 101(3) CJA 2003** the court must not admit evidence under **s. 101(1)(d) or (g)** if on an application by the defendant to exclude it, it appears to the court that the admission of the evidence would have such an adverse effect on the fairness of the proceedings that the court ought not to admit it.

Although evidence admitted under this head goes mainly to credibility, following *R v Highton* it may also be evidence of propensity (see also *R v Randall* [2004] 1 WLR 56). If Fred chooses not to give evidence, it should be borne in mind that **s. 35 of the Criminal Justice and Public Order Act 1994** allows the court or the jury to draw such inferences as appear proper from the accused's failure to give evidence without good cause. Thus, there is a risk that the jury may draw adverse inferences from his failure to give evidence in court (see *R v Cowan*). Under **s. 35(5)** a failure to answer questions is presumed to be 'without good cause' unless the accused is entitled under statute not to answer particular questions or enjoys a legal privilege not to answer them or alternatively the court grants discretion not to answer. The judge should follow the Judicial Studies Board Guidelines on Fred's non-appearance to testify. The directions follow those in *Cowan* and are different from those under **ss. 34, 36 and 37**. In particular the jury is restricted to considering the prosecution's case in deciding whether it should draw an adverse inference. The points covered should remind the jury of the following: the burden of proof was on the prosecution; the defendant had a right to silence; silence alone could prove guilt; the jury must first consider whether there was a case to answer and if the answer was 'yes' then ask if the defendant had an answer would he not have gone into the witness box. In *Birchall* (1999) Lord Bingham CJ stated: 'Inescapable logic demands that a jury should not start to consider whether they should draw inferences from a defendant's failure to give oral evidence at his trial until they have concluded that the Crown's case against him is sufficiently compelling to call for an answer.'

In *R v Becouarn* [2005] UKHL 55 the House of Lords held that the Judicial Studies Board Specimen Direction was sufficiently fair to defendants. The jury could be directed that they could draw an adverse inference if they considered the accused to have no answer to the prosecution case, or none that would stand up to cross-examination, even though an additional reason might be that he would have his criminal record revealed if he testified. The House rejected any direction along the lines of *Lucas* pertaining to lies by the defendant that there might be other reasons for the defendant's silence. (This situation, of course, is less likely to arise now since criminal record may be revealed in certain circumstances even if the defendant does not testify.)

 Question 6

Jeremy, Harold, Christine and Joan are on trial for supplying illegal drugs. They share a flat in which the police find quantities of heroin, £50,000 in used banknotes, and a large quantity of designer clothes. The defendants claim that they had won the money at horse-racing. They claim that the heroin must have been left by a student they had put up for the night, who has now disappeared. At the investigation stage they all have the same solicitor, Good

& Co. Before the trial Christine changes solicitor. Jeremy pleads guilty and gives evidence for the prosecution. Christine's counsel has sought leave to produce a statement that Jeremy had made to Good & Co. which is inconsistent with evidence he gives in court and which would help Christine's defence. Harold had made a confession of his responsibility for the drug dealing in a statement to the police, in which he said that Christine was not involved in the offence. Harold's confession is, however, excluded by the trial judge beforehand in a voir dire. At the trial, in giving evidence, Harold claims that he had seen Christine selling drugs outside a school. Christine's counsel wishes to question him on his statement to the police. Joan refuses to answer a number of questions at a police interview with a solicitor present. She does say, however, she was not a user of drugs. She claims at trial that she was a user, not a supplier of drugs.

Advise on the admissibility of Jeremy's statement with Good & Co. and whether Christine's counsel is likely to be able to question Harold on his pre-trial statement.

 Commentary

You will need to show first, an awareness of recent case law dealing with legal professional privilege when it appears to conflict with the interests of a defendant. The question also requires an appreciation of the tricky situation arising when a defendant wishes to adduce a co-defendant's confession or to cross-examine a co-defendant on a confession which has already been ruled inadmissible as part of the prosecution's case. This question requires familiarity with the concept of relevance and in particular a knowledge of case law on the relevance of 'lifestyle' in drugs cases.

 Answer plan

- Relevance of 'lifestyle' evidence in drug offences.
- Legal professional privilege will apply to Jeremy's statement—see **R v Derby Magistrates' Court, ex parte B (1995)**.
- Counsel for co-accused may cross-examine maker of inadmissible confession to undermine credibility.
- Excluded confession may be available to co-defendant—**R v Myers**, CJA 2003.
- Joan's statement at trial—whether inference may be drawn from earlier silence; **Lucas** direction on lies.

Relevance and 'lifestyle'

All evidence must be relevant, although of course not all relevant evidence is admissible. The test for relevance is a matter of experience and common sense. A number of cases have shown the application of the concept of relevance in connection with drug dealing. In *R v Wright* **[1994] Crim LR 55** the Court of Appeal held that the finding of a large quantity of cash was capable of being relevant to the issue of whether the accused was supplying drugs to others. It is clear, however, that the judge must direct that the jury must not treat that evidence as evidence of propensity. In *R v Grant* **[1996] 1 Cr App R 73** guidelines for directions to the jury were set out. In order for the finding of the £50,000 to constitute evidence the jury would have to reject the explanation that it was a result of success at the races and accept that there was no other innocent explanation. If the jury were to conclude that the presence of the money indicated not only past dealing, but an ongoing dealing in drugs, then finding the money together with the drugs in question would be a matter which they could take into account in considering whether the necessary intent to supply had been proved. £50,000 is likely to be considered a large enough amount to be relevant but the admissibility of the evidence of designer clothes is less certain. Further information is needed to establish how exclusive they are (Nike, Gap or Versace?). It has in any case been held that evidence of lavish lifestyle will only rarely be relevant to an issue of intent to supply (*R v Halpin* **[1996] Crim LR 112**). In the controversial case of *R v Guney* **[1998] 2 Cr App R 242**, on the other hand, the Court of Appeal said that whether evidence is relevant depends on the particular circumstances of each case. Evidence of cash and lifestyle might even be relevant to possession, but more likely to intent to supply. In that case the Court of Appeal held that the evidence of finding nearly £ 25,000 in the accused's bedroom near to the drugs was admissible, relevant evidence on the question of possession. The accused had claimed the drugs were planted on him. The court stated, however, that evidence of a lavish lifestyle or possession of large sums of cash was not without more proof of possession.

Privilege

There is no general privilege attached to confidential statements made between professional people and their clients. However, the major exception to this is legal professional privilege, which covers certain types of correspondence between a lawyer and his or her client and certain communications between a lawyer and/or client and third parties. The privilege belongs to the client, who can insist on non-disclosure by the lawyer or third party in question. The scope of the privilege is given in **s. 10 of the Police and Criminal Evidence Act 1984 (PACE)**. This section, however, does not regulate its use in general but sets limits on police powers to search for and seize evidence. Jeremy can thus claim legal professional privilege for his statement to Good & Co. He may waive this if he wishes. However, if he fails to it will be impossible for Christine to challenge it successfully in the light of a House of Lords ruling. Christine might reasonably argue that a refusal to disclose harms her defence and in the case of *R v Ataou* [1988] QB 798, that claim was heard sympathetically by the Court of Appeal. However, in *R v Derby Magistrates' Court, ex parte B* [1996] AC 487, the House of Lords overruled *Ataou* and the earlier case of *R v Barton* [1972] 2 All ER 321. The House held that 'no exception should be allowed to the absolute nature of legal professional privilege once established.' The House also held that the privilege is the same whether it is sought by the prosecution or the defence and the 'refusal of the client to waive his privilege, for whatever reason, or for no reason, cannot be questioned or investigated by the court.' The court considered that 'if a balancing exercise was ever required in the case of legal professional privilege it was performed once and for all in the 16th century.' In that case a witness, B, who had previously been acquitted of a murder, could not be compelled to produce a confession made in the presence of his solicitor in a subsequent trial of his stepfather for the same offence. This decision has been much criticised. Choo, for example (2012, p. 237) comments that it 'is open to criticism on the ground that it overlooks the importance of the need to protect the innocent from wrongful conviction.' The House of Lords limited its scope in *Re L (A minor)* [1997] AC 16 when it held that it was confined to legal advice privilege and did not apply in care proceedings. It is assumed that Jeremy's statement concerns legal advice privilege. Christine is unlikely to be allowed to adduce the document.

Confession

Evidence of Harold's confession is clearly relevant to the trial since it conflicts with his evidence in court. He had previously absolved Christine but now he is implicating her. Christine's counsel is advised to apply to present Harold's confession not as to the truth of its contents but in order to demonstrate the inconsistency of Harold's testimony and thus to undermine his credibility. In *R v Rowson* [1986] QB 174 the Court of Appeal held that a trial judge did not have a discretion to prevent counsel for a co-accused from cross-examining the maker of an inadmissible confession. Such questioning is for the purpose of showing that the witness has made a previous inconsistent statement and thus undermining his credibility. The judge must make it clear to the jury that any evidence of the confession is not evidence of guilt. The only pre-condition is that the evidence be relevant, as the Privy Council held in *Lui-Mei Lin v R* (1989) 88 Cr App R 296. The right to cross-examine is thus unfettered. An alternative, and perhaps better approach, however, would be an application to sever the indictment. This is illustrated by *R v O'Boyle* (1991) 92 Cr App R 202, where a joint trial would be harmful to the defendant subject to such cross-examination, whereas a separate trial would not harm the co-defendant and the prosecution.

In *R v Myers* [1998] AC 124 the House of Lords went further and held that a confession excluded by s. 78 PACE might still be available to a co-defendant. A defendant in a joint trial has the right to ask about a voluntary statement made by a co-accused outside court even though it is not relied on by the prosecution as long as it is relevant to the party who wishes to rely on it. Thus Christine may be allowed to cross-examine Harold and the officer to whom he made the confession if it had been excluded under s. 78. The evidence adduced would be relevant both to credibility and the facts in issue. The judge would have no discretion, as between co-accused, to exclude it. Further information is required as to whether Harold's confession was excluded under **s. 78 or s. 76 PACE. Section 76A(1) PACE** now states that 'in any proceedings a confession made by an accused person may be given in evidence for another person charged in the same proceedings (a co-accused) in so far as it is relevant to any matter in issue in the proceedings and is not excluded by the court in pursuance of this section.'

The court will apply the tests for oppression and reliability, as formulated for evidence tendered by the prosecution but the standard applied to the co-defendant will be the balance of probabilities. As defence evidence it cannot be excluded by s. 78. The court may consider **s. 126(1) of the Criminal Justice Act (CJA) 2003**, which provides an exclusionary discretion for hearsay statements, but it is unlikely it will be applied to prevent Christine producing evidence of her innocence.

Silence

The contrast between Joan's statement at trial and her earlier silence at interview raises the possibility of inviting the jury to consider **s. 34 or s. 36** if the issue at interview was explaining the presence of drugs. More information is needed on the circumstances of the interview, particularly the nature of the legal advice and how much Joan was told of the case against her. In *R v Compton* **[2002] EWCA Crim 2835** the court considered that it was sufficient for the police questioner to say that he was investigating drug trafficking, without being specific about the offence. Joan's explanation appears to go to the central issue, i.e. she is denying dealing in drugs. It is established that **s. 34** may apply even if the jury in drawing an adverse inference would effectively determine guilt. Lord Woolf CJ in *Gowland-Wynn* **[2002] 1 Cr App 569** stated that **s. 34** applied when a 'defendant could be expected to comment about something which goes to the heart of his defence.' If other conditions apply then Joan's silence may be admissible.

Lies

The final issue to consider here is that in the interview room she said she was not a user of drugs. If the prosecution had used this it is arguable that a *Lucas* direction is required, since Jane appears to have told an out-of-court lie. In *R v AO* **[2000] Crim LR 617** the Court of Appeal held that 'where the same response was relied upon both as a lie and a failure to mention a fact relied on by the defence, then both directions should be given.' The judge should therefore give a *Lucas* direction as well as one on failure to mention a fact if the conditions apply. The lie by Joan must be admitted or proved beyond reasonable doubt and the jury told that the mere fact that the defendant lied is not in itself evidence of guilt since defendants may lie for innocent reasons. So only if the jury is sure that Joan did not lie for an innocent reason can the lie support the prosecution case.

Question 7

Hilda is charged with two counts of criminal damage. The prosecution case on the first count is that she painted slogans on the wall of a local factory farm which she considered was treating chickens cruelly; the second count refers to damage caused to walls on a local dog kennels. There had been a spate of such desecrations and police had set up watch in a neighbouring house and identified Hilda as the offender. Hilda suspects that the surveillance took place and wishes to cross-examine the prosecution witness about the quality of his observation because she contests the identification. The police have searched Hilda's lodgings with a search warrant and find pots of paint identical to the colours used on the factory farm wall slogans. No paint was found to match that on the dog kennels. The police wish to call Norman, Hilda's estranged husband, as a witness. He still lives in the same house as her and had made a statement to the police that Hilda came in very late on the night in question and her hands were covered with paint. He is called at the trial for the prosecution but refuses to give any evidence. There is medical evidence to the effect that Hilda is in any case unfit to stand trial because she suffers from a mental instability. The defence lost the plea, having been told by the judge that they should reach the standard of proof on the issue of beyond reasonable doubt. Hilda plans not to give evidence at trial. The defence have discovered that the police had secretly recorded a conversation between Hilda and her solicitor while Hilda was in police custody.

Advise on evidence.

Examiner's tip

This tip applies to all your answers. Examination questions rarely give you unnecessary information so you should question every fact you are given. You will see, for example, in this question that you are told there are two charges on the indictment. This should alert you to an often overlooked aspect of propensity evidence that the bad character may be simultaneous as well as previous. Here you need to discuss whether the evidence of disposition on one count can be used in assessing guilt on the other. The answer is generally yes.

Commentary

A potpourri of issues, which means that you must have the law relating to them at your finger tips. Make a list of the areas and then work systematically through them.

Answer plan

- Can the police be compelled to disclose the identity of the surveillance? This turns on the question of public interest immunity and the protection of informers, including how far this stretches to surveillance sites. Consider also witness anonymity.

- Is evidence arising from the search admissible? Consider whether the evidence is relevant.

- Is Norman a compellable witness? What is the status of estranged spouses? Consider **s. 80 PACE** and appropriate case law.

- If Norman does not appear as a witness, may his evidence be presented in any other form, for example under the hearsay exceptions of the **CJA 2003**? Do the provisions of **s. 80 PACE** on compellability apply?

- What is the burden and standard of proof on the issue of Hilda's competence to testify?

- What view will the court take of the secret police recording? Will the prosecution go ahead?

- Can the evidence on the chicken farm charge be used in assessing guilt on the kennels charge?

- Was the direction on burden of proof on the unfit to plead correct?

- How will silence provisions of **s. 35 CJPOA** affect Hilda?

Suggested answer

Secret recording

The secret recording by the police of the conversation between Hilda and her solicitor is likely to be taken very seriously by the court. In *R v Grant* [2005] 3 WLR 437 the court held that a prosecution should have been stayed for abuse of process since the police had, by recording a conversation between the accused and their solicitors, interfered with the right to communicate in confidence, even though there was no prejudice to the accused as a result. (See also *Brennan v UK* (2001) 34 EHRR 507 and Re McE (2009).) In the event the trial does go ahead, there are a number of issues arising from the evidence.

Observation post

The police may wish to keep the identity of the house they are using secret, either because the people who allowed them to use it have been promised confidentiality or in order not to deter other possible assistance. However, the identity of the premises may be important to Hilda's defence so she can cross-examine the police witness on the quality of the identification evidence. The rule in *Marks v Beyfus* (1890) 25 QBD 494, allows the identity of informers to be protected as a matter of public policy. In *R v Rankine* [1986] QBD 861 this rule was held to apply also to the identity of persons who have allowed their property to be used as an observation post. However, if the owners do not wish to maintain secrecy, there would be no objection to identifying the premises. In any case, the prosecution must lay down a basis for the anonymity if it is required. In *R v Johnson* [1988] 1 WLR 1377, the Court of Appeal said it was necessary for the prosecution to satisfy the court that there was a particular need for the observation post and for anonymity before suppression would be accepted. In the event the identity in that case was not revealed. In *R v Brown*, *R v Daley* (1987) 87 Cr App Rep 52, the Court of Appeal held that the extension of the exclusionary rule to surveillance sites was intended to protect the owner or occupier, not the post *simpliciter*. Here details of an unmarked police car ought to have been revealed. It is necessary then to see whether on the facts the address is relevant information and to establish the attitude of the occupier. In view of these authorities it may be possible for Hilda to have discovery of the identity of the premises. If the prosecution wishes to refuse disclosure then depending on the sensitivity of the material it must follow the procedures set out in the **Criminal Procedure and Investigations Act 1996**. The House of Lords considered this in *R v H*, *R v C* [2003] UKHL 3. This is an area where the Strasbourg Court has had considerable impact (see *Rowe and Davis v UK*). In some cases partial disclosure may be possible. It is possible that the undercover police officer may be able to give evidence anonymously under the provisions of the **Coroners and Justice Act 2009**. The law was considered in a series of conjoined appeals in *R v Mayers* (2008) (see page 46). There the knowledge of the true identities of undercover police officers was of no importance to the defendant.

Paint as evidence

It is arguable that the evidence of the paint is relevant if it goes to support other identification evidence, as it does here. In *R v Reading* [1966] 1 WLR 836 the court held that if otherwise innocent-seeming articles, in that case walkie-talkie radios and imitation police uniforms, could be used for criminal purposes it is not necessary that any particular occasion on which they were used be identified. It thus appears sufficient that there is identification evidence linking Hilda to the offence to make the submission of the paint as real evidence relevant in the case. The evidence may be admitted under **CJA 2003, s. 103(1)(a) and s. 101(1)(d)**. One difficulty facing Hilda is that she has two charges. The evidence on the chicken factory appears stronger than that on the kennels. The prosecution will rely on the cases of *R v Freeman* (2009) and *R v Chopra* (2007) where the judge held that evidence in relation to one count was capable of being admitted in relation to any other count if it met any of the criteria in **s. 101(1)**. Here the evidence is likely to fall within **s. 101(1)(d)** as it did in *Freeman*.

It is assumed that Norman is a competent witness. Under the **Police and Criminal Evidence Act 1984 (PACE), s. 80(5)**, former spouses are treated as any other witnesses. However, that only applies if the marriage has been ended by divorce or if it was voidable and has been annulled. The common law position remains that a marriage is treated as subsisting even if there has been a judicial separation, as the court held in

Moss v Moss [1963] 2 QBD 799. Thus Norman is a competent witness for the prosecution by virtue of **s. 53 of the Youth Justice and Criminal Evidence Act 1999**. He is not, however, compellable, since the offence in question does not fall within the categories of **s. 80(3) PACE**; that is, an offence that involves a violent or sexual attack on the spouse or a person under 16 years.

If he persists in refusing to testify the prosecution may need to consider whether the evidence can be adduced in any other way. His statement to the police is clearly hearsay in that the purpose of adducing it is to suggest it is true. The prosecution will be aided by *R v L* [2009] **All E R (D) 137** where a pre-trial statement of a non-compellable spouse was admissible under **s. 114(1)(d)**. The court held that **s. 80 PACE** did not preclude a witness from giving evidence of a voluntary statement made in the past by the defendant's wife. Whether it was just in such instances to admit the statement depended on the specific facts.

The statement is arguably endorsed by him and therefore would fulfil the requirement of firsthand hearsay in **s. 116 CJA 2003**. However, there is difficulty in adducing it since on the facts there does not appear to be any reason for not calling him as a witness. The lack of one of the acceptable reasons listed in **s. 116(2)** is likely to be fatal to admissibility. One final point on this is that the prosecution cannot use Hilda's failure to call Norman as the occasion of an adverse comment, by virtue of **s. 80A PACE**, nor should a judge invite a jury to draw adverse inferences from her failure to testify. With regard to the possible plea of unfitness to plead, the defence has the legal burden of proof to the civil standard, as held by the Court of Criminal Appeal in *R v F* [1960] **1 QB 325**. The judge therefore wrongly directed on this, making grounds of appeal. One final point is that if Hilda does not testify she runs the risk of an adverse inference being drawn under **s. 35 of the Criminal Justice and Public Order Act 1994**. Although s. 35(1)(b) has the potential to protect a vulnerable defendant like Hilda in that it refers to 'the physical or mental condition of the accused' as making it 'undesirable' for him to give evidence, it has been restrictively interpreted. In *R v Friend (No. 1)* [1997 1 WLR 1443 an adverse inference was drawn when the defendant had a mental age of nine. However, in a later appeal, *Friend (No. 2)* [2004] EWCA Crim 266, the conviction was quashed on the basis of consideration of the effect his mental condition might have on his ability to give evidence. Nonetheless, the case law suggests that Hilda will face difficulties. In *R (on the application of the DPP) v Kavanagh* [2006] **Crim LR 370** the Court of Appeal stressed that it was not enough for a defendant to suffer from a physical or mental condition, it had to be such that it was undesirable for him to give evidence.

SELECTED BIBLIOGRAPHY

Allen, C., *Practical Guide to Evidence*, 4th edn (London: Routledge-Cavendish, 2008).

Ashworth, A., 'Criminal Proceedings After the Human Rights Act' [2001] Crim LR 855.

Ashworth, A., *Human Rights, Serious Crime and Criminal Procedure* (London: Sweet & Maxwell, 2002).

Ashworth, A., 'Criminal Justice Act 2003: (2) Criminal Justice Reform: Principles, Human Rights and Public Protection' [2004] Crim LR 516.

Brooks, P., *Troubling Confessions* (Chicago, IL: University of Chicago Press, 2001).

Choo, A.L.-T., *Evidence* (Oxford: OUP, 2012).

Dennis, I.H., *The Law of Evidence*, 4th edn (London: Sweet & Maxwell, 2010).

Doak, J. and McGourlay, C., *Criminal Evidence in Context*, 3rd edn (Abingdon: Law Matters, 2012).

Durston, G., *Evidence: Texts and Materials*, 2nd edn (Oxford: OUP, 2011).

Emson, R., *Evidence*, 5th edn (Basingstoke: Palgrave Macmillan, 2010).

Kadri, S., *The Trial: A History from Socrates to OJ Simpson* (London: HarperCollins, 2010).

Keane, A. and McKeown, P., *The Modern Law of Evidence*, 9th edn (Oxford: OUP, 2012).

Langbein, J., *The Origins of the Adversary Criminal Trial* (Oxford: OUP, 2005).

McEwan, J., *Evidence and the Adversarial Process*, 2nd edn (Oxford: OUP, 1998).

Munday, R., *Evidence*, 5th edn (London: Butterworths, 2011).

Murphy, P. and Glover, R., *Murphy on Evidence*, 12th edn (Oxford: OUP, 2011).

Roberts, P. and Zuckerman, A., *Criminal Evidence* (Oxford: OUP, 2010).

Sharpe, S., *Judicial Discretion and Criminal Investigation* (London: Sweet & Maxwell, 1997).

Tapper, C., *Cross and Tapper on Evidence*, 12th edn (Oxford: OUP, 2010).

Taylor, R., Wasik, M. and Leng, R., *Blackstone's Guide to the Criminal Justice Act 2003* (Oxford: OUP, 2004).

Zuckerman, A., *The Principles of Criminal Evidence* (Oxford: OUP, 1989).

Introductory Note

References such as '178–9' indicate (not necessarily continuous) discussion of a topic across a range of pages. Wherever possible in the case of topics with many references, these have either been divided into sub-topics or only the most significant discussions of the topic are listed. Because the entire work is about 'evidence', the use of this term (and certain others which occur constantly throughout the book) as an entry point has been minimised. Information will be found under the corresponding detailed topics.